THE GROWING SEASON

THE
GROWING
SEASON

How I Built a New Life—
and Saved an American Farm

SARAH FREY

BALLANTINE BOOKS
NEW YORK

Published in the United States by Ballantine Books, an imprint of Random House, a division of Penguin Random House LLC, New York.

BALLANTINE and the HOUSE colophon are registered trademarks of Penguin Random House LLC.

Library of Congress Cataloging-in-Publication Data
Names: Frey, Sarah, author.
Title: The growing season: how I built a new life—and saved an American farm / Sarah Frey.
Description: First edition. | New York: Ballantine Books, [2020]
Identifiers: LCCN 2019048607 (print) | LCCN 2019048608 (ebook) | ISBN 9780593129395 (hardcover) | ISBN 9780593129401 (ebook)
Subjects: LCSH: Frey, Sarah. | Frey Farms. | Women farmers—United States—Biography. | Women chief executive officers—United States—Biography. | Produce trade—United States. | Agricultural industries—United States.
Classification: LCC HD9010.F74 A3 2020 (print) | LCC HD9010.F74 (ebook) | DDC 338.7/63092 [B]—dc23
LC record available at https://lccn.loc.gov/2019048607
LC ebook record available at https://lccn.loc.gov/2019048608

Printed in the United States of America on acid-free paper

randomhousebooks.com

2 4 6 8 9 7 5 3 1

First Edition

Title page art: photo, iStock.com/SimonSkafar; illustration, iStock.com/ilbusca

For the girls who steal thunder
and the boys who help them do it

Contents

Social Graces

L ast night it happened again. At a cocktail party teeming with some of the most successful people in the country, a man assumed we came from the same place. I understood his mistake. On the outside, I looked—aside from being one of the few women in the room—as though I belonged. He wore a custom-made suit; I a designer skirt, blouse, and heels. He sported an expensive watch; I had on pearls. As we gazed out of the floor-to-ceiling windows over the sea of skyscrapers, we both held glasses of champagne.

The latest notches on our resumes, too, were similar. We both ran companies that earned millions a year in revenue. I'm the CEO—or, as I prefer to be called, the founding farmer—of Frey Farms, which sells, among other things, tens of millions of pumpkins and watermelons a year. My company, which has its headquarters down the road from my childhood and current home in a tiny Illinois town called Orchardville, manages thousands of acres of farmland coast to coast.

In recent years I've enjoyed expanding our agribusiness into the beverage and consumer packaged goods markets. Harvard Business

School used one of my first major deals as a case study in the art of negotiation. If you've ever bought a melon or a pumpkin in America, chances are you are my customer. Thank you.

Where the man made a mistake was in his belief that we shared a past as well as a present. I could see him struggle to figure out where we might have intersected. Boarding school? Martha's Vineyard vacations? Ivy League college?

He asked the inevitable question: "Remind me, Sarah, where you went to school. Was it Harvard Business? Wharton?"

That simple, common question once terrified me. I was afraid that if I answered honestly, I would be judged unworthy, and that it would be clear to everyone instantly that I didn't belong, that the pearls and heels were a costume. At one time, whenever I was asked anything about my past, I would immediately change the subject. That way, someone like the businessman at that party could continue to assume that we'd attended the same institutions of higher learning, that we had roughly the same background, that I'd found my way into this room the same way he had.

Now, though, I have a new response: the truth.

"I went to Frontier," I said confidently, and looked him right in the eye with a smile.

Then I took a sip of my drink and enjoyed a moment watching him silently wonder about Frontier. Was it some elite private institution? If he called the right people, could he get his kid transferred there from Columbia?

Frontier is a community college in Fairfield, Illinois, about half an hour's drive from my family's farm. It offers degrees in, among other things, automotive technology, fire science, and electrical distribution systems. It's one of the top two or three Illinois Eastern Community Colleges, of which there are four. Go Bobcats.

As a child, I was a good student with dreams of heading off to a major university, just as I had seen my four older brothers do. But I was also living on my own at age fifteen and needed to make money. While I was still technically in high school, I started taking college classes at Frontier at night while also working various jobs.

At many events like the one last night, I often have the least formal education of anyone in the room—including the busboys. I'm also often one of the youngest people there and one of the only ones who are female or from the middle of the country. I am *definitely* the only person there who was born into a house with no indoor plumbing, grew up skinning deer, and was driving big trucks and tractors by middle school.

When I talk about my company, I say that Frey Farms is a family business—which it is. But the words "family farm" usually provoke another round of uncomfortable questions.

First, people assume that I inherited the company: "A family farm? That's great! Did your father put you in charge? Or did your grandfather start it?"

I understand how this assumption is made. I don't exactly look like the image people usually have in their heads of a farmer—or a CEO, for that matter. On nights like this, I am frequently mistaken for someone's wife. I come across, they tell me, as elegant and well-spoken, with a warm smile. What no one there knows is that on that very morning I was clad in grubby jeans, my unbrushed hair pulled back under a ball cap, yelling over the noise in the sorting room. No way I'd be mistaken for a Wharton alum.

How much should I share about my past and my family? That's been a tough call my whole life. When people ask, "How many brothers and sisters do you have?" I might give the short answer: "I have four older brothers in the business."

It's not a lie. I do have *four* older brothers *in the business*.

Sometimes I open up a bit more and say, "My mother had eight children." This is also technically true.

"Yep!" I say to their inevitable astonishment. "I come from a big family."

Rarely do I admit the full truth: "Including my half-siblings, I'm the youngest of twenty-one."

Yes, you read that right: twenty-one.

In most rooms, it's best to just talk about my four older brothers. They were, by far, the biggest influence on me. They taught me to hunt, fish, and live off the land. That knowledge gave me the confidence to believe that I could take care of myself no matter what happened. Those four know where I came from as no one else ever will.

Another thing people ask when they hear where I'm from is, "You're from Illinois? I love Chicago!"

"Chicago is a wonderful city," I reply. But I'm actually from *southern* Illinois.

My home turf, Wayne County, is much closer to Kentucky than it is to Chicago. It has a culture, a way of life, and a mindset that are completely foreign to people who grew up on the coasts or in any major city. Where I come from, success is measured not by your educational attainment or bank balance but by the size of your truck tires, the speed of your four-wheeler, and the variety in your gun collection. In my part of the state, there are no street signs, no lights on the roads, no stores for miles.

As a child, I wanted nothing to do with our rural way of life. I couldn't wait to grow up and move far away to a big city. I counted the days until I would leave our eighty-acre piece of rolling clay dirt in the middle of nowhere, what we called the Hill. For years I kept hoping my time there was over. I wished my childhood away. Sometimes I didn't think I would make it out alive.

Today I have a greater appreciation of where I'm from. Although we were dirt poor by most measures, in other ways we were rich. We had a piece of land, a big family, and freedom to roam in nature. We ate food we grew and caught ourselves. Ironically, that diet is now coveted and promoted as the ideal: clean, healthy, sustainable food, with nothing going to waste. We had the original farm-to-table lifestyle—we'd pull things out of the ground minutes before cooking them. We would take what we called "the ugly fruit" and turn it into the most delicious dishes and beverages. We were eating organic, hyperlocal, freshly prepared foods out of necessity long before it became a trend.

Because I'm one of the younger CEOs in my business circles,

and my company's founder, people often ask me, "How have you done so much in such a short period of time?"

The truth is, I started doing everything for myself early because no one else was going to do it for me. On the Hill, by the time I was seven or eight years old, I was doing things most teenagers wouldn't even consider doing on their own, taking on projects that most adults wouldn't venture. I do not advocate deprivation as a parenting strategy, but I can't deny that, ironically enough, being disadvantaged gave me a huge head start. Even though I was sixteen years old when I founded my company, it was more like I was thirty-six, because of the lessons I'd already learned growing up where and how I did. By grade school, I understood how to take care of myself and the people around me.

That said, I do sometimes wonder what a normal childhood would have been like. And these days, given the choice, I'd much rather grow my food than hunt, gather, fish, or scavenge. As a result, I don't always fit in back home. I can track an animal for miles. But I don't like to do it just for sport. I'm a crack shot. But I'm not a member of the NRA. I know the woods and the fields like the back of my hand. But I prefer using Google Maps.

The one thing that I do not regret is how much where I come from made me love the earth. With every part of my soul, I love the soil, and I love owning plots of it. In that way, I am a typical farmer. It's the farmer's mentality to buy land and hold it, then buy more the second you can, even if it takes the last bit of cash that you have. The term for that is "land-poor." Even if you can't afford to do much with it, you don't let go of that land, no matter what. Ever.

The land is part of me. I love the sounds of the countryside, the smells. The air in the country is lighter and fresher. The food tastes better. The water is cleaner. The sunsets are more colorful. You can see every star in the sky at night. I can't even explain my connection to this land except to say that I need the feel of the dirt under my feet the way I need oxygen and water. Every American has agrarian roots. I don't care how disconnected you might be from the earth in your day-to-day life. Our ancestors grew, hunted, harvested. It's in our bones.

As difficult as my early life was, the land has always been good to me. I wouldn't trade it for anything. What I went through at an early age gave me the grit to grow from a pigtailed little girl in dirty overalls to the founder of a company that's sold more than a billion dollars' worth of fresh produce.

I marvel at how much has happened to me right here on this one piece of land. It was here that my restless spirit was born and that I conjured dreams of far-off places. I spent the majority of my early years planning my escape. And yet when I had the opportunity to leave, I didn't take it. As my company grew, I began to travel on business constantly. I've been to some of the most amazing places. I've worked with some of our country's most powerful people. And yet my soul is rooted here on the same piece of earth where I grew up. I hate it and I love it, and I suspect that I would wither like a harvested plant if I ever left.

Well-meaning advisors have told me that I should hide certain parts of who I am—either to conceal my humble origins or to minimize my current success. When I started my business at age sixteen, most days I wore jeans, work boots, and a baseball cap. People said, "How can she be a businesswoman dressed like that?" Now when I wear heels and a skirt, people say, "How can she be a farmer?"

I'm sharing things in this book that for a long time I never dreamed of sharing with anyone, much less the world. Confronting colleagues with the more complicated truth would have taken time and energy. It was easier for me to let people believe whatever they wanted or needed to believe in order to accept me as someone who belonged at the negotiating table or the cocktail parties.

Over time, though, I've become brave enough to be myself no matter where I'm at and who's in the room. I have a newfound appreciation of where I come from, what I've experienced, and where I am now. My community is filled with those I care deeply for. We don't hear enough from people who come from the humble small towns of America, from people who know what it is to work with their hands from morning until nightfall, and who find ways to thrive without abandoning their roots.

Looking back on last night's gathering, I know I belonged there as much as anyone did. In fact, my hardscrabble background gives me the advantage of perspective. I've done just about every working-class job you can think of. I've been the truck driver. I've been the cashier. I've been the field hand. Today I'm the boss. My story is the story of America, rich and destitute, raw and polished, damned and blessed. And it starts in a poor, tiny village in the middle of the country.

THE GROWING SEASON

Chapter 1

Hunting and Fishing

The clay-rich farmland of southeastern Illinois sits between the New Madrid fault line and the Wabash River Valley. Earthquakes have rattled this land over the centuries, but no one seems to mind. There have never been many buildings over two stories high, and the plants don't object to being shaken around.

When I was a little girl, I felt like part of the earth. I was usually filthy, with dirt under my nails and all over my clothes. In the fall, I jumped in piles of leaves. In the gray of winter, I made ice cream from sweet condensed milk, snow, and sugar—always from the second snowfall, because my father didn't trust the first one. He believed in the old wives' tale that the first snow cleaned the air and was full of toxins. In the spring, I picked flowers and helped the mares through labor.

My favorite season has always been summer. The daytime air smelled like honeysuckle. At night, the fireflies came out in great swarms of flickering light. The first evening they appeared, I ran out into the night and spun my arms, my body gently bumping into the lightning bugs as they flashed on and off. I spun until they blurred.

Dizzy, I collapsed in the field, then stood up to do it again. If I could bottle that feeling—that goodness and magic and hope and lightness—I could cure the world of every ill.

At that age, my greatest wish was for my four older brothers to take me with them when they went on adventures. For what felt like eternity, they didn't let me go along when they went fishing in the pond or the creek, or when they went hunting for deer, rabbits, or quail in the woods near our house. I had to stay behind by myself.

Our farm was isolated, even by southern Illinois standards. The nearest major town, a thirty-minute drive away, is Mount Vernon, with seventeen thousand inhabitants. Orchardville, the unincorporated village about five miles from us, has just twenty-eight houses inside the town limits. Few they may be, but Orchardville residents have contributed a lot to the country. They've fought in every American conflict since the Revolutionary War.

Orchardville's nineteenth-century nickname was "the Big Red Apple." Today in addition to fruit trees there are a few hog and turkey farms, thanks to some new Amish and Mennonite neighbors, and a few large grain bins that hold corn and soybeans, but not a whole lot else except an excellent diner called the Skillet Fork Grill (order the curly fries). What hasn't changed is that anyone you meet would give you the last dollar out of their wallet. They're good people who fiercely love our country and choose to keep to themselves unless they're called upon to help others.

Wayne County has been declining in population for the past hundred years. The median household income is around $45,000 a year. In many parts of the country, you might be poor with that salary. But here, middle-income standards are different, and the bounty of nature is there for the taking. The woods and fields are full of animals to hunt and wild fruit to forage. The frogs, crickets, and coyotes perform free concerts every night.

My father, Harold, was born outside St. Louis in 1929. He was spoiled rotten by his grandmother Sarah, after whom I'm named. In 1934, when he was just five years old and automobiles were still rare in the United States, she bought him an actual truck. Not a toy truck. A Ford. His parents let him quit school when he was in the seventh grade. He couldn't stand being cooped up indoors. Plus, he thought he was smarter than most of his teachers. I think he probably was.

Dad worked as a steelworker and farmer, and then eventually bought into the Dixie Feed franchise, for which he controlled a couple of feed mills. After marrying young, he had thirteen children with his first wife. The marriage was unhappy. She said he philandered; he said she drank too much.

Then he met a woman named Elizabeth, the wife of one of his mill employees. She was beautiful, with dark hair and dark eyes. Everyone said she looked French. Like Harold, she was dissatisfied with the way her life was going. Elizabeth had become pregnant and married at sixteen to escape a terrible home life. Her father had lost his hand in a corn picker and carried a lot of anger, which he took out on his children. And yet that early marriage didn't provide the escape she was looking for. Her young husband drank heavily, just like her father had. After her second child was born, she began to look, again, for a way out. That's when she met Harold.

Ready for a new life, Elizabeth and Harold made plans to run away together. My father was famous for his charisma. He could make you believe almost anything. Harold, Elizabeth believed, would whisk her away into a fanciful new life, full of excitement and adventure. She had every reason to hope that he would take care of her and her two children, and keep their life interesting, too. He was a hard worker with an entrepreneurial spirit. Unfortunately, he was also, as she would come to learn, a hustler and a bit of a con man.

With Elizabeth's two preschool-aged children in tow, the illicit couple left Illinois and moved to Tennessee. As you would think, running away from a large family and starting from scratch in the hills of Tennessee is not a recipe for amassing wealth. So why did my father do it? Simply put, he needed to get out of town. A perfect storm of bad business decisions and personal drama made the decision to leave an easy one.

While no one ever said a word, I knew from an early age, simply because of the company he kept, that my father was some sort of "fixer" for men who didn't want to get their hands dirty. He was someone they trusted with their secrets. He didn't have many friends in Wayne County, where we lived, but he had plenty in St. Louis. Down around the racetrack there, he had a network of associates and a whole secret life far removed from our isolated farming community. To me, his St. Louis associates all seemed either really wealthy or really poor. I watched him glide effortlessly between the two worlds.

Recently I learned the lengths to which my father would go to "fix" things: the day he left behind his former life, my father staged a car crash to make it look like he had died. His car was found smashed at the bottom of a cliff, burned to its shell and covered in rabbit's blood, which resembles a human's. No body was found. His own mother thought he was dead. I've seen photos of her before and after this episode. It looks as though she had aged a hundred years. She died not long after—relatives say the cause was a broken heart, her will to live having left her when she believed her adored son to be dead.

On the run, my parents took refuge in Tennessee with horse-racing buddies of my father's. Back at home, for months my father's thirteen children also believed Harold to be dead, but there was no body, and they didn't have a funeral.

In the coming years, Harold would resurrect himself and pay his original family visits from time to time, sometimes handing the children bags of coins for spending money. But for them there would be a clear before and after to their childhoods: before, when they had two parents and enough food to eat, and after he covered that car with animal blood and pushed it off a cliff, when they were left to fend for themselves.

Harold and Elizabeth began their new life in Tennessee with high hopes, but they had awful luck from the start. They doted on the first child they had together, Lana. While my mother was working in the house, Lana, just two and a half years old, was playing outside when she was run over and killed by a truck driven by a farmhand.

Guilt-stricken, my mother, pregnant at the time with my brother Leonard, took to her bed. By all accounts, on that day she changed forever. The light went out of her eyes. Defeated in Tennessee, my parents left the state once Leonard was born. They returned to Illinois to try to rebuild their lives, but at a distance from where they'd lived before.

The family of three settled first in a country home in Wayne County. A tornado lifted it off them as they cowered in the root cellar. Then they found the Hill, which would be their home for decades to come: eighty acres of rich farmland, with fields spreading away from the farmhouse in all directions. I think my father liked owning that much elevated land. He knew he could grow crops and keep livestock. I also think he liked that from that perch he could see an enemy coming from miles away. Terrified of another tornado, they turned the musty cellar into an emergency shelter, stocking shelves along the sandstone walls with canned goods.

My father was desperate for a girl to replace the one they'd lost, and so my mother had one baby after another, hoping for a daughter. She gave birth to three more boys after Leonard: Harley, John, Ted. At last I was born on July 24, 1976, the hottest day of the year. I was the twenty-first and final child produced by their various marriages. Seeing that her husband's wish for another daughter had finally come true, my mother greeted my birth with the warm, maternal words "I'm done," and immediately had her tubes tied.

My earliest memories aren't of my parents; they're of my brothers. As I was growing up on the farm, there was too much work for playdates or sports teams, for board games or skipping rope. For entertainment, I tagged along watching my brothers work all day, every day, as they learned skills: rewiring electric systems, putting a new engine block into a car, building stairs, mending a fence, constructing a barn, fixing leaks, patching holes. My father taught my brothers how to do everything. I was their eager apprentice, always looking forward to the next task.

Our father worked the boys hard, and it was rare that he gave any of them a compliment. Behind their backs, though, he lavished praise on his boys. I wished my brothers could have heard some of the good things our father said about them to other people. He would brag about how smart Leonard was, how strong Harley was, how hard John worked, how Ted could fix anything. He never told us such things to our face. We still knew, deep down, that we did him proud. We understood that there was no time for niceties or for kind words; we were fighting for survival.

As the youngest child, I became everyone's assistant. I learned by helping—handing them a channel lock while they were under the jacked-up truck or flipping the breaker so they could unscrew an outlet. My brothers taught me how to survive—whether that meant cultivating the earth, caring for livestock, or cutting firewood to stay warm. By the time I was approaching kindergarten, I had my own full schedule of chores, some of which had to be completed before breakfast. Each of us was expected to do the work of a full-fledged adult, no whining or complaining—and certainly no questioning—allowed.

My easiest chore was my least favorite. I dreaded gathering eggs. I didn't like the chickens, especially not the laying hens—always frantic, always shaking, billows of dust flying from their feathers. I hated the smell of the chicken coop, and I had to wander around there in the musty darkness to find the eggs in the hens' nesting boxes. When people think of chickens, they think of decorative little hens in the pretty little houses that you see on Instagram. No. We had a shadowy henhouse full of spiderwebs, mice, and the occasional egg-sucking varmint—a raccoon or possum. The henhouse was a scary place.

One time when I was a little girl, I was with my father on a neighbor's farm to collect hay for the horses. The farm's mean rooster was chasing me around, so I sprayed him with water. This made him furious, and he attacked me, flogging me with his wings and scratching me with his spurs. From that moment on I was terrified of chickens. My experience taking care of the hens did nothing to make me like them more.

Dad scolded me for only wanting to collect the eggs that I could see. He insisted that I reach under the nesting chickens, too.

"She won't bite you," my dad said of our biggest and most productive black-and-white hen. He stood over me in the henhouse and commanded me to get all the eggs, including any that were under her. It was a standoff. I'd already taken all the exposed eggs. He said I had to slide my hand under the hen.

"She *is* going to bite me," I said.

"You get those eggs," my father said. "Slowly slide your hand under her and she'll let you take it."

I reached my little hand under her as slowly as I could. As soon as I approached the egg, the black-and-white hen pecked me hard, drawing blood. I yanked my hand back and bit my lip to hold back tears. I held the back of my hand up to my father. Even then, I never became hysterical. It was a joke around the house, as it would later be around the office, that I stay cool and collected no matter what lunacy surrounds me. I was, however, furious with him.

"I told you so," I said, pointing to the blood running down my arm.

"It's too far from your heart to kill you," he said, grinning.

He was enjoying it. He pushed the chicken out of the way so I could get the eggs. He wouldn't let my age, my fear, or my bleeding hand keep me from doing the task he'd set for me. I would have rather weeded fields every day than deal with the chickens, but it was my job, and he insisted I do it right. I grumbled the whole time, but from that day on I never left another egg behind.

As children, we worked long hours on that farm, and after they did their farm labor my brothers often went out and hunted for our dinner. My brothers will tell you that there were plenty of times when they didn't catch anything in the woods, which meant the livestock ate dinner and the kids did not. I never remember going to bed without eating anything, but sometimes our meals were just a bowl of mush.

But most of the food we did eat was delicious—even the mush. We'd usually have bacon for breakfast, making sure to save the bacon grease for cooking everything else. My mother would make jelly rolls, or a simple pudding from eggs, milk, and vanilla. Sometimes she sent us out to collect goose eggs, which made baked goods taste especially good. The cornmeal mush had little leftover pieces of meat in it, usually salvaged from a boar's head. In the summer we would muddle fresh mint, wild blackberries, and fresh spring water to make delicious drinks. One of our favorite meals was simple white rice and milk.

Given how many mouths my mother had to feed, it's probably no surprise that she made a lot of soups and stews. She also found ways to be creative with whatever we had fresh, and found ways to make it stretch. I loved seeing whatever was on the table and watching my mother figure out what could be made from it. And I loved being sent out to gather ingredients. I also enjoyed processing meat in the smokehouse (after which I'd go to school smelling like smoke) and canning.

My father usually prepared Sunday dinner, or at least started it while the rest of us were at church. He didn't attend services with us, but we didn't mind, because we always came home to something delicious-smelling cooking in the kitchen.

Once, in the middle of the night, my father and I were both awake. I couldn't sleep because of a throbbing finger that I'd smashed earlier that day between a chunk of firewood and the stove I was throwing it into. Dad didn't sleep a lot—I think probably because he was so addicted to cigarettes that he would wake up and want to smoke. When I couldn't take the pain any longer, I found him in the kitchen and showed him my smashed pinky finger. He pulled out his pocketknife and told me to place my hand on the kitchen table as if he was going to cut the pinky off. He took out his lighter and began to heat the blade.

"No, Dad!" I shouted. "It's okay, really! I'm fine! I promise!" I was certain he was going to amputate my finger.

"Put your finger on the table," he repeated.

I did what he said, grimaced, and closed my eyes to wait for the sawing to begin. Instead I felt the blade on my nail where the throbbing was the worst. I decided to peek. He carefully twisted the tip into my nail until blood bubbled up from the puncture. The throbbing stopped immediately.

Then, rather than shooing me back to bed as I expected, he said, "Sis, do you want me to teach you how to make biscuits?"

I said yes. Together, at two in the morning, we made biscuits. We did that four or five times that year, always in the middle of the night. It was some of the most special time I've ever spent with anyone. And it's a recipe I've never forgotten.

During the winter, our house barely kept out the cold. We'd huddle for warmth around the woodstove in the living room. Even then, you could see your breath indoors, and the windowpanes were caked with frost. We'd bring in the clothes from the line—jeans that had frozen solid as wooden planks—and we would hang them on clotheslines strung from wall to wall. You'd have to bob and weave through the wet clothes to get from one end of the room to the other.

One time, my brother Ted and I smelled burning flesh. We screamed at my brother Harley to step away from the stove. Cold and naked after a bath, with just a towel in front of him, he'd backed up into the stove and not noticed because his skin was so numb. To us back then, it was just another hilarious Frey kids story: the time our brother literally caught his ass on fire.

For many years I didn't realize quite how poor we were. Occasionally, though, I would catch a glimpse of an alternative life. Once or twice we found ourselves visiting modern homes near St. Louis. It was there I noticed a magical device on the wall that could adjust the temperature up or down. I learned the name for this wizardry: a thermostat. As a little girl, I had to carry in wood every morning and every night. Keeping the house warm was my most important job.

After that St. Louis visit, I kept wondering, *Why can't we just sell a horse and buy one of those little magic boxes so that we can be warm too?*

As much as I loved our farm and my family, though, I never felt that I quite fit in on the Hill. I felt like I was made for adventure and glory that were impossible out there in the middle of nowhere. As I grew older, I thought someone in my family had made a mistake and confused the Big Red Apple, Orchardville, with the Big Apple of New York City, where I surely belonged.

My father said we lived in "God's country," and that the Hill was where we should be. We needed to keep to ourselves in this rural paradise, he told us, because we were special. He and our mother taught us to have good manners so that the world would know we weren't like the other kids, the ones who cussed or talked while they ate. No, we were different, our parents insisted. As a marker of our specialness, we needed to call everyone sir and ma'am and to put our napkins in our laps.

Later in life, I would learn another reason why my father always told me things like "Stay away from southern Illinois boys—they aren't good enough for you." The real reason for this isolationism was that he had eighteen biological children that he acknowledged, and he feared we might someday end up accidentally dating someone we were related to. When he died, he had at least fifty-two grand-children and great-grandchildren—many of them around my age or older than me.

My father benefited in many ways from keeping us sequestered on the Hill. There he had his own secluded kingdom—and his children were a captive workforce. It took money we didn't have to put gas in a vehicle and go anywhere, so we just stayed put. My brothers joked that if they ever missed the school bus, they would chase it down, because it was the only way to get off the Hill. Brainwashing us into believing we were special was Dad's way of offsetting whatever insecurities we might have had based on how humbly we were being raised.

My brothers thought I had it easy. Compared to them, I didn't have to do as much backbreaking physical labor. But I envied them right back. They had so much more freedom than I did, because they could do everything. With their shirts off in the summer, they hopped on tractors and took off. Grabbing a rifle and a sack, they went into the woods by themselves and came back with dinner. I often wished I were a boy, too, though in retrospect, most of my lack of opportunity there had nothing to do with being a girl; it was simply a function of being the youngest.

When I was four, my brothers taught me to swim. Well, I learned to swim. It was a hot day, the chores were finished, and the boys ran to go swimming in the pond. I chased after them with great enthusiasm. From in the water, Harley said in a sweet, kind, convincing voice, "Come on, Sis, jump! I'll catch you!"

I should have known better, because he was my most mischievous brother. With a glint in his eye, he held out his arms. I ran down the dock as fast as I could, jumped high into the air, and . . . Harley didn't catch me. He let me crash alone into the pond. Down, down, I went. Then I kicked my way up. By the time I reached the surface, I was swimming. Spitting mad, but swimming. From that day on, I swam all summer.

For the first five years of my life, each September when the first day of school came, I had to watch my brothers in a line, one by one, like ducks, getting on the big school bus. I was too young to go, and it made me sad. I had to spend the whole day by myself or with my parents, waiting for the bus to bring my brothers home to me.

I made my own fun. There were vehicles everywhere with the keys in the ignition. Starting when I was four or five, whenever my parents took the truck into town and left me alone at the farm, I'd hop into their old two-door Mercury Grand Marquis. I would hot-lap around the farm, driving in circles, looking through the little half-moon shape between the steering wheel and the dash, because I couldn't see any higher. I knew I was burning precious gas, so I'd watch the gas gauge and quit as soon as I saw the needle move toward the E.

Or, on foot, I would roam the farm alone for hours, spinning out elaborate fantasies. I pretended to be a soldier, a veterinarian, a

Viking, or the president of the United States. I had long conversations with myself, imagining another person was there listening to me. I loved to watch the news, and I would imitate the way leaders talked and carried themselves.

One day when the boys were off at school and my parents were working, I strapped my BB gun to my back and headed out onto the farm. Guns were a necessary tool growing up. It wasn't unusual to have a gun leaning against our kitchen table. We were taught to respect guns and understood the consequences of not doing so. We handled them at all times as if they were loaded even if we knew they weren't. We never picked up a gun unless we had the full intention of using it. Along with a healthy sense of fear of firearms, I was given my first BB gun about the time I was old enough to lift it.

On that day, I imagined that my BB gun was an old rifle. I was hunting game in the mountainous desert. In my mind, the free-range chickens pecking in the dust were bison, any one of which would feed my whole village. It was my job to provide. The brave and noble hunter stalked her prey. I hid behind trees and darted behind rocks. I spied the mightiest beast of them all. Silently I drew my weapon. I looked down the gun, judging the distance. My rational mind thought: *It's too far. There's no way I'll hit her. The BB is going to drop before it ever gets anywhere close, so it's safe to aim right at it.*

I allowed my imagination to take back over while I took my time aiming. Filled with the adrenaline of the big-game hunter, yet steady and confident, I squeezed the trigger.

Bam.

Shot straight through the head, our great big black-and-white speckled hen keeled over and flopped violently.

I panicked. *What the hell! I didn't mean to actually shoot the chicken!* That was a really good chicken, a fat laying hen that gave us several eggs each week. *I'm going to be in so much trouble!* This was the very chicken that had pecked me and drawn blood, so I thought my father might think I'd killed it on purpose.

I swiveled my head around.

Should I go tell my mother or father? I wondered for a split second.

No, I thought. *Either one would kill me.* Then came the clear thought: *I have to hide the body.*

Terrified that I would have to wring its neck to put it out of its misery, I approached the hen warily. My heart was pounding. I knew the farm dogs could come running any second to see what was happening. My parents would be right behind them. There would be a scene. Finally the hen stopped flopping.

I didn't want to touch her at all, but I closed my eyes and wrapped my little hands around the firm, waxy legs. The gnarly claws brushed against my body as I hefted the corpse. I was so little and the chicken's body was so fat and heavy.

Now the clock was ticking. I had to hide the body before anyone saw what I had done. I could have redeemed the murder by giving us all dinner that night, but no—my father would have made me chop off the chicken's head and pluck its feathers. I shuddered at the thought.

I took off running with the evidence. Finally, about a quarter of a mile down the back road where we picked five-gallon buckets' worth of wild blackberries for preserves and pies, I reached a ravine. Near what we called the Bottoms, the swampy area that filled each spring with rainwater and flooded the roads, I flung the chicken into the tall weeds, sure that the coyotes would find it there before my parents did. I went home and told no one what I'd done. Nobody suspected me. Small livestock went missing all of the time. Everyone assumed a raccoon had gotten the hen. I kept the secret for more than twenty years.

In the house where I grew up, everyone had secrets. Our biggest shared secret, one we all worked hard to keep from everyone in the county, especially the authorities, was how brutally poor we were. Our house didn't look terrible from the road. It was just a big old white farmhouse with a circular driveway. There was a large, shaded front porch with sturdy support posts. In the back there was a screened-in summer porch. Coming off it were poured-concrete steps. I sat on those steps for hours at a time, holding court for the animals.

To visitors, I believed it didn't look like we were quite as badly off as we were. The new aluminum siding made it resemble a farmhouse like any other, with four bedrooms and two chimneys. But up close, you could see that the house was crumbling, the window frames so rotted that there were big holes underneath the sills. The porch's boards were warped.

The house's old plaster walls breathed. The floors were a combination of wood and worn-down carpet the color of dirt. There was no fiber left. They had to be swept with a broom. There was no central heat. There were bedrooms, but in the winter, we kids slept in the living room, where the large woodstove was. We hung old horse blankets in the doorways to keep the heat concentrated, and gave up on much of the rest of the house until spring.

When I was five, my family finally installed indoor plumbing. Before that, there was an outhouse. Every drop of water we used for that or that we drank, or gave to the animals, or used to wash, had to be hauled up by one of us from the spring-fed well or the pond. Even once the indoor plumbing was installed, it was broken half the time, and then we had to go to the well to get water to flush the toilet or to the pond to get water for the livestock. We either took five-gallon buckets two at a time or backed the truck up to the pond and filled up fifty-gallon drums.

Living this way was all I knew, and to the extent I thought about it at all when I was very young, I considered our house cozy. I loved growing up close to my big family. I never wanted to be alone. I felt sorry for kids who didn't have a lot of siblings. My brothers were my best friends.

Whenever people came in from the outside, though, I sensed we weren't growing up like other children. One day when we were little, Ted and I were running the chainsaw and stacking wood in the front yard when a salesman came up. He asked if our parents were home and we said no. He said we shouldn't be using a chainsaw without them there. We told him we did it all the time. The man hung around and waited to scold our parents when they came home.

"Let's just get this done, Sis," Ted told me. "He'll leave eventually. They all do."

Ted was right. After a while the man seemed to grow tired of waiting and left.

When I wasn't carrying water, I was carrying wood for the small kitchen stove or the big living room one. Carrying buckets of water and wood for the house was mind-numbing work, but I couldn't complain, because my brothers, among other things, butchered meat, cleaned stalls, mixed feed, and hauled water for the animals.

At one point we had as many as sixty horses and one or two of nearly everything else. Every animal was free-range. Unless a horse was getting ready to foal, our animals were never penned up. The large horse pasture had a fence around it, and the chickens had a house for nesting at night, but otherwise every creature on our farm roamed free—the ducks, geese, sheep, and goats. There were always lots of dogs, and usually at least one litter of puppies. The only animals we never had were cats. My father didn't like cats, especially because they killed rabbits, which he liked having around for food. He told me we couldn't have cats because I was allergic to them, which I later found out was not true—he'd just made that up.

I didn't have many friends outside the farm, so I hung out with the animals. We had two goats, Billy Jack and Shirley. Shirley was a white Swiss Alpine goat, and I had to milk her. If my parents weren't home, I'd lead her into the kitchen and up on top of the table so that I could milk her from the comfort of a chair and wouldn't have to lean over. Otherwise I'd milk her on the back porch. If one of my brothers ran out of the house carrying a sandwich, Shirley would follow him through the yard and onto the school bus trying to get the food from him. Cathi, our school bus driver, would laugh and curse at the goat while pushing her back out the door.

It was difficult having to slaughter animals we'd come to care about. Usually Dad would do it, or friends of his would come over to take care of it and then leave with some of the meat as payment for their services. It was normal to come home and see a hog head sitting on the kitchen table. My father would make head cheese from meat he pulled off the skull. We sometimes ate brains in our scrambled eggs, though they tasted like mushrooms and I wasn't a fan.

I never could have eaten Shirley. Happily, she was a milk goat, so she was safe. Baa-Baa, the ram I bottle-fed and who thought I was his mother, was fortunately a pet, not there to eat. The boys, especially Harley, thought it was the most fun game to torment me and make me scream so that the ram would come running to protect me. That ram was my guardian, one of the most highly intelligent animals that I've ever cared for. He would never smash into my brother if he was holding me, but as soon as the coast was clear the ram would go after him. Who needed guard dogs when you had Baa-Baa the ram? Once a tall, dressed-up Mennonite came to leave religious literature. Alarmed by the stranger's presence, Baa-Baa chased after him in a fury out of our yard and down our long driveway. We giggled as the man tried to hang on to his hat.

I loved Baa-Baa. We rarely sheared him, so his fur was long and matted. We could hold on to it when we rode him around the farm, which we did often. It felt like sitting on a mattress. One day when I was five, Baa-Baa went missing. It broke my heart. Two days went by and no Baa-Baa. I was suspicious of my father and began to think the worst had happened, but he, too, seemed genuinely concerned. Another suspect was Harley. He was capable of all manner of mischief. Hiding my favorite pet was within his capabilities. But it was unlikely that even he could hide a 250-pound ram from me for very long.

I was sitting under a shady tree, missing Baa-Baa, when Harley crept up behind me and gave a great werewolf howl. I shrieked. Then I started yelling at Harley about how he shouldn't sneak up on people like that.

"Shut up!" Harley said, shushing me. "I hear something."

I was quiet for a second and then, off in the distance, we heard "Baaaaaaa!"

"That's Baa-Baa!" I yelled.

We looked across the field and saw our ram in the distance, running through a field of wild prairie grass, jumping like a deer. When he reached us, we saw there was oil all over his neck and sides from sleeping around the oil pumps. It seemed that he must have followed the pumper man off the farm, or been taken. It looked like he'd had a rope around his neck, though he may have just gotten his head caught in the sucker rods around the pumps.

Whooping and cheering, we brought him through the living room into the kitchen to show our parents. My mom was shocked to see Baa-Baa marching through the house, but I think she understood that this was a moment of true joy, so she didn't yell at us. I felt grateful for Harley's jerkiness. If Harley hadn't been a werewolf that day, I wonder if Baa-Baa would ever have found his way home.

Finally, the fall after I turned five, my brothers let me tag along when they went hunting. Maybe they sensed that I'd taken down the mighty bison-chicken. Maybe my father was sick of hearing me complain about not getting to go with them. I didn't care why. My day had come, and I was ecstatic. *If we see a rabbit, I'll kill it,* I vowed to myself. *I'll show everyone that I'm not so little. They'll never leave me behind for a hunt again.*

My father came along with us. He handed me his .22 and walked behind as I quietly prowled through the brush. Suddenly our beagles started barking and running around. They'd found a rabbit. *This is my rabbit!* I decided.

My heart pounded as I raised my weapon. My father leaned down and helped me hold and aim the gun. He made sure the stock was tight against my shoulder. Adrenaline pumped through my small body. This was my chance to prove that I was capable. If I succeeded, I would never be doubted again. I'd show them all that I was as good as if not better than the boys—and the adults, too. I would finally prove my greatness. I squeezed the trigger. A moment later, my brother Leonard reached into the brush and pulled out . . . a dead rabbit!

"You got it!" he shouted.

"Wow!" my other brothers chimed in. "You got the rabbit! Way to go!"

"Of course she killed the rabbit," my father said. "She's a born hunter."

Bursting with pride, I handed my father back his gun, then ran and grabbed my rabbit by its back legs. I held it high into the sky like a trophy.

Deep down in my heart, I thought, *I'm the queen of hunting. This is how you do it, everyone. Follow me from now on and you'll never go hungry. I'll take care of us all.*

W hen I went fishing for the first time the following April, the scene was almost identical. I went with my brothers and father to a tiny pond. I was handed a pole and plunked down on the bank.

Moments later, the line tugged, and then tugged harder.

"Somebody help me!" I screamed.

They all smiled, but nobody helped me reel in this fish—and it felt like I had a whale at the end of my line. *How incredible to find a fish so big and strong in such a little pond!* I thought. I started to reel it in, shouting, "My line's going to break!"

Still no one came to my rescue.

I began to worry that I'd be pulled into the water and down under the surface. So much was at stake: my reputation as my brothers' equal, my pride. I also didn't want to drown trying to get this giant fish ashore.

I twisted the reel, and I was pulled into the water up to my waist. But I stayed on my feet, standing in the pond. Finally I was able to pull the line in and to wrestle the fish onto the shore. It was a massive channel catfish—what we used to call "all mouth and no brains." A beast.

Again I puffed with pride. I was convinced that everyone needed me. I told my brothers I was sorry they would never be nearly as good a hunter and fisher, but that they were welcome to come along with me. I would never again have to beg to be taken along. I was their equal. They would be the ones tagging along from here on out.

It wasn't until I became a teenager that my brothers confessed they'd staged both episodes at our father's direction. They'd killed the rabbit and put it in the brush. The catfish they'd caught in the river and attached to my hook before handing me the pole. I was too young to know then that it was a river fish and not a pond fish.

For my own good, my father and brothers insisted that I, as the only girl, learn how to keep up. They knew that what I lacked in physical strength could be compensated for in confidence. When I was just a little girl, they nicknamed me "Queen Bee." They pushed me again and again to learn what I would need to know to be independent, to be strong. And they refused to accept excuses.

Their strategy worked—and then some. At the age of five, I was convinced that I was capable of feeding my family, which made me feel powerful, brave, and destined for a life of greatness. And yet, if anyone had looked my way, they would have seen nothing more than a scrawny, gritty little country girl, utterly unremarkable save for her flashing green eyes.

Chapter 2

Growing Wild

The few southern Illinois girls I knew when I was young envisioned their future selves as happy homemakers. Each one liked to decorate and bake, dreamed of her wedding day and the boy she would marry. For me, all of that sounded like a fate worse than death. I didn't want to do housework, and I *really* did not want to be responsible for cooking or cleaning or taking care of babies. My mother, to her credit, didn't even attempt to make me. My whole childhood, I washed the dinner dishes just once. My mother took a picture, it was such a special occasion.

Angela, my mother's oldest girl from her first marriage, had helped take care of the babies, and she did housework in addition to doing outside chores. Angela was out of the house by the time I came along. I didn't remember meeting her until I was nineteen. I learned that, being the oldest, she'd shouldered untold responsibility as a young woman. She worked as hard as, if not harder than, the boys.

I also realized why my mother was so disappointed that I didn't care more about my appearance. Angela was gorgeous. She'd somehow managed to do everything she did around the house while working to keep up her appearance. For years my mother tried to lay out girly clothes for me to wear, but I was stubborn and wanted to choose my own clothes. At some point she gave up on trying to reason with me. It helped that I was the youngest, so there were no babies to look after—just the pressure to feed seven people three meals a day on almost no money.

Not only wasn't I domestically inclined; I wasn't domesticated, period. My mother sometimes tried to brush my hair in the morning. It would hurt because I had very fine hair that would tangle easily. I'd only let my father do it, because he'd make it fun. He'd get a tangle out and throw it on the floor and shout, "Sis, stomp the rat!"

I was wild, like a weed you can't kill. I craved raw freedom and despised rules. I accepted my father's authority but nobody else's. While my mother would occasionally protect one of the boys from our father's wrath, she never interfered with the way he raised me. My father loomed so much larger than my mother did that I can think of few childhood moments that I shared with her. I know she was there the whole time, but in my memory she is always in the background, hanging up the wash or cooking. My father was in the foreground, every word he said as significant and memorable as gospel. He taught me to believe I was the best and didn't need any teachers or friends—just my brothers, who served both roles.

My older brothers and I were all born exactly two years apart on either a twenty-fourth or twenty-seventh of the month. In chronological order, from oldest to youngest, they are Leonard, Harley, John, and Ted.

Leonard was the smart one—our resident researcher and intellectual. He worked hard and was always on the honors list. He served as a role model of first-child studiousness—not that we all particularly followed in his bookish footsteps.

Harley was the strongest. He was a tough guy, and the only one among us to get in trouble at school. The rest of us turned the other cheek when we were teased, but he never would. In that way, he was like most of the people from our community. A history of Orchardville reads: "Orchardville has always been known for having pretty girls and boys who wouldn't back down from a good fist fight."

In our house it was different. My father had a rule—you only fight for two things, your life or money.

One day Harley broke my father's rule. A kid had been teasing him about his hair. We'd nicknamed Harley "Clark Gable," because he spent so much time combing his hair. Finally this kid mocked Harley's hair one too many times. Harley met him in the parking lot to settle things, damaging both a car and the other boy's head in the fight that ensued. Harley was suspended. We thought our father would be furious, but when he arrived at the high school to pick Harley up, he looked him over and, noticing an absence of serious bruises, said, "You don't look like a loser."

"That's because I didn't lose," Harley said.

"If you didn't lose, where's the money?" our dad said.

Everyone was still alive, my father figured, so surely cash could be the only motivator for this kind of scrape. For some reason, my dad let it slide. I've often wondered if that was partly because Harley's storminess served a greater purpose: it was a sign to everyone at that school not to mess with the Freys—never mind that the other boys, mild-mannered as they were, wouldn't have hurt a fly. Harley fought everyone's battles for them.

That's not to say Harley went easy on us. He teased and taunted me and our brothers incessantly, calling us names and pranking us. At the same time, deep down I knew that he had the softest heart. I suspected that he was acting out because he had to do a lot of the worst jobs around the farm.

You'd especially see his soft side when he was dealing with the animals. When he was fourteen, one of our farm ducks hatched. Because the first living thing it saw was Harley, it became convinced that he was its mother. That duckling followed him everywhere and Harley took care of it as if he really was the duck's adoring parent—until John ran it over with the tractor. Poor Harley—he brushed off the loss, but we knew he was distraught. He was probably the most sensitive of us all, but he covered it up the best.

Harley fretted over me as if I were a duckling, too. He was always worried something bad would happen and I'd get stuck in Wayne County forever or that I'd turn wild. Once he left the Hill for work in Chicago, he would come home and give my father money. The boys all gave our father most of what they earned off the Hill. But Harley would always slip me some, too. It was never a loan. He would hand me cash for food or gas, no thanks required.

Harley's antagonism toughened us up. And he made the rest of us closer to one another. He and Ted, the youngest of the four, butted heads the most. Ted was like a little bull and rarely backed down. When it came to his physique, Harley was proud, to say the least. One Sunday afternoon he raised his shirt to display his incredibly muscular abs and taunted Ted with his manliness: "Hit me as hard as you can!"

Looking up at his older brother and shaking the moppy blond hair out of his face, Ted made a fist and reared back. Then he sucker-punched Harley in the nose. Harley screamed, horrified that he had almost been knocked out by his youngest brother.

Our father, sitting nearby at the kitchen table, just smirked. Without looking up from his racing form, he said dryly, "You told him to hit you. And you didn't say where."

As a rule, no one could take on Harley alone. Once we figured that out, Ted, John, Leonard, and I ganged up on him. One day we used our belts to tie him up to the metal frame of the pullout couch in the living room. Then we tortured him long enough to make him genuinely afraid of us.

"Don't ever pick on us again," we said, "because we know that no one person can take you down, but if the four of us get together, we can." It had an effect. Harley chilled out quite a lot and never picked on any of us much after that. That's when I learned the value of teamwork.

John, had he been born later, surely would have been diagnosed as hyperactive. In his frenzy, he could fix anything, and he was a whiz with computers. He was also so kind and had such a big heart that we teased him about being a saint and nicknamed him John the Baptist. He hates to see anyone suffer, even people who definitely deserve to. Children love John because he glows with a fundamental goodness.

Ted, also known as "Teddy Bear," was two years older than me, and I spent most of my early childhood at his side. Ted has always been a solid guy—thoughtful, kind, considerate. He was responsible, too—never missed a day of school. He won a Presidential Physical Fitness Award in high school, though you wouldn't guess it if you saw him now. He jokes, "I might look like a water buffalo, but I can run like a gazelle."

Together my brothers got into countless scrapes. One time they even blew up one of our barns. It started innocently enough. We had several hound dogs on the farm; in the summer, they would get loaded with ticks. One day my brothers were in the barn pulling ticks off the hounds and throwing them into a steel Folgers coffee can. Soon there were so many ticks in the can that they were starting to crawl out.

One of my brothers came up with a solution: pouring a little gas in the can. But the ticks just swam around in the gas and kept crawling up the sides, trying to escape. Harley, of course, decided to take it to the next level: "Let's light 'em on fire."

As the four little boys looked into this can, watching the ticks, Harley dropped in a lit match. A fireball blew up past their eyebrows, all the way to the hayloft. The dried-up corn stalks immediately caught on fire. The boys leaned back in wide-eyed astonishment as the flames spread throughout the loft.

I was taking a nap in the house when I heard the fire truck zoom into our yard. The whole barn was ablaze. My brother Leonard charged back into the barn to rescue our stallion.

I ran outside to find my mother talking to the fire chief, who had arrived in no time. He said to her, "Mrs. Frey, does Harold have any explosives in the barn?" Many farmers keep TNT around for demolition purposes, and my father was no exception.

Before she was able to answer, the barn exploded. Leonard and the stallion made it out just in time.

We were always experiencing near misses like that. Ted saved my life once when I was nine. It was springtime and the creek had risen with the heavy rains. The water was freezing, but we were too excited to wait for warmer weather. Patty Creek looked better than a raging water ride at a theme park. We could float down the stream on our backs for miles, then trudge home along the banks. One time a heavy tree branch trapped me in such a way that the water was rushing over my face. I was pinned under the limb and couldn't break free. I was drowning. Just as everything began to go dark Ted pulled me up and lifted off the log. Had I been alone, I would have drowned for sure. I know the boys, who did more challenging work and took more risks than I did, saved one another's lives a hundred times over.

Danger lurked everywhere. It was no surprise we were always covered in scratches and bruises. Even the fish could hurt you. Once my brothers and I were swimming around in the lake with the turtles and catfish. The boys hung around by the banks trying to "noodle" fish—that meant that you'd feel for fish underwater around the rocks and then grab them out of the water by their gills and mouths. Harley yelled that he'd caught one. Then he screamed and pulled his hand out of the water with blood running down his arm. He'd noodled a catfish, but then the catfish had started to spin. The skin of Harley's hand had come off on the fish's sharp little teeth.

When the work was done and the weather was bad, we did sometimes get to watch TV just like other kids. We had one television station growing up, ABC, channel 13. We'd watch it on our tiny little black-and-white TV. Reception wasn't good, so whenever we watched, one of us would have to go outside and hold the antenna in a certain position. From inside we'd yell, "Turn it to the right! Turn it to the left!" When the snow finally gave way to a clear picture we'd yell, "Stop! Stay right there!" The person on antenna duty couldn't watch TV, but we would take turns.

We loved baseball. Even though we lived in southern Illinois and most of the people around there are Cardinals fans, channel 13 aired only Cubs games, so we became Cubs fans by default. When we played baseball in the backyard, for the longest time I refused to walk or strike out. I was so spoiled by my brothers that they'd go along with it and just let me stand there until I got good at hitting. The only position I never played was pitcher, because my brothers were so much bigger than I was. They worried that a line drive might kill me.

I had a crush on Ryne Sandberg and liked Mark Grace, but my favorite player of all was Andre Dawson. As a little girl, I might not have resembled the six-foot-three Awesome Dawson in any way, but in my heart he and I had something important in common. He was the first player to be named MVP while on a last-place team. People might have doubted that anyone from my family could be destined for fame, fortune, and Hall of Fame induction, but I knew I would prove them wrong. The only question remaining was how I would manifest my greatness.

One night my father gestured to Geraldine Ferraro on the TV and said, "See, Sis? Girls can be anything they want to be."

I was bewildered by that comment. *Why would you even say that?* I thought. It would be like remarking that the sky was blue. Of course women did incredible things. Why was it important to point that out? Clearly this was supposed to be another of my father's lessons, but it had an effect opposite from what he'd intended.

It wasn't until that moment that I realized that off the Hill, my kingdom, things were different. Before that, I believed I could be anything I wanted to be. My imagination let me step into any role— great hunter, leader of the free world, warrior, master of my own universe. I didn't even consider my gender. I had been conjuring my future without restraint. At five, I already considered myself a powerful individual. On the Hill, I was treated like royalty by the animals, like a worthy deputy by my father, and as an equal by my brothers. I was every bit as powerful as a boy, if not more so.

So when my father pointed out the female vice presidential candidate, my imagination was met with a reality check for the first time. Now, watching the news, it dawned on me that the people who wielded real power were mostly men. I went to bed thinking I didn't want to watch TV anymore.

As I rode shotgun in the family pickup one afternoon with my dad, suddenly he hit the brakes. I went into the dash. (This was in the days before the mandatory seatbelt law; even when it passed, my family took it as more of a suggestion.)

In the middle of the gravel road was a snapping turtle the size of a trashcan lid. I stared at the enormous creature in disbelief. It was the biggest turtle I'd ever seen. I knew my brothers wouldn't even believe it. My father pulled the truck around in front of it so that it was near the tailgate.

I'd seen plenty of snapping turtles in the area. Supposedly you could eat them, but as a rule we stayed far away from them. They were my biggest fear when swimming in the pond. We knew they could take off a finger or toe if you came too close. I was about seven and small, so this one could have taken off my whole hand.

"Get out and put that turtle in the truck," my father said, his voice as casual as if he were asking me to bring him a cup of coffee.

By this point in my childhood, my father was not as strong as he'd once been. He was still tall, dark, and handsome, with his olive skin and his beautiful green eyes. But now his hair was thinning on top and he combed it over. He had a bit of a belly. My dad was an older dad, and much older than my mother. But I thought that made him distinguished. I knew he'd aged quicker because of the hard life he'd had. Maybe the reason I'm not judgmental of people today is that I spent so much of my early life trying to look for the good in my father.

There was so much I loved about him. I was fascinated by what went on inside his mind. I knew it wasn't good all of the time. He was a complex person. I watched him do deals that I knew were shady, and I also witnessed incredible acts of kindness. He was an interesting man in so many ways: he had only a seventh-grade education but read racing forms, books, newspapers, everything he could get his hands on, all the time.

He read the whole encyclopedia and encouraged me to do the same. When I was in the third or fourth grade, our school board donated a set of encyclopedias to our little country school to be given to a deserving student. Mr. Brower, who taught all the Frey kids in fifth and sixth grade at Orchardville, advocated for the Frey family. Because there were so many of us, he reasoned, they'd get the most use at our place. I'm so grateful to Mr. Brower. Like my father, I read all those books cover to cover. They were navy blue, brand-new, and the most beautiful books I'd ever seen. I even remember the way they smelled. That first month they were in our home, I probably smelled them as much as I read them.

He would speak deeply on some topics, but he had many secrets. He was a contradiction. You'd hear glowing things and terrible things about him—sometimes from the same people.

For my father, it wasn't an option for any of us not to go to school. Education was important to him. He had two primary pieces of advice that played on repeat: Go to college. Don't get married young. His hands were always dirty, but he had the most beautiful handwriting you ever saw. He had a soft spot in his heart for people who didn't have much, especially if they were polite kids or old people. In many ways, he was kinder to strangers and animals than to his own family. He'd feed the horses before his kids, and some said he loved them more, too.

I was Dad's acolyte; I was spoiled with his love and attention. He had particular rules. Some were trivial. For instance, he looked down on women who wore makeup, which he called "war paint." More unusual, he never wanted me to write anything down. I had to memorize everything from numbers to instructions. He was so paranoid that a piece of paper was going to bear witness against him one day that he avoided paper altogether. I had to learn his sayings—Harold Frey's rules of life—by heart.

"Never write a love letter because someday when you run for president, they'll pull it out and embarrass you."

"Don't ever sign your name to anything."

"Don't let anybody know how smart you are."

Decades later, I still hear those rules in my head all the time.

He was trying to teach me the same lessons that helped him get by in life, and I followed him without hesitation. My father was the only person from whom I gladly took orders. As he became older and weaker, he sat at the kitchen table in what he called his stall. From earliest childhood, I had an adjoining stall—the chair closest to him. He had a magnificent view of the farm from where he sat and could monitor all of the action without ever getting up from his chair. It was at that table that I would receive my daily briefings about what needed to be done. Then I would be dispatched outside to go relay the information to my brothers.

From as long ago as any of us can remember, my brothers were used to me speaking for my father, being his voice. I channeled him so often, I began to think like him, too. It became hard to know where his will ended and mine began. He never yelled. His voice deepened when he was serious. When he spoke in that tone, it was hard not to listen. You knew there was no talking back to it. You didn't argue with that deep, confident voice. I'd never tried to before, in any case.

But this turtle thing? Surely, he was joking.

I laughed.

"I said get out and put it in the truck." He wanted to take it home and have my brothers kill it and clean it for our mother to cook. They say turtles provide seven different kinds of meat depending on the part of the animal. I did not want to eat any of them. I wanted nothing to do with this monster, dead or alive.

"You want it?" I told my father. "*You* get out and put it in the truck."

I never said no to him, but he was sending me on a suicide mission. Snapping turtles bit sticks in half. Scary as my father could be when he was angry, I'd rather take my punishment from him than from a snapping turtle.

The tension inside the truck grew thick.

"I want you to go out there *right now*," he said, "and put that turtle in the truck."

Tears, I thought in a panic. *I need tears.*

Stonewalling was not working, so I tried another tactic, one I almost never used: I threw a girly fit. I huffed and puffed, insisting I was too demure to ever confront such a dangerous creature. "Daddy," I whined, "it will bite me and it won't let go!"

When I ran out of steam, he said, "Now that you're done, go on out there and put that turtle in the truck."

This was a real showdown. I had challenged my father's authority. As his deputy, I knew this was extremely dangerous. Discipline was my father's forte. He knew that he didn't have to lift a finger to inflict pain when it came to me, but I'd witnessed the beatings that resulted when my brothers had tried standing up to him. He kept staring me down, though, and I realized that it was a test—a test of how strong and how brave I was. My father wanted me to be fearless, to face a mean, hissing, violent animal head-on. I knew I couldn't play the girl card now. The message was clear: either you're a girly girl and you have to do housework or you have to pick up the turtle. I weighed the thought of doing dishes against the threat posed by this terrifying animal.

I got out of the truck, and my father did, too. He stood there and watched as, angry and fearful, I approached the snapper. It was an ugly, muddy brown, with sharp contours on its shell and a leathery, hooked snout. As I approached, it hissed, its mouth open wide enough to fit a baseball inside. I gave my father one last fleeting glance. His expression was serious. In that moment I might have gotten out of it. There was, I could see, concern on his face. Once he was out of the truck, he could tell that he'd underestimated that turtle's size. He knew now that it was truly dangerous. I thought about pushing back again. But the mission was already under way. I was doing it. The turtle was eyeing the tall weeds at the side of the road. I only had seconds to make my move.

And so I moved. Fast. I was Sarah Frey, Almighty Killer of Chicken, Rabbit, and Fish! I could do this. I gathered up every ounce of courage. In one swift motion I grabbed the turtle by its thick, scaly tail with both hands. Then, with closed eyes, I hoisted the hissing thing off the ground, swung it over my head like a lasso, and hurled it toward the pickup. I didn't open my eyes until I heard the thud of the turtle landing in the bed of the truck.

My eyes popped out in disbelief. To this day, I don't know how I managed to heave that giant snapping turtle. No way did I have the strength to even lift it. It was pure, heart-pounding adrenaline, inspired by fear. Fear can be one of the best motivators. It's worked for me my whole life, ever since. Fear is an incredible incentive—fear of not having money to buy food, fear of being stuck, fear of cruelty. Fear is natural and normal. How do you take that fear and turn it into a tool in the war chest? How do you envision success while letting yourself be afraid? Of course that turtle was scary. Touching it was one of the worst moments of my life—and then one of the best.

High from the rush of my triumph, I climbed back into the truck. For the rest of the ride, I was careful to direct my gaze out the side window, so my father could not see the proud look on my face. I didn't want to give him the satisfaction of realizing that his nasty plan had worked. Small as I was, I'd trapped our dinner. I don't know that in my whole life I've ever felt prouder of myself. I could do anything at all. I was unstoppable. I was free of fear.

Frankly, had I known about beer at that age, I might have demanded one. Ever since, every time I've faced a new challenge, I've attempted to replicate that moment. I've never felt quite as proud. You're always chasing that first high. For me, that was it.

Chapter 3

Betting the Farm

We always had horses for racing and riding, and we boarded other people's horses, too. But when I was six, my father acquired a truly magnificent racehorse. The stallion's name was Singing Unimack. He was jet black with just a few white hairs on his face. My brothers and I gathered around his stall to marvel at him: a beast so world-class elegant that we could hardly believe he was ours.

Our father loved that horse and insisted that Singing Unimack would be our deliverance. This gorgeous horse would make us all rich. At first we didn't mind that Dad was spending all his time and money on that animal. He believed that in addition to all the little races in which he was competing, Singing Unimack would win a stakes race coming up, one with a $75,000 purse. Hearing that, we all grew excited.

Then an even bigger opportunity came along, and, unlike the race, this was a sure thing. Someone saw the horse one day at the racetrack and offered my dad several hundred thousand dollars for him—or so my father said.

"Take the money!" my brothers and I begged him.

Dad refused. He believed the horse would win that $75,000, then many more races, and then who knew? Maybe one day the Kentucky Derby.

My mother and brothers and I were more realistic. Horse racing is a rich people's sport for a reason: it takes a lot of money and a lot of time, and true payoffs are very rare. We wanted to sell the horse and invest the money in more practical aspects of the farm. But my father was determined to see his adventure through. He thrived on taking risks. The deacons at the little country church said it was sinful to race horses for gambling. This is probably part of why my father avoided going to church. When confronted about it, he'd respond, "Don't you farm? Isn't that gambling, too?"

Riding horses is a gamble as well, even around the farm. If we ever had a free hour, Ted and I would saddle up a couple of horses and ride. The horse I loved to ride the most was named Independent. His name pretty much summed up his personality. He loved to run free. Ted's filly was happiest in her stall, a condition we called being "barn sour." We would ride away from the farm having to kick and urge them the whole way, but once we turned them around, they raced back to the stalls as fast as they could. One time we were down on the back road riding up the side of the cornfield, through the clover. We came upon some deer down in the creek. As thoroughbreds that had spent most of their lives on the racetrack, our horses had never seen deer before. I felt Independent quiver nervously. In a flash, both horses bolted. They started racing even faster than usual back toward the barn.

Unfortunately for me, a fence had grown over with honeysuckle vines. It looked like brush, but there was a taut wire hidden inside. My horse was fast and out of control. When it tripped on the hidden fence, the horse flipped over headfirst and busted its mouth and lip, tossing me like a ragdoll into a tree. Worse, we crashed near a group of broodmares. They can be aggressive when other horses are around their foals. I had the breath knocked out of me, but Ted was screaming and hollering at me to get my gelding out of the enclosure before the mares attacked him. I was covered in snot and blood, but I managed to get my horse out of there fast.

Sometimes going out for a ride, wind rushing through your hair, felt like true freedom. But in a second, even the most glorious of rides could turn tragic. Those thoroughbreds Ted and I rode were fine animals, but they had nothing on Singing Unimack. With him, the possibility of a terrible accident was greater, but so was the potential for winning—and a change of fortune, at last, for the Frey family. Our father made sure that horse ate like a king even on days when we only had mush. My brothers and I may have lacked basic necessities, but Dad took out loans and hustled for cash to keep Singing Unimack a contender.

I had to admit that he *was* a beautiful horse. And taking him to race did give us an excuse to drive to the racetrack in Chicago, which I loved. Our father would leave for the track in the middle of the night with a truckload of feed and hay. I begged to go every time. We had a CB in the truck, and as we traveled north up I-57 he let me talk to the truckers: "Breaker. Breaker 1-9 for a radio check. How 'bout them smoky bears?" (In CB slang, smoky bears are code for the police.) My handle was Queen Bee, and the amused truckers always responded to me, stifling their laughter and thanking me for my tips.

Sometimes we drove downtown. Looking out the window of our truck at the crowded sidewalks, I studied the women I saw walking by and pictured myself in their suits and high heels. Just as I'd played at being a big-game hunter, now I imagined myself in Chicago, all elegance and sophistication. I would be a businesswoman, living and working in towers high above the city. I would shop in department stores and eat at restaurants. There wouldn't be any more dirt under my nails. I wanted to believe that we could all ride to this new life on the back of Singing Unimack.

That was the dream. The reality of the racetrack couldn't have been more different. It was a dangerous place for a curious little girl. One time I was with my mother and my father's aunt Maybelle. I slipped away from where my mother and great-aunt were sitting inside to go to the track and pull myself up on the guardrail to watch the horses work.

As I was waiting for the horses to come by, I was overtaken by an eerie feeling. I climbed off the ledge. When I turned around, all I saw were giant man-hands about to grab me. They were the biggest hands I'd ever seen. When the man saw my alarmed eyes, he spun around very quickly and ran away. I watched him leave and then I ran toward the big doors and told my mom. "Mom, a man tried to grab me!" She jumped up, took hold of my arm, and said, "Where is he? What happened?" Then she took me to tell a security guard.

The guard never looked for the man, only told my mother that she should watch me better.

Finally, Singing Unimack's biggest race came. Dad didn't take me with him to Chicago that time, but I wished him luck as he drove off. I had come to believe him that our horse would win, that my father would return in glory, carrying a briefcase overflowing with cash and leading Singing Unimack festooned with wreaths . . .

My father and the horse returned late at night. I heard the truck pull into the driveway and raced to the window in my pajamas. I stood there trying to catch a glimpse of a trophy glinting in the moonlight, but I didn't see one.

The second my father's face came into view, I knew they hadn't won. When I saw the horse hobbling out of the trailer, I knew something terrible had happened. The animal, his front leg in a cast, appeared to be in great pain. I couldn't believe they hadn't put him to sleep the way they usually did with injured animals. Given the extent of the bandages, he would never race again, I was sure. I watched from the window as this majestic horse, so relieved to be back on the farm, knelt down and rolled around in the dust.

The next morning I would learn what had happened. A horse from California on an inside lane had been "blowing turns," meaning he'd run straight instead of turning properly, and he had careened into our horse.

That was the closest in my father's life that he ever came to having a real win with a horse. Instead, from the stands, he had to watch as another horse nearly killed his own. There would be no more big-stakes races. There would be no more offers to buy Singing Unimack. Losing all that money was hard on Dad, but I think what made it even worse was that he truly loved that horse. He was sorry for the horse's suffering as much as for his own.

After that, my father had to go to the bank and take out yet another mortgage to keep us from losing the farm. For me, those trips to the bank were like Groundhog Day. Every year, it seemed, we were back there in that bank, waiting to find out if we could get more credit. He took me, his deputy, with him so I'd learn how to play the game. But what I saw was a cautionary tale. Pay the debt off, borrow more money, pay the debt off, borrow more money . . . Around and around like a merry-go-round, with no way to get off, no way to ever own anything outright or to ever feel safe.

Every time Dad would somehow convince the bankers to give us another loan. *You can't possibly be buying this,* I'd think, watching the banker accept whatever line my father was feeding him. And I was so ashamed that we had to keep asking.

Why do we keep doing this? I'd think. *Why can't we get off this ride? We shouldn't have to live like this. We should sell all the horses, for goodness' sake!*

"You probably heard," my father said to this year's gullible young suit-clad banker, leaning in, his green eyes twinkling, "that our son Buddy won the lottery, so we'll be paying off the mortgage in a few months?"

The banker had not heard. No one had heard, because Buddy, my father's oldest son from his first marriage, was working as a trainer at the racetrack and had received no such windfall. Dad had just made it up in that moment.

Watching him weave these lies, I swore that when I was old enough and owned something, I would never put it in peril. I would be smarter about debt. I would never have to beg another person to let me keep my own home. Most of all, I would never own another horse. Horse racing seemed crazy. If we couldn't afford any new clothes, what business did we have spending thousands of dollars on racehorses?

Could things get any bleaker? I wondered, watching this same scene unfold yet again between my father and a banker. Little did I know that things would get much, much worse.

Chapter 4

Through the Eyes of Jesus

At last, I was finally old enough to start school. I was so excited. On my first day, I bounded to our front door to race out to the school bus. I flung open the door onto a glorious September morning. At that very moment, a man had his hand on the outside doorknob. We collided in the doorway. I looked up.

For six years, I'd been a happy, confident, fearless little girl, teeming with midwestern moxie, but now I felt a sudden, stabbing terror. The man had long hair and a huge red beard, and eyes that peered down at me through that face full of hair. In those eyes, I could see that this man wanted to hurt me. I somehow knew, deep down, that he would.

The man was basically a bum. My father had met him at the racetrack in Chicago. Even after Dad gave him a haircut and cleaned him up, I could tell he was a bad man. But I also knew that he was strong. That meant he might be able to take some of the grueling physical labor off my brothers. I was conflicted. My brothers worked so hard on that farm. No one works as hard as those young boys had to. Every day. Day in. Day out. No rest. So I kept silent.

Two months into his time boarding with us there on the farm, he started coming into my room at night. His excuse for being up and walking around at two or three in the morning would be that he was putting wood in the stove. When I heard the stove door close, I froze in fear, because after he put wood in the stove he came into my room. I did not move as he touched me. I lay there, scared and confused, until he'd done what he wanted. Then he went away.

I began to dread the night. There was nowhere safe. I knew I didn't want to be in my bed anymore. I started sleeping between my brothers on the pull-out couch or with my parents. But one night the farmhand came into the room where my brothers and I were sleeping and put his hands on me. I was in shock. He was so bold and so brazen, and he would find me unless I was sleeping with my parents.

Never had I felt so confused and so disappointed in the world. I'd been off of the farm before. What I knew about the outside world wasn't all good. I'd seen urban poverty around Cicero Avenue when we went to the racetrack. I sensed the danger there. But at home on the Hill, I'd always been the master of my own universe. Now this man, this invader, was trying to take that power from me.

What consumed me most was the cost of telling my parents what he was doing: *If I say something, my brothers will suffer,* I thought. This thirty-year-old man was dumb as a rock but hardworking. He made things easier on my brothers, I saw that. I worked hard, but it was nothing compared to what they had to do. Not only that, the farm was always in trouble. *Without his work,* I thought, *the farm might fail. And then it will be my fault if we're thrown off the Hill.*

We were conditioned to remain quiet about any injuries we received on the farm. There were almost always negative consequences if you told. The dog that bit you while playing might get put down. The fun part of the river where you almost drowned could become off-limits. You could be scolded for climbing the tree from which you fell and told not to try it again. Dealing with your physical pain in silence was almost always better than coming forward to our parents and explaining that you needed help.

One day when he was seven Ted broke his arm falling off our huge goat, Billy Jack. It was his own fault. Billy Jack ran through the cedar trees and the brush trying to get Ted off, but Ted would not be thrown. He yelled, "John, spray him with the water hose and make him go faster!" Ted rode him like a bronco, and finally Billy Jack ran under the clothesline, catching Ted. He put his arm out to break his fall and suffered the consequences.

In this case, there was no way to hide the injury. His options were limited. After much deliberation, he and John went and told our mother. She was right in the middle of the time-sensitive job of canning tomatoes. She scolded Ted for being careless. He stood there, his arm dangling as she put her jars down, took off her apron, and grabbed her car keys. My father was not always so lenient. With him, the margin for error was far slimmer. Everyone knew that if you made trouble for Dad, you would come to regret it.

My best friend was still the ram, Baa-Baa. Baa-Baa was a good ram. I'd bottle-fed and cared for him when he was a baby. Now he was the size of a Shetland pony and a strong, highly intelligent animal. He roamed free on the farm and he would never attack—unless provoked. His two guiding concerns were my happiness and when he was going to eat next.

Once when I was seven, my father was mending fences. Dad walked around the back of his truck and Baa-Baa was in his path, so my father took his jersey gloves and smacked him out of the way. Baa-Baa cocked his head, walked off fifteen feet, turned around, took a running start, and knocked Dad over. I knew immediately that Baa-Baa's days were numbered. My father put him into a stall. The next day, he told me and Ted to put Baa-Baa in the back of the truck.

"He's gotten aggressive," my father said. "That means it's time for him to go father some babies. We'll take him to a farm where he'll be able to live with girl sheep. Maybe one day Baa-Baa can come home, along with one of his babies."

This sounded a little suspicious, but I liked the idea of Baa-Baa having babies, so I coaxed him into the truck. Ted and I rode in the back of the truck with Baa-Baa to a farm near Mount Vernon. There I watched as my father traded Baa-Baa for some alfalfa to feed our horses. The other farmer put Baa-Baa into a chute.

The second the door closed in front of him, Baa-Baa started screaming his head off. Ted and I sat in the back of the truck as we pulled away. Over and over, Baa-Baa bleated and kept trying to climb over the chute to get back to me. I'll never forget his screams and the scraping sounds of his hooves trying to break the wooden planks of the chute. I could hear them for miles. Ted and I stared at each other, our eyes full of tears. We knew Baa-Baa was never coming home.

On the way back to the farm, my father stopped at a convenience store and bought me and Ted cans of Orange Crush, the first soda I could remember tasting. That was his way of trying to make it better for us, but it tasted like acid in our mouths.

One afternoon, a social services caseworker showed up at our house. He had a slight frame and was wearing black horn-rimmed glasses that kept sliding down the bridge of his nose. He and my father stood together on the front porch while I leaned against a post and listened to them talk.

He wasn't there because of me. He couldn't have known about the farmhand. I hadn't told a soul. He must have heard from one of our teachers how shabby the house was, or how hard my brothers were working back home, or how they frequently showed up at school with bruises, some of which seemed like they were made by an adult hand.

I was afraid. I had heard that social services sometimes came and took children away. As unhappy as I was with what was happening at night when the farmhand was there, I didn't want to leave my home. I loved my brothers. I knew my parents loved me and would protect me as soon as I told them what was happening.

The caseworker asked my father a lot of questions. I longed to butt in and deliver a speech about how well we were being raised. I thought, *This social services guy doesn't seem very smart. I bet he will be easily impressed by how grown-up I act and how well-spoken I am. I can assure him that I'm very happy, well fed, and cared for.*

You might think we'd be wild, untamed animals given how hard we worked, how much time we spent outside, but we called all adults Mr. and Mrs. We never talked back, and when we were asked to speak, our vocabulary was expansive, with no distinctive dialect or noticeable accent. Our parents encouraged good enunciation, and we didn't pick up slang from other kids—perhaps because we spent so little time away from the Hill.

I thought of what I would say when the social worker asked me a question. I would say, "Yes, the house could use some work, but does that matter? Yes, we work very hard, but we are happy doing it." I would show him my excellent grades. *But what if he asks what grades my brothers are making? Hmm, maybe school achievement isn't the platform I should stand on.*

"Mr. Frey," I heard the man say, "we've been getting calls. People are saying that it's not right to make your children work this hard and that your methods of discipline are too severe." As he glanced around the farm, I could tell he also disapproved of our living conditions.

Finally my father held up his hand to let the man know the conversation was over.

My father is fighting for us! I thought. I knew he would make this okay.

"You think you can do a better job raising them? You take them," my father casually said to the man. "You can take my children, but if you do, you have to take all of them, and you can't ever bring them back. I won't want them after they have been ruined."

Dad truly believed that putting us into what most of the world considered a normal, healthy environment—whatever that was— would change us for the worse. We would never be able to return to the way things were on the farm. Perhaps he thought we'd question everything. I began to suspect that he kept us isolated because he didn't want to know that some kids came home from school to television rather than chores. They ate Pop-Tarts rather than cow brains. That was okay. I didn't want TV and Pop-Tarts. I may have had questions about our father's horse obsession and his money management, but this was my family. I wanted to grow up with my brothers on the Hill.

I looked at my father in disbelief. He loved us, didn't he? Surely he didn't want us to go away. And even if he didn't love us, he couldn't run the farm without us! He needed us. What was he doing?

I stood as still as a statue looking up at him, waiting for one of the many lines on his face to move. Nothing. Oh, God, he meant every word. He told the Department of Children and Family Services to take us. *All of us.* Not just one of my brothers, but all of them. *Me too.*

The man turned pale. He evidently didn't know what to do with this.

I'm sure I looked at least as shocked as he did. *What are my options?* I thought. I knew that if the man tried to take me, I would run. That was it. *I'm out.* I began to slowly sidestep away from the man and my father. Keeping my eyes on both of them, I started to look around to decide which direction I would run. Then I caught sight of the man's car. He had driven out to the farm in a tiny Volkswagen Rabbit. I almost laughed out loud as I thought, *My father knows that we aren't going anywhere with this guy today. He's bluffing, because he knows there's no way the caseworker is going to fit all five of us into that car! That's why my father demanded he take us all.*

That day should have made me realize that there was something unusual about the way we were growing up. Instead, it made me admire my father even more. He seemed in that moment not like a callous father whose methods were being challenged by the community but rather like a wise strategist, a genius who had outwitted the authorities yet again.

N o matter how bright the day, at night, I had just one question: *Where do I sleep tonight so I'll be safe?* Many nights I crawled in with my parents and slept on the edge of the bed next to my mother.

The farmhand persisted. I resolved to get rid of him, even if it would mean more work for my brothers. Telling on him was out of the question. I'd learned well that we all had to handle our problems ourselves, and this was no one's problem but mine. My family had taught me to hunt, and I began to think of the farmhand as prey. I looked at him and thought, *I'll kill you and tell God you died.* I thought I could have a talk with God, making it clear that murdering him was not, in fact, a sin, but that I was just ridding the world of evil— sort of helping God out.

There are a million ways to die on a farm. He would be in a risky situation at some point, and I would take advantage of it. Maybe he would be working on a vehicle that would roll over him. Maybe he would be operating a piece of machinery and he would fall into it. I knew I could make it happen. I drove big equipment. I could run him over. When he took water out of the pond, I could back the tractor over him, drown him with the weight of the tractor. I could shoot him and say it was an accident, cry when the sheriff came.

And yet the perfect opportunity never presented itself. From when the abuse started, when I was seven, weeks went by, then months, with me hiding and running and wondering how no one saw what was happening. I would have a reprieve when he left the farm for the racetrack; I'd think, *Maybe he won't come back.* But he always did. There was no telling if it was over, or if he was just taking a break, maybe even planning something worse.

M y relationship with God became shaky. He was the only one I could talk to about what was happening, but he wasn't getting rid of the man. My mother was a Catholic and my father was, in name at least, a Baptist. Every Sunday he stayed home as my mother took me and my brothers to the closest house of worship, a little Baptist church. My brothers sang every Sunday in front of the congregation. The preacher would say, "Let's get the Frey boys up here," and they would do two or three songs. Their repertoire included "I'll Fly Away," "Blessed Redeemer," "Dear Lord," "Old Rugged Cross," and "Victory in Jesus."

For me when I was little, church was a great place to catch up on my rest. It was hard for me to sit still and focus on a sermon without falling asleep. I wanted God in my heart, but I wondered why we had to go spend two hours in church every Sunday. At first I thought you should be able to just learn the lessons you needed and then graduate, like it was school. God created the world, everything and everyone in it. *Check.* God is good. *Check.* The Devil is bad. *Check.* Live by the Ten Commandments. *Got it.* Jesus is born and then he dies and then he comes back again. *Check, check, check.*

And yet I struggled to match the lessons I learned at church with the reality I lived. I struggled with the question of how God could have let this happen to me up until now if he had any control over things.

Finally I let my parents know what was going on. I thought my father would get rid of the man right away. If you have a father prone to violence, the one advantage should be that he will avenge you in situations like this one. Certainly he should protect his youngest child, a little girl he always said was the apple of his eye, so much like him, his favorite. Instead, he merely told my mother she should watch me better.

That day after I told, when I realized the farmhand was still on the farm, I only saw him at a distance. He didn't eat at the table. On the second day, my luck ran out.

Doing evening chores, I made my way from the back porch to the old barn, my favorite place to go. This was where the horse stalls were, and where we mixed the livestock feed, and where when a song I loved came on the radio I danced with abandon. On that day, the big barn doors were open. Dusk light was pouring through the west-facing windows. I came from the east entrance of the barn. The yellow light hit my face, so I was momentarily blinded. Then my eyes adjusted, and I saw the farmhand standing in the middle of the barn, in partial shadow. We both froze and looked at each other. He was finishing mixing the oats and corn and molasses for the horses. He had a pitchfork in his hand. I knew he was about to take the bucket and wheelbarrow out to feed the animals.

I thought: *You can't run away. Where would you go? This is the way it's going to be. You have to face it.* And so I stood there and I did not move.

In his eyes, I saw something worse than the evil I'd seen when we first met. Now he looked like he had nothing left to lose. His face didn't move, but it wasn't blank, exactly. It was like a still, shallow pool. It was void of emotion. He looked like a ghost.

I was afraid at first. But I stayed calm. I knew that I had to face him. He wasn't leaving and I wasn't either. I kept my arms at my sides. I kept telling myself that there was nothing else to do but stare him down. The longer I stared, the more my resolve strengthened. I felt my face harden. He did not move or speak for what felt like an hour. He knew I was strong enough to tell and strong enough not to hide afterward. Then he looked away. Without a word, he picked up the bucket and wheelbarrow and went about his work. I began to feel a lightness. I would never be the prey again. My courage had been there waiting the whole time. I remained alone in the barn, my barn, as the sun set.

Around this time, a ten-year-old girl named Amy was brutally raped and murdered nearby. Her body was found near an oil well on an access road. They caught her killer. He was not the farm-hand on our farm, but I saw the murderer on the news and he had the same chilling look in his eyes.

Hanging on my bedroom wall to the left of my dresser was an oil painting of Jesus. One afternoon after school, when everyone else was outside working and I was alone in the house, I looked up at that picture of Jesus to have a conversation with him about the farmhand, who was back working on the Hill for a period of time. I asked him why he would have let that happen to me if he was so good and was supposed to protect all the little children of the world. I was a little older now, and that was a question that I wanted answered.

Jesus glared back. *Glared.*

Is Jesus mad at me? I wondered.

Jesus looks scary! I thought.

I looked harder, and there was a little hole in the painting where one of Jesus's eyes used to be. I climbed up on my dresser and removed the painting from the wall. I looked at the picture and saw that there was a perfectly round hole drilled into the painting of Jesus. Behind where the painting usually hung, there was a bigger hole. I looked through and saw darkness.

I went out my door and into the room next door—the farmhand's room. I moved fast, because I was afraid that he or someone else might come back inside unexpectedly, and also because his room was a disgusting place. It was filthy, with dirty clothes everywhere. I jumped up on a barrel and felt along the wall until I found a jagged break in the paneling. I removed the panel and looked through the hole in my room's wall. I could see my whole room. I could see where I stood when I emerged from the bath, where I changed. He had been watching me through the eye of the Jesus painting.

Here was proof of what kind of person he was. He wasn't touching me anymore, but he was watching me. Until now I'd shown mercy by not hurting him and not bringing it up again with my parents. The time for mercy was over. I was ten. Amy had been murdered. I had to be vigilant. I couldn't forget how strong I was, how I could kill and skin a deer on my own if I needed to. This man could not stay on our farm another minute.

I went to my mother and showed her the hole in the wall.

I spoke calmly, but inside I was raging. I could let a lot of things slide. I knew the way we were living wasn't normal. I accepted that as part of keeping our family together. By this age I knew that someday I would leave home and build my own normal life. But for now, I was done with this. As I held the painting, I assured her there would be a reckoning. She could see the resolve in my eyes.

At last my parents acted. I don't know what they said to the farmhand, but within twenty-four hours the man was gone. I never had to face him again. His departure went a long way toward restoring my faith. In a way, Jesus did help me get rid of that man after all.

Chapter 5

A Proper Education

From first through sixth grade, I attended the nearby Orchard-ville School, a one-story, one-hallway cinder-block building. Two grades were combined in each classroom, and the class size never exceeded about eight. I'd been so excited to start school, but to my dismay I found out quickly that school was all about fitting in. I was already too far gone for that. The time spent alone on the farm surrounded by my animals and the freedom of space, nature, and imagination was replaced by walls plastered with rules and deco-rated in primary colors not usually found in nature. To add to my misery, all the children there seemed so *normal*.

I realized quickly that my early experiences had made me differ-ent from what I called normal children. The very idea of trying to blend in exhausted me. I couldn't tell them about my life outside school. They would never understand. Meanwhile, their talk of backyard barbecues, MTV, shopping trips, and vacations was so for-eign to me, it was like they were speaking another language. My method of survival was to turn inward and escape to a place in my mind where I was free. I did my work and counted the days until each school year was over.

At school I was well behaved, but if anyone told me to color the cow brown, I would grab the purple crayon. I would color the cow whatever color I wanted to, thank you very much. I struggled with doing things that I didn't want to do. I grew terribly bored.

I hated structure and authority and being captive those hours of every day when I could have been outside and alone. To me, those painted cinder-block walls felt like a prison. When I was in that building, I felt like I was suffocating. I was also learning that outside my own imaginary kingdom I was a pauper. Our bright yellow free-lunch cards had to be picked up at the principal's office. When you presented them in the cafeteria, everyone knew you couldn't pay for your lunch. Many of us in that community were poor, but I felt private shame at my inability to buy my own meal. I started to feel conflicted about accepting the food. I was hungry and wanted to eat, but it felt embarrassing that I wasn't paying and other children were.

My father expected me to get straight As. He'd dropped out of school at age twelve. That didn't matter. For him, rules were for other people. When I brought home my first B, in some class that I didn't care about, my father said with that low voice of his that he was disappointed in me. He never laid a hand on me, but his words hurt me more than the physical punishment he gave my brothers. To me, a whipping was nowhere near as bad as that look of disappointment in his eyes.

That evening I packed a bag to run away from home. I thought he hated me. I thought I should just leave. I got halfway down the road but thought better of it when I heard the coyotes howling. I went and hid in the barn, wedged tightly between bales of alfalfa, crying my eyes out. When it grew dark, I could hear my brothers calling my name. I stayed hidden in the hayloft until I was so hungry that I couldn't take it any longer. Inside the warm house, they were eating dinner. Finally I went inside.

So much of my daily life was spent worrying about what my father thought of me. When a boy tried to kiss me once by the back door of the gym, I was petrified that someone would find out—scared, in particular, of what my father would think of me if he heard I'd kissed a boy at school. The thought of his disapproval made me flee. As a result, it would be many more years before my first kiss.

The other children talked about their love of fast food, but I had no idea what it was. Not once did our entire family ever go out to a restaurant together. The first time I ever had fast food was when I was taken to McDonald's in third grade. The honors kids were taken there from school one day for a treat and allowed to order whatever we wanted.

The other kids had eaten there a million times before, so they all ordered a Happy Meal or some McNuggets. My eyes wide, I recalled the instructions the teachers had given us and followed them to the letter. They did say "Order *anything* you want . . ." I ordered a McRib, a Quarter Pounder with cheese, french fries, a Happy Meal, and a caramel sundae with nuts. The other children looked at me like I was a freak. I didn't care. I ate every last bite. I thought it was the best food I had ever tasted in my life.

The first time I had steak I was twelve or thirteen and hunters were visiting from Chicago. The men who came to the farm had brought a prime rib to cook. I thought I'd died and gone to heaven. It replaced the McRib as my favorite meal. I vowed that someday, when I lived and worked in a city, I would eat steak every day. From that point forward, I craved beef over sweets.

We did have cows and pigs on the farm, but if we ever slaughtered one, we would take the livestock meat, grind it up, and blend it with venison to make it last longer. I never grew up eating straight beef. The lunches provided at school, too, contained a blend of mystery meat. There may have been ground burger in a spaghetti sauce or on a sloppy joe, but it certainly didn't taste like prime rib. Can you imagine my surprise and disappointment as a young woman when I found out that in the best restaurants they serve venison, rabbit, and quail?

One day, for the first time ever, I was allowed to visit the home of the only other girl in my grade. Dawn lived in what I thought was the nicest house in the county, a *brick* home. To me, a brick house was the height of prestige.

I wanted very badly to be friends with Dawn. But our lives were so different. She became a daily reminder of how I was not a normal girl. We were Nellie and Laura in *Little House on the Prairie*. I was Laura, with the same mousy hair. Dawn was Nellie, from her haughtiness to her blond ringlets. She didn't even like animals. She bought her clothes at J. C. Penney. One time she spilled paint on her outfit and she said, "no, now we're going to have to throw this away." I said, "Throw it away? Are you kidding me?" Even with the stain, it would have been the nicest thing I owned.

In sixth grade, a second little girl moved into the area, just about a mile from my house. Finally, another girl! This girl was the second youngest of five children. Her little ranch house was one of the nicer places in our part of the county, with a pretty white barn and a big maple tree out front. They only had wood heat, like us, but they had hardwood floors, asphalt shingles, aluminum siding, and drapes. Their place always seemed cleaner than ours.

We became very good friends, but I wouldn't have traded my life for hers. I could just tell something was wrong in that house. I was learning that all of the little country homes held their own secrets. The family eventually lost their home and small farm to the bank.

I was struck by the lack of hope that little girl seemed to have. Like so many children I knew growing up, she seemed to have given up on having a good life by the time she was out of elementary school. I ask myself all the time, why didn't I give up? Was hope something I was born with? Did I find it in the encouragement of my father and brothers? Did working on the farm instill it in me somehow, make me realize that a life could change as quickly as the weather?

All I know is, I had just as many reasons to have low expectations as that girl did. And yet from the time I was little, I knew in my heart that there would be some path for me. I would wait for the right moment and then I would escape. I would go places.

I was overcome with joy when, in fifth grade, I was told that once or twice a month they would let me out of the Orchardville Grade School to attend a "gifted" program in a bigger town nearby: Wayne City, which had a population of more than a thousand.

Great, I thought, *this will expedite my freedom! I will meet kids like me.* Everything was moving far too slowly. *Maybe the gifted program would speed things up,* I thought. They might even see that I didn't need to go to school anymore. I could be released, given a diploma, and sent on my way.

Yeah, not so much. The kids were smarter but, alas, still normal.

My mother fielded a phone call from the director of the program. "Mrs. Frey, your daughter is extremely intelligent, but she is antisocial."

When she asked me what that was about, I said, "I'm not antisocial, Mom. Those kids are stupid." For the record, none of them were remotely stupid. It was just that, compared to the adult situations I was dealing with at home, their interests seemed trivial to me, even absurd.

My mother didn't take the teacher seriously, in any case. She shrugged and went back to work. But hearing about that call made me think the gifted program wouldn't be my golden ticket. The teacher was blind to the truth: I never lacked social skills or confidence. I could hold a conversation with any adult on just about any subject. I just felt out of place when I was around kids because we had so little in common. My brothers and I were hunting in the woods, keeping livestock alive, and rebuilding truck engines. These kids at school were obsessed with who had a boyfriend and listing their favorite Hubba Bubba flavors.

I pounced on the next opportunity that came along. There was a regional speech contest coming up, and you could submit a three- to five-minute audio tape to enter. The teachers would listen to the tapes and pick students to participate in the contest. This was my chance to prove that I wasn't antisocial. People who are comfortable speaking in front of crowds aren't antisocial! I would prove them all wrong! As it turned out, I was the only middle schooler chosen. Almost all of the other contestants were in high school.

My father helped me practice for the big day. He said, "When you get up there, imagine all the people in the audience are animals."

For weeks I stood on the tailgate of our old Ford pickup truck and orated to Shirley and Billy Jack. Sometimes I practiced while I sat on back steps and pulled ticks off the beagles. By the time my preparation was complete, every animal on the farm knew all about the lives of Helen Keller and Annie Sullivan.

The day arrived. The speech contest was at the high school library in Wayne City. The other contestants looked worldly, like people whose houses had thermostats. One was the beautiful daughter of the superintendent, Mr. Sutton. Everyone there was so much more mature and so much better dressed than I was. They had normal families, you could tell. No one knew what my life was like when I disembarked from that school bus. It was my first time, apart from singing at the General Baptist Church, that I would have to speak in front of a large crowd. *Don't screw this up,* I told myself. *This is your shot.*

There is something to be said for believing everything you might ever dream of is out there waiting for you. When you have nothing, it's only upward from there. I knew it was all up to me. I was solely responsible for my future. Me and only me. My fear vanished.

When my name was called and I took the stage, it was like an adult master communicator stepped into my body. From voice inflection to posture, I delivered the performance of a lifetime. I looked everyone in the eye. I hit every mark. It was an out-of-body experience for me.

Looking into the audience, I saw the pride on my father's face. His eyes sparkled when he watched me deliver my speech with confidence and conviction. Dad never came to anything except graduations. He had no meaningful relationships in the community. But he'd put on a suit to watch me in the speech contest. That was one of my proudest moments: seeing him sitting there watching me command the attention of the room.

After everyone gave their speeches, we went to the gym for the award ceremony. At this point I didn't care if I won. I figured the superintendent's daughter would win. *That's who wins these things*, I thought, *someone in a pink dress. She looks like a winner.* Still, I felt like I had won already, because my dad saw me knock it out of the park.

I lost track of my parents inside the crowded gymnasium, so I took a seat next to my Orchardville grade-school teacher, Donna Leyva, and her husband, who was a hairdresser. How I loved Mrs. Leyva. She was so beautiful and so pulled together, but she didn't mess around. She was a smart, witty, strong, and capable woman. She dressed up to go to work in that country school, her red high heels crunching through the gravel parking lot. In that little gym, she played rag-ball wearing a crisp blue cotton dress and a red beaded necklace. Her strength, elegance, and sophistication made her stand out, and she made no apologies for it. I believed she was magic. She was who I wanted to be.

I could look through everyone, but not her. There was just enough mystery in her eyes that I knew she had an edge. She was who I wanted to be. On the surface, she appeared to have stepped right out of a fashion catalog with a million-dollar smile. But you could talk to her for five seconds and realize that she was tough as nails. She didn't care that she was teaching at a little country school; she was going to dress and talk any way she wanted. She didn't give a flip about what anyone thought.

In the middle of the award ceremony, Ms. Leyva suddenly turned to me and started shouting something. It took me a minute, but finally I heard her: "Sarah! Sarah! You won! Go get your award!"

I went up onstage, and the contest emcee handed me a big wooden and metal plaque.

When I sat down, Ms. Leyva said, "Do you realize who you beat? So-and-so is a sophomore! So-and-so is a junior!"

After it was all over, I climbed into the backseat of the car with my plaque. My dad turned around in the driver's seat and smiled at me. "See?" he said. "You can do anything."

Chapter 6

The Melon Route

Most of the year, my parents struggled to turn a profit on the farm. They grew hay and corn, and had what's known as a "truck patch"—about a hundred times bigger than a garden but not a full field—of fruits and vegetables. But only one thing made real money consistently: my mother's summer melon route.

Every summer, my mother liked to buy us melons from a nearby farm, and when she did, she always picked up extras to give away to our neighbors. One time she came home with more than anyone we knew could eat, so she took the extras to the local grocery store. When the shopkeeper sold out in half an hour, he called her up and said, "Elizabeth, can you bring me more of those melons?"

She went back to the melon farmer, bought a carful of cantaloupes, and drove them to the grocery store. Those, too, sold out immediately. Soon she was visiting several melon farms and bringing trucks full of melons to the shop every summer, making gas money and a little extra cash. As the years went by, she added several more stores to her route, turning a better profit each time she expanded.

Whenever I saw her preparing for her deliveries, I would follow her around so she'd be sure to take me along. I'd chase her truck down the road if she tried to leave on her own. Oh, I loved those trips. I loved any opportunity to get off the farm, but the melon route was special; it meant going to farms and then from grocery store to grocery store, town to town.

The farms where we went to buy melons usually kept livestock because they fed the animals the rejected fruit, so those farms often smelled like a sweet-and-sour perfume of fresh cantaloupes and pigsties. At one, the farmer's kids had a plastic Big Wheel trike that they rode around on a patch of concrete. John and I had never seen a bike like that. We were allowed to try it out, even though we were technically too big for such a toy. We couldn't believe how fun it was.

Many of these farms used high school kids as their labor force. The teenagers would arrive at dawn to harvest the melons. They'd be in a line, three or four on each side of the hay wagon, and then a couple of kids riding on it. They'd fill up six or seven wagons before the sun set. My brothers were hypnotized by the Indiana girls, who withstood the hot sun by working in the fields wearing only bikinis. Walking in the sandy Wabash River Valley to pick the melons was like walking on a beach. Most pickers would go barefoot—in spite of the risk posed by prickly sandbur weeds.

My brothers and I stacked the melons as high as we could in the truck beds. When we finished with that, we loaded the cab with however many melons we could fit without displacing any human passengers. We spent many summer evenings driving between farms in Indiana and Illinois, napping atop the heaps of watermelons. I was usually asleep before we crossed the Wabash River. The hot summer wind blowing into the cab of the truck and the sweet smell of cantaloupes was bliss—though these reveries were often interrupted by the sound of a tire blowing out or the acrid smell of the engine overheating.

I didn't even care that our trucks were old and broke down nearly every day. We were usually prepared for just about any type of mechanical failure. I could change tires along the interstate, charge batteries, cool off overheated radiators, you name it. Everyone in our household knew how to take an engine out of a car and put it back together again. We never went to a mechanic; we were the mechanics. And one thing I learned early: there's almost nothing that a little WD-40 can't fix.

With starts and stops, we kept moving forward. On the way to the grocery stores, we filled up with gas and got a Slo Poke or a Chick-O-Stick, sometimes even a Dr Pepper.

Going with my mom on her delivery route was a dream come true. For me, getting off the farm and having those interactions was one of the most empowering things that I could have done as a child. My size was actually an advantage. When meeting me for the first time, most adults were taken by surprise to hear a confident voice come from such a tiny person. They would follow me with curiosity to find out if I really had fruit to sell. I was practically a carnival hawker. In my mind, I had a spiel going: *Behold the melon truck filled with the most amazing melons! Fresh from Posey County, Indiana! Available for a limited time only!*

I would walk right up to produce managers at shops and say, "Hey, how are you doing today? Mom is out back there in our melon truck. I've got jumbo cantaloupes for a dollar! Are you sure you only want twenty-five? We're not going to be back for about three days, so if I were you, I'd make it forty."

I carried myself with such confidence that no one ever said, "Get out of here, kid." They dealt with me as one businessperson to another. Even when I wasn't yet a teen, I upsold everyone, chattering away like some pigtailed Dale Carnegie, with an innate sense of how to phrase my pitch so people would respond the way I wanted them to.

With every sale, I would go through the front door, find the manager, take the order, and then walk through the back of the produce department to the dock. By that time, my mother had driven around to the dock. I would open the door. We would quickly load the melons into a grocery cart. I'd push it back through the store to the produce manager. We'd sign the paperwork and I'd say, "Thank you very much."

Then I would go to the front office, hand him the ticket that was signed by the produce manager, and he'd pay me. I'd stuff the bills in my pocket and walk out the front of the store, where my mother would already have pulled up.

I don't know that the truck ever stopped moving, to be honest. I was always jumping out of a moving truck or running alongside a moving vehicle to jump back in. We were always trying to beat the clock. Hauling melons around in the open air and under the hot sun meant you only had so long before they became ripe and then turned. We kept that constantly in mind. It was drive up, tell the manager to "Get them while they're hot! *Literally,*" unload, then on to the next store.

We often hear about how women struggle to find the courage to ask for a raise or a higher salary when they take a new job. That luckily hasn't been a challenge for me, because I've been asking for more money since I was eight years old. I guess it helps to start when you're young. I give my mother credit. Sometimes she told me matter-of-factly, "We had to pay the farmer more money for these melons, so we have to raise the price to the grocery stores. When you go in there, you say that we need more money than last time."

At the first store I went into after she told me that, I made the decision not to ask for more. When I walked into the grocery store and through the produce department, I saw that their display was nearly full. They hadn't sold that many since we'd last been there. They needed a few more, but not a lot. I made the calculation in my head at the time that the time wasn't right to ask for more money.

"How much did you get out of him?" she asked as we drove out the parking lot.

"Same as last time," I said.

She was hot, sweaty, and already aggravated from the heat. "That tight-ass never wants to pay for what anything is worth," she groused.

"That's not it," I admitted.

"What do you mean? You didn't ask for more money?" She sounded incredulous.

"Nope, I didn't," I said. "Not today, at least."

"I don't understand," she said, her voice taking on an edge. "I *told you* to ask for more money!" She was mad.

"We'll get more money, Mom, when the time is right," I said, hoping I sounded reassuring.

I did understand her viewpoint. She was at the back of the store looking at a truckful of hot cantaloupes—cantaloupes we'd paid for—baking in the sun. She was focused on our problem, while I had the luxury of strolling through the air-conditioned store.

The next grocery store along the delivery route that day was a different story. She dropped me off in the front of the store and I walked through the front and into the produce department, where I saw that their melon cart was down to the last two or three. The produce manager was anxious to see me. I knew he was going to place an order.

"We have great melons today!" I said with a big smile. "They're a little bigger than normal and they're really fresh. We just picked them up last night." Then I told him that not only did he need to pay a little bit more money for them, he needed to go ahead and buy more because we didn't know how long they were going to be this size and this good. He believed me. That day he not only paid more but felt like he'd made a good deal. Not only was this my first lesson in asking for money, but it was my first negotiation and lesson in customer service. I learned to look for the need.

When we weren't on the melon route, my mom was mostly invisible to me. I was always outside working with the boys. My father was the one who taught me almost all of the skills I needed. And yet when it came to what would become the most important skill of all in my life—the ability to get off the Hill and make money—it was my mom who showed me the way.

I had so many new experiences on that route. We never ate out as a family, but on the melon route we might get food from the grocery store or we'd barter in the parking lot with the guys delivering Frito-Lay products or Bunny Bread. We'd give them melons in exchange for bags of chips and dinner rolls.

I loved the other delivery drivers. And, frankly, they wanted fresh fruit after being around processed food all day. I would approach them with a cantaloupe in my hand, twirling it around like a basketball. Then I would offer it up to them like it was a precious gem. "You know you want it," I'd say. "Now hand over the Doritos."

Sometimes it felt like my own personal shopping experience. I would climb into the back of the Frito-Lay truck and browse the racks of chips and snacks. The first chips I ever tasted were in a supermarket parking lot after doing a melon deal. Between what I hustled from the drivers, I had all the ingredients needed to make a meal: Doritos smashed between two slices of Bunny white bread, with a Hostess cupcake or fruit pie for dessert. It tasted to me like the ambrosia and nectar of the gods combined. And the drivers seemed to feel the same way about the produce I traded them. They'd pull a knife out of their pocket and cut a slice right there.

If we had a few ripe melons left over, we might try to sell them at a restaurant or a nursing home, where they'd cut them up immediately and serve them. In exchange, we could have a meal. Mom's melon route opened my world to normal things like eating at restaurants and going to real supermarkets. I was probably eight the first time I saw a real, big supermarket, not just a little discount market, like the kind where we bought 25-cent bags of bread.

We stopped off at a Hometown IGA in Centralia, Illinois. The store smelled like a combination of their meat case (which I noticed had a huge commercial meat saw like the one in our kitchen) and the earthy scents coming from the various displays of fresh produce, along with a hint of packaging and the distinctive odor of old cooling equipment from the open refrigerator cases. I was instantly overstimulated looking around at all the packaged food. It was like going to Disney World. I walked down the cereal aisle as if at the best museum in the world.

That is where my love of consumer-packaged goods began. I was in awe. The colors! The slogans! Someone had killed it or grown it or prepared it *for* me! How easy!

From then on, I went with my mom on her melon route every year for July and the first part of August. Those were the best six weeks of every year. I was proud that this was a job I was good at. I especially loved how at the end of the day you could see the profit so clearly. I learned about the most fundamental form of commerce. You'd buy something, sell it for more, subtract the cost of gas, and you'd see exactly how much you'd made. On the drive back, my pockets bulged with cash. There was no A/C in the truck, so I'd roll the windows up to keep the money from blowing out. With sweat dripping down my face, I'd make stacks: ones, tens, twenties, fifties, hundreds.

"Look at all of this money!" I'd say to my mother.

To me, those piles of cash looked like independence and power. Let my father have his horses. The way I saw it, the answer to our prayers was my mother's melon route, not horse racing. Melons weren't glamorous like winning horses. Going from town to town in a dusty truck peddling fruits and vegetables wasn't as exciting as a one-in-a-million shot to have a winning thoroughbred. But I found it more exciting, not less, because it took me off the Hill and to so many new places. Plus, it was a sure thing.

I knew it was something I could do on my own as soon as I was old enough to drive legally. I never questioned my plan. From a very early age, I felt like when that day came, I could take off, buy a truck, buy produce, and drive hundreds of miles away to resell it.

I loved meeting people, making deals, and I also knew that this was something that could be scaled up exponentially. My mother only went to a handful of grocery stores. I wanted to keep going to the next town, the next county, the next state. I knew someday I could accomplish even more. A lot of people I grew up around never expected to leave home. I never expected to stay. I'd read the encyclopedia in our home; I knew it was a great big world, and I knew that I belonged out in it.

Driving on the melon route, I felt free. I loved how you could smell those melons, loaded loose in the back of the pickup truck, from way up in the cab. Back then, the sweetest smell in the world was the aroma of cantaloupes, hot in the back of that truck. They smelled like freedom, like money, like my ticket out of southern Illinois.

If, for me, the melon route meant adventure, for my mother it was just another job—one of the many she worked at tirelessly. Still, I think she enjoyed it because it was her way off the Hill, too. It was a way for her to shine. She always had a gift for business, in her own way. She had no problem asking for things. When it came time to collect donations for the school raffle, she collected more door prizes than all the other mothers put together. Of course, after all that work on the road, she still had to go back home, give my father control of the earnings, then do all the cooking and cleaning.

I like to think those trips were a respite for my mother, but the truth is, she was stressed out and unhappy for many of those years when she and I shared the melon route. I tried to never give her any cause for further grief. Aside from believing I was a grown-up, I was actually a pretty good kid. I didn't have a sassy mouth and didn't need to be told what to do.

I managed to avoid setting her off until I was in seventh grade. Ted had succeeded in getting a busted old riding lawnmower to work. He wanted to drive the mower while I sat on the wagon behind it, throwing hay to the horses. It seemed idiotic to me. I didn't trust the mower, and Ted always drove too fast. I was sure the thing would stop short and I'd fall off the back, or he'd speed up climbing a hill and I'd tumble off. Either way, I would get hurt for no reason. The wheelbarrow worked just fine. This was one time I was against innovation.

"I'm not doing it!" I said, and started walking back to the house.

"You are!" Ted said. He caught me and dragged me back to the wagon.

I pretended I was going along with it because I knew I could escape once he started driving. The second he got in the seat and hit the gas, I jumped off the wagon and outran him back to the house.

"Mom!" I yelled as I burst through the door. "Ted's making me do something stupid!"

"She's not helping with the chores!" Ted shouted as he raced in, seconds behind me.

I think we caught her on a bad day. She had a broom in her hands. Not just any broom. It was an old, sturdy one, with a thick wooden handle. She might as well have been holding a fence post. No sooner had I breathlessly stormed into the kitchen than she started hitting me with it. I tried to escape, but wound up stuck between the wall and the kitchen table, and she kept going. I was trapped. I held my arm up so she wouldn't get me in the face, and that arm wound up taking a lot of punishment. I couldn't help but believe, even while I was getting pummeled with the broomstick, that her wrath had nothing to do with me. I wasn't even mad at her for losing it. It was Ted I was furious with. If only he hadn't tried to make me ride his stupid redneck lawnmower-trailer contraption, I wouldn't be in this mess. The worst part was that he lied when he said I wasn't helping him. I just wasn't helping in the dumb way he wanted me to.

By the time I reached school the next day I'd forgotten about the broom incident. Getting hurt and keeping your mouth shut about the pain was customary in our household. Besides, it seemed like farm kids always had some kind of scrape or bruise, so I didn't think much about it.

That afternoon, my math teacher, Mrs. Richardson, was walking through the classroom looking down at us as we worked our math problems, and she paused at my desk, hovering over me while I worked the problems. *Back off, lady,* I thought. *I've got this. No need to judge my work until I hand it in.*

Then I looked up and saw her staring in shock at my arm where it rested on my desk. I looked to see what had made her go white. Her lingering presence had nothing to do with my work. My entire forearm was badly swollen with massive welts and black bruises.

The pencil froze in my hand. I could feel her judgment and concern. I continued to stare down at my paper, but the math problems blurred on the page.

Not today, I prayed. *Please, God. I'm so close to getting into high school, which would make me old enough to move out of my parents' house.* The farm was declining rapidly, but I felt like things were starting to look up for me. I would have a driver's license in a few years, and then I could do anything. I could go anywhere. The path was becoming clear. All I had to do was work hard and remain on good behavior. *I had a plan, damn it.*

"Sarah," Mrs. Richardson said, her voice stern. "What happened to your arm?"

I heard the gasps of my classmates as they began to look over at me.

"Nothing happened." *Okay, that was dumb. Clearly something happened. My arm looks like it's rotting.* "Oh, you mean this arm?"

"Yes, this arm."

"Well . . . ," I began. *Think. Think. Fell out of the hayloft. Fell off a horse. Fell into the well. Blame Ted.*

"I fell off a wagon and Ted accidentally ran over me," I said in a nonchalant tone, as if everyone's older brothers ran over them with wagons every day and what was the big deal?

She didn't say a word. Not one tiny muscle in her face moved.

Oh, boy. Quick! Roll your eyes for more credibility. Good. Now give her the "My brother is an idiot" look. I shrugged and went back to working the math problems. *Okay, I think she bought it. Nothing to see here, folks. Math is fun! Ignore her. Has she left yet?*

I peeked up. She had not left.

"Go to the principal's office," she said. Her voice was steady, without emotion.

Great. The normal kids are staring at me now. This is just fantastic.

I rose from my seat and gave her a look that quite clearly said she was wasting her time. *Stay calm. Stay cool. Just breathe.* I paused in the hallway just outside the classroom door. *The teachers are out to tear our family apart,* I thought. *They're in touch with the Department of Children and Family Services, just waiting for their chance to take us.*

The way I saw it, I only had two options. I could turn right, stroll down to the principal's office, and try my luck at convincing Mr. Draper that Ted had run me over and it was an accident. *But what if they go find Ted? His story won't match. Ugh.* Or . . . I looked to my left and spotted the big red double doors leading outside. *I could run.*

The afternoon sun was pouring though the panes of glass. As much as I wanted to step right out of that building and into the light, I knew there would be no coming back. *The timing is bad. Everyone still thinks I'm too little. They still call me Small Frey. They will find me and make me live in a children's home or with strangers.* I thought about my mother and how this would add to the stress that had made her snap in the first place. She had no idea she had hurt me so badly. My choice was clear: I had to make the principal believe my story.

Thanks to my time with all the produce managers, I was comfortable dealing with male authority figures. Mr. Draper was a kind man and he seemed pretty reasonable. He was also what I now know to call emotionally intelligent. As I made my way to his office, I decided it was best to pop in like a happy ray of sunshine, say as little as possible, and then create a diversion. This needed to be chalked up to a quirky little farm accident so we could all get on with our lives.

His door was open, and I poked my head inside.

"Hey, Mr. Draper," I said. "I'm sorry to bother you. Mrs. Richardson asked me to come down and see you real quick."

"Come in here and take a seat, Sarah." His voice was warm and inviting. I didn't want to sit. I wanted to stand. I wanted to run, truth be told. Mr. Draper was a well-meaning man, but even with the best of intentions he had the potential to blow up my world. *You can do this,* I told myself. *Act like you're happy to be there. You love visiting Mr. Draper.*

I sat there in front of Principal Draper trying to seem nonchalant and poised. He asked me what had happened, and I said, "Oh, this arm thing. It's nothing really. Ted hitched a riding lawnmower to a rickety cart. I told him it was dangerous, but he wouldn't listen. You know how Ted is. I was on the back, throwing hay to the horses. When he sped up, I fell off the wagon." I had to make it believable, so I said that when I fell off the front of the wagon my arm got caught under the tires. I said Ted then backed up over it again by mistake, trying to get it off me.

He looked at me with what I took to be sympathy.

This is a good man, I thought. *I'm going to hell for lying to him.*

"Okay, Sarah," he said after staring at me for a minute. "Swing by the nurse's office on your way back to class."

I stood up and thanked him. I was relieved—until I turned around to see Mrs. Richardson and the school nurse standing there. Mrs. Richardson was taking in the situation, and it was clear she wasn't letting this go so easily. Her questioning eyes moved back and forth between me and Mr. Draper. Then they landed squarely back on me. She could tell he believed my story, but she wasn't having it.

"Show the nurse your arm, Sarah. And tell us all again what happened." Her arms were folded now. *Not a good sign. Why don't my tricks work on her?*

Mrs. Richardson had taught nearly every one of the Frey kids throughout the years. Oftentimes she would call me Angela, the name of my mother's daughter from her first marriage, by mistake. It happened so often that I wondered if at times she did it on purpose. Did she enjoy seeing my reaction to being called by the name of an older sister I hadn't even met?

We were already on the radar of DCFS. If this new injury was blamed on my parents, I knew a caseworker would take action. Ted and I were the last kids left on the Hill, as John was graduating soon. If we were taken away, he and I would be split up and sent to different families in town. I would be trapped until I was eighteen. I couldn't let Mrs. Richardson's misguided attempt at justice ruin my plans.

The nurse looked at my arm again while I spoke. They made me tell the story three times. I kept all the details straight. Mrs. Richardson still didn't believe me, I could tell. She wanted me to spill my guts. She wanted to be the one who finally proved there was a reason for her suspicions about the Hill.

I joked. "That brother of mine . . . he couldn't just run over me once." What I hoped they would pick up on, even if they doubted my story, was my determination to stay on that farm.

Finally they let me go back to class, and no one at school ever spoke of it again.

I returned home that day and spoke sharply to my mother.

"I just want you to know I had to lie for you today," I told her.

I was angry, but on the other hand I did empathize with the emotional pain she felt. She'd given birth to eight kids, and raised us while living hand to mouth. She worked tirelessly. She was completely under the emotional and financial control of an unpredictable husband who was obsessed with horses and couldn't get the family out of debt. He never raised a hand to her, but he ran roughshod over her boys, so much so that she sometimes had to step in to protect them from his wrath. And one day, while she was cleaning the kitchen for the millionth time that week, her little girl had come tromping through the house screaming something about how she didn't want to ride on the back of the wagon on a bale of hay? Her life was in shambles and she had no patience left. I was old enough to see that and forgive her. I also knew that I needed her as an ally if either of us was going to make it out of there.

The more I tasted independence and freedom, the less tolerable my daily life became. Now that I was a young teenager, the summer melon route was what I lived for—the sunshine, the meals on the road, the bills bulging in my pockets. Its polar opposite was the short days and long nights of winter, when the ground froze solid and the wind whipped through the house. To survive during those lean months, we engaged in what most people would call poaching—what we called a "night ride." When there wasn't enough to eat, we drove to a field and shot deer out of season.

Shooting deer when we weren't supposed to wasn't noble, nor was it legal, but to us it wasn't exactly poaching; it was harvesting fresh meat when we needed to eat. We lived off the land. If we weren't growing our food or finding it, we were killing it. We considered it the same as when we would go into cornfields where a mechanical picker had been through, leaving behind stray cobs. Our father would drop us off in the field with gunnysacks and buckets and we'd collect the leavings for our livestock. It was just like how we would gather up bullfrogs by flashlight, then bring them home for my mother to fry so we could eat frogs' legs.

We had no choice, but we were still always afraid of being caught when we broke the rules. We knew you could go to jail for poaching deer. The game wardens would confiscate your trucks and guns. Our father didn't care. If he was ever challenged on the morality of the night rides, my father would say simply: "Poor people have poor ways."

One winter when I was twelve, my brother Ted and I climbed into the old Ford pickup truck with our father at eleven o'clock at night and drove into the cold darkness, frost crunching under our tires.

About two miles away was an open field. As we arrived, our headlights landed on a huge buck. My brother Ted lifted the rifle and dropped the deer with one shot. I scurried out of the truck while my dad turned off the headlights. We ran through the frozen field. The ground was full of iced-over tilled earth, so it was like big frozen rocks. I tripped and fell several times. It was so cold that breathing made my chest hurt. We had to work fast, quickly grabbing the deer and dragging it back to the road to load it in the truck before anyone found us.

Ted and I ran up on the deer, prepared to drag it back to the truck, but it wasn't dead. It was thrashing its head and antlers around in agonizing pain, grunting. It had been wounded pretty badly. My mind was racing. I was in fear of the animal. It had a big rack of antlers; we could be gored. And yet the clock was ticking. If we watched it bleed out slowly for an hour, that would give the game wardens time to find us. If it tried to run, we could be out there all night tracking it.

Ted and I decided that the best course of action was for one of us to run back to the truck and get a handgun so we could shoot the deer and end this quickly. I got back to the truck, out of breath. "Dad," I said, panting, "it's still alive. We have to kill it now. I need the pistol."

My father pulled out a hammer.

"Dad," I said, thinking he must have misunderstood me, "it's not dead. It's a *buck*. A ten- or twelve-point buck."

"Can't waste another shot," he said. "The neighbors will hear. Just hit it in the head with the hammer."

Of course I didn't question him aloud, though in my head was the thought *You have no idea what it's like out there in the darkness with a wounded buck trying to kill you.* I turned around and ran back to my brother and the deer. Ted was standing near the poor creature, which was still writhing around on the ground. Ted didn't even look at me. He just put out his hand, thinking I was going to place a pistol in it. I put the hammer in his hand. He looked down at it, then up at me, then down at the hammer.

"Dad said we can't have another shot go off," I said.

I'd never felt so bad for any of my brothers. I'll never forget the look of shock in Ted's big blue eyes in the moonlight. He looked from the hammer in his hand to the flailing animal. I put my hand on his. I didn't want to find out how my father would react if he refused. I also didn't want to find out what would happen if I ran back and tried to renegotiate for the handgun. I reached for the hammer in Ted's hand and said, "I can do it."

"No," he said, "it's too dangerous." The buck's antlers were flying.

And he did it. He bashed in the deer's skull. It was one of the most gruesome things that I've ever had to witness. After several blows between the animal's eyes while he was trying to gore us, the deer finally died. We grabbed it by the antlers and dragged it over the frozen ground all the way back to the truck. We put it in the back, without looking at our father or each other.

Driving home, looking down at my gloves, the deer's warm blood soaked into them, I vowed that no matter what it took, I would get out of that house and off the Hill for good.

Chapter 7

Chomping at the Bit

Holidays on the Hill when we were young were spartan but cheerful. The Easter when I was six, I came out of the house with my basket to see that Ted, who was eight, was still hiding the hard-boiled eggs for me. I pretended that I hadn't seen him doing it so I could find them faster when it was time to look. My brothers ravaged their chocolate bunnies and wound up with sticky smears all over their faces. I would leave my bunny in the box and hide it away. Occasionally I would take it out and admire it. I was dying to eat the bunny, but saving it was a self-inflicted test of willpower. The temptation to eat it was great. *I want the bunny. I need the bunny. Oh, the bunny looks so delicious. Maybe just one ear. No. Maybe I'll taste it tomorrow.* I waited until melon season, July. By then I would be getting off the Hill and I would have money in my pocket to replace it at one of the grocery stores along our route. That way, I would always have something sweet in reserve.

Christmas was my favorite holiday—better than my birthday. I loved to hunt in the woods for the perfect cedar tree. We created our own wintertime fun sledding down hills and building snowmen. My dad would get a friend to dress up as Santa and peek through the window. It was so exciting when we saw Santa's face appear. Dad might also get a horse to run around on the porch after we were in bed and tell us that it was reindeer. One year we built a sled for our team of horses to pull. Presents were usually communal and tended to come in the form of sweet treats like an orange or a bag of nuts. One year Ted and I each received a great big lollipop.

When it came to toys, I didn't really know what I was missing because no one around us had any to speak of and we weren't around other children very often outside school. Our father often reminded us that having animals was better than having toys. The village fire department sometimes dropped off Secret Santa presents when they had a toy drive. One year, from a raffle at the school cafeteria I won a real Game Boy with Tetris on it. Another year, I won a Cabbage Patch Kid at a department store, but that was in the fifth grade, so I was too old to really enjoy it.

The one Christmas morning that there was actually a toy just for me under our tree was when I was five years old. I couldn't believe that there was a colorful package with my name on it. I unwrapped it. Brand-new and in its original packaging was a Baby Alive doll! I was so happy. Then the doll peed, which startled me. I dropped it on the floor and put it away for the day. The next day when I went to play with it, I found that it had disappeared. I suspected that my parents had put it back in the box and returned it for a refund. I knew better than to ask. After the doll went missing, I pretended that I didn't like playing with dolls.

By the time I was thirteen, my parents had abandoned all pretense of us being a normal happy family. Leonard, Harley, and John no longer came home for the holidays. After a few visits, they'd realized that our parents' downward spiral was accelerating. My father was getting desperate as his health and his kingdom crumbled, and he lashed out at anyone who came near. My mother was beginning to realize that once Ted and I were out of the house she would be free. She was eager for that day and no longer tried to keep up the pretense of an orderly home.

Off the Hill, our older brothers' lives were expanding. At school and work, they made friends easily, and they were especially popular with girls. They were handsome, well-mannered, hardworking men now. People they met assumed that they were from a well-off family. They were warmly welcomed by families of girlfriends and classmates as they quickly acclimated to the outside world. I did not share their joy. With each brother who packed his belongings to leave, I felt a loss of our camaraderie and a sense of abandonment.

I understood why they left. Resources were so limited. My brother Leonard, when he was sixteen, attended high school and college simultaneously. We lived about thirty minutes from the town of Fairfield, where Frontier Community College was, and that's where he went to night school. It took a lot of gas to get there and back, and you couldn't pay for gas with food stamps. And so we had to devise a plan. What we would do was that Leonard and I would drive to Fairfield with the food stamps. He would drop me off, and while he went to his college classes, I would walk around the town and go into various grocery stores.

If you bought something that cost $2 and paid with a $5 food stamp, you would get $3 in food stamps as change. To get cash back you had to buy something that cost less than $1. The plan was to go in and buy the lowest-priced item possible. Only it couldn't be a 10-cent piece of bubble gum because that didn't qualify, so you had to buy an actual food item. And the food item that was cheapest to purchase at the time was Campbell's soup.

At each store I would buy a 21-cent can of chicken noodle soup. I'd go to the register, put one can down, and give the cashier a $1 food stamp. She would give me back 79 cents. Doing that several times at each store, I'd get $6 or $8 worth of change by the time Leonard was out of class. He would pick me up and then we could go to the gas station. Paying entirely in coins, we would fill up the tank.

Leonard was ashamed that that's what we had to do so he could get to and from school. On those long drives home, we often talked about how our lives would be different one day. Once he tasted life off the farm, there was no bringing him back.

One year, when I was thirteen or fourteen, Christmas Day came and went and there was no holiday dinner. There were no presents. I didn't say anything about it to my mom that day, though. The next day, December 26, I climbed in the truck with her to go to town.

Oh! I thought. *She and I are going to go shopping and do something special. We're still celebrating Christmas, just a day later!* I knew we didn't have money but I still thought maybe we'd get something in town. I asked if that's what was happening. From the driver's seat, she unloaded on me about how terribly broke we were. My whole childhood, we received paper food stamps in the mail every month—ones, fives, tens, and twenties. You always knew when the food stamp envelope came in the mail. When I was little, we received a big, thick envelope. As the number of kids under the roof dwindled, so did the size of these envelopes.

But I asked the question that was on my mind anyway. "Mom, am I going to get a Christmas present?"

I regretted asking as soon as the words left my lips. I knew better. She had just told me that our home and land were in jeopardy of being taken away. My father's health was getting worse. They struggled to afford hay for the few horses Dad was desperately holding on to, let alone make the farm payments. My brothers were sending less money home and keeping more of what they earned in order to build their own lives.

"Yeah, you have a Christmas present," she said.

She reached behind her into the backseat and grabbed something and tossed it to me. It was a blue stocking decorated with a snowman face. The stocking was empty.

My mother was as tired of living hand to mouth as I was. Christmas was nothing more than a reminder of how truly miserable her life had become. She was just as trapped as I was. We drove in si-

lence all the way to town, where we ran an errand for my father, then returned, still in silence. I vowed to do what my brothers had done, to disappear and never spend one more Christmas on the Hill.

When I was fourteen, a high school freshman, I had my first sleepover, at my girlfriend Christy's house in Wayne City. We tried on clothes and she showed me how to style different outfits. We played with makeup—a major no-no in my dad's eyes—and I realized how liberating it could feel to make yourself look different. Her mom brought us delicious snacks. We stayed up late talking and being silly in her cheerful room. Her walls were plastered with posters of rainbows, unicorns, and cute boys who I understood to be pop stars, though I didn't recognize them. I wanted to stay up all night because I didn't want this magical day to end.

It was the first time in so long that I'd had fun. Real fun. It turned out the whole being-a-kid thing wasn't all that bad. I actually *liked* being a girly girl. As I drifted off to sleep, gently rocking on Christy's waterbed, I wondered if this was what it was like to have a sister. The next morning, Christy and I were sleeping in when I was woken up by Christy's mom. Her voice sounded serious.

"Sarah, wake up," she said. "We have to leave. I have to take you home right now."

I took in the cheery room through my sleep-filled eyes and refocused on Christy's mom. I was confused and disappointed. *Wait. I really like it here. I don't want to go back to the Hill. Please. This is like heaven.* I told her I thought I was going to spend the day there.

Christy's mother assured me that they would love to have me stay longer but that she'd just received a call. My parents wanted me back at the farm. My brother Harley had been shot. Harley had always been the tough guy among my brothers, the fighter, but I still didn't believe the news. *Shot? He lives in Chicago! You don't have hunting accidents in Chicago! Wait. Shot on purpose?* I jumped out of my bed and threw on my farm clothes.

. . .

Harley had moved off the Hill just a year or so earlier, as soon as he'd finished high school. He found a decent-paying job in Chicago. As with all the boys, he sent much of what he earned back to our father.

As a result, it was taking a long time for Harley to save up enough so he could go to school for a degree. He thought about joining the military so he could get help paying for college. My parents had discouraged him from entering the army, though. My mother was afraid he'd get hurt. So instead he found a job at the racetrack, putting the horses in the starting gates. And, in 1990, he got shot anyway.

After taking a wrong turn, he was driving with his girlfriend through a notorious slum, Cabrini Green, known since the Civil War era as "Little Hell," when they realized they were lost. He pulled over to ask a pedestrian couple for directions back to the freeway. This turned out *not* to be a good place to stop. For decades famously vicious gangs like the Vice Lords had battled over this turf. By the 1980s heroin and crack had made things even worse and some residents carried Uzis. But what did he know? He was just a naive country kid. The couple Harley asked for directions attempted to carjack him. In the process, they shot once into the car at close range. Harley sped away and made it two blocks before bleeding out into unconsciousness.

An ambulance rushed him to the nearest hospital, Northwestern. He arrived legally dead, but, as luck would have it, a renowned heart surgeon named Dr. Axel Joob happened to be making his rounds. The doctors cut him open and found that the bullet had gone through his arm, heart, and lung. Dr. Joob massaged Harley's heart with his hand and brought him back to life. Harley died again on the operating table, but again he came back. I've always believed that he survived because his body was so strong from all the work he'd done.

I went back to the Hill from Christy's house, where I found Ted

waiting for me. Our parents were already on the way to Chicago to see Harley. I felt helpless. Ted and I both did. I could tell he was thinking the same thing I was. On one hand, we were scared. On the other, we both wanted to leave and find whoever did this. The realization that bad people could get away with such things was crushing. Ted said we should pray, so we did.

Ted and I worked together all that day on the Hill in silence—cleaning stalls, feeding the animals, and exchanging the occasional nervous glance. We were both anxious to hear the ring of the old rotary phone bell that was attached to the outside of the house.

The second the ringing came we threw down our rakes and bolted toward the house. Harley was alive, our mother told us. But there was no telling how long he would be in a coma.

The coma would last a week, it turned out. Ted and I did all the work on the farm while our parents stayed with Harley and waited for him to wake up. When he finally did, the cops put one book of mugshots in front of Harley after another, but he never could identify who shot him. They never caught the shooter.

In time, Harley returned to the Hill to recover. He may have been a bit of a brute when we were growing up, but he was *my brother*. I was sure happy to see him. I was really missing all of my brothers and the way things used to be before they began leaving home. I could understand their desire to get far away from the life we had lived, but I still wanted us to be together. I wished his return could have been under different circumstances. I also wished that there had been more to come home to. I noticed him looking around, seeing how bad things had gotten.

His face was pale as he unbuttoned his shirt to show me the damage. I wasn't prepared for what I saw. A solid strip of metal staples held his breastbone together all the way to his groin. He had been essentially field-dressed by the surgeons at Northwestern who saved his life.

He needed constant care, so I pitched in as an amateur nurse. When I first unwrapped the bandage from his arm to change the dressing, he began to explain in gruesome detail how the bullet entered his arm. He described how it had damaged each of his organs before becoming lodged in his lung. I felt woozy.

"They patched my heart with pig, Sis," he went on.

I could have gone my whole life without knowing that, Harley, I thought. But I smiled and said, "That's really cool!" Even if he *was* badly wounded, I wasn't going to give him the satisfaction of grossing me out.

He held his arm up, and I could see how thin the skin was around his wound—so thin that light shone through. I could smell rotting flesh as I cleaned the bullet wound in his arm. He was sweating out the drugs they'd given him for pain, too; the opioids smelled to me like poison. I thought Harley had been naive to stop in a bad neighborhood like that—talk about fresh off the farm.

Harley's car was eventually sent back to us. There was still dried blood on the seat. I sat there for a moment staring at the blood and thought back on all the other times we'd all almost died.

This wasn't even Harley's first gun-related casualty. He'd once shot a gun that had dirt in the barrel; it exploded in his face. I was beginning to realize how fragile life was. Given the odds with that number of kids, we'd been really lucky so far.

Harley had been away long enough to build caring relationships with others outside our community—mainly attractive women. Harley had a couple of these female friends from the city visit him one afternoon. From behind the closed door of Harley's room came a chorus of adoring moans as the women loudly expressed their gratitude for his recovery. At just that moment, the preacher from our little church showed up at the door. *God must have heard those women calling his name,* I thought. I did what any mischievous little sister would do. I let the preacher walk right into the house.

Brother Brookman had presided over the baptism of several Frey brothers in the small pond on our farm. The baptisms scared me when I was little. I felt like everyone prayed a little too long while holding my brothers under the water.

Now the preacher called out, "Son, where are you?" as he walked from room to room. I tried to contain my laughter as I heard the women scrambling to pull themselves together.

By the time the preacher opened the door to Harley's room, Harley was in bed playing the convalescent and the two women were sitting on the edge of the bed pretending to be concerned visitors. The preacher made himself comfortable sitting on the edge of the bed alongside Harley's girlfriends. He asked Harley to describe his experience of twice dying and coming back to life. As they prayed together, I began to giggle under my breath. *Harley was such a pain in the ass that God kicked him out of heaven twice.*

Within a year of that tragedy, Harley had healed and, at age fifteen, I was ready to move out of my family's home and to take charge of my own life. I'd had enough. The only path on the Hill led downhill. I asked Ted, then a high school senior, if he wanted to move out, too, and live with me. He was working off the farm, bailing hay and doing other work for local farmers. I liked being around Ted. We were the closest in age. Besides, he had a driver's license. I had Harley's old car, but it would be another year before I could legally drive it.

There was a house on another property that my parents had bought years earlier and deeded to my oldest brother, Leonard. The house needed a lot of work and was sitting empty, so it would be rent-free. Between our various after-school jobs, I knew Ted and I could afford to make some repairs and cover the electricity and other bills. Our parents didn't object. They knew we could take care of ourselves. Besides, their relationship and finances were unraveling so rapidly that I don't think they wanted us around to witness the death throes.

I loved my little house. When I moved in, it had tacky orange carpeting and outdated appliances, but I didn't care. My bedroom had a twin bed for me and another one in case I had a friend sleep over. It even had a thermostat! At Christmas we had a real fir tree and wrapped presents stacked underneath. I went from sweeping grit off a threadbare brown rug as a child to cleaning, organizing, and decorating my way into something resembling worthy of a home décor magazine.

I loved any excuse to run errands. To me, a big supermarket was a magical wonderland. Looking around, I remembered that I no longer had to grow, hunt, or find my food. I could walk through an air-conditioned store and choose whatever I wanted. I became obsessed with a Birds Eye frozen meal called Voila! chicken. You throw it in a skillet and you have a chicken and broccoli dish in about ten minutes. I cooked it all the time, even though it wasn't as delicious as when we cooked chicken and vegetables on the farm. It was so different in taste, but I became obsessed with the convenience. Ted begged me to get a crockpot because he was so sick of Voila! chicken, so we added pot roast and other slow-cooked meals to our at-home menu.

"What mother lets their kid leave at age fifteen?" you may ask. In this case, I say a smart one. I needed to get out of there, and she knew it would be the best thing for me. Everything I did was getting me closer to leaving southern Illinois forever. I felt there was so much more. My leaving was also the best thing for her. Once I was out of the house, she could begin the process of seeking more work off the Hill and discovering her own independence. As she came into her own, she became a lot easier to be around.

You might think my newfound freedom would have set me on a fast course for destruction, but just the opposite happened. Ted and I worked hard to create a normal environment, and I found that having everything under my control made me feel calm and happy. I kept the house clean to the point that it was almost sterile. Clutter be damned. I organized the bills, calculating how much we needed each month. We kept the propane tank full. In the winter, that house was warm and cozy. For the hot summers, my buddy Joe gave me an air conditioner. I kept that little house the exact temperature I wanted it to be, all year round.

. . .

Everything came to a head one holiday season after we moved out. I hosted Thanksgiving that year, cooking the entire meal, from the turkey to the pies. I called my friend Penny for advice on what to buy and what recipes to use.

Ted and I had ripped out the carpet, replaced windows, and painted. Leonard came home with his girlfriend and her parents, who wanted to meet his family. Leonard arrived early and was shocked at all we had done with that little house. I was so proud of it and was showing off all the work Ted and I had done. Leonard said, "Act like this is how we always lived."

"Of course," I said. "This old thing?"

I was thrilled by my Thanksgiving meal, but still, the mood around our table was somber. By now, the Hill was a joyless and childless place. My mother was gone most of the day, too. She'd started work selling housing at the University of Illinois, and then found a job at a radio station—both for the money and for her own sanity. It was the first time she'd been out of the home for any length of time. When we were growing up, she'd substitute for the bus driver or help out at the school, but mostly she raised her kids and kept the home fires burning.

My father was ill and frail, left at home on his own. He didn't trust doctors and wouldn't seek treatment, even though he had a number of things wrong with him, including diabetes and cancer. I pleaded with him to go to the hospital when he was at his worst. His standard response: "No way. People die in those places."

The boys were away, so there was no more workforce. It takes money to buy hay and feed. The farm was down to just a couple of horses and one old Saint Bernard. Even with his disability checks, my father didn't have the means to fix up the place, and my mother had decided for the first time in her life that she wouldn't hand over her paychecks to Dad anymore. She said she would no longer throw good money after bad. My father, sick as he was, started to feel lonely. While my mother was away at her job, a woman who worked as a home health nurse started coming around to see him. She got it in her head that he had money, and they began having an affair.

This only made my parents' financial situation scarier. A divorce seemed to be looming, so neither of them wanted to make a payment on the farm. Mom was saving as much as she could, but she wasn't willing to use her own money to make a payment. If you make your monthly payment in that kind of situation, you're technically giving your spouse half of it. And so month followed month, the two of them waiting each other out, not paying the mortgage.

In rural America when I was young, the day you were given your driver's license, almost always on your sixteenth birthday, was the day you felt truly free. Until then, all I had to legally ride was an old bike with "Evel Knievel" emblazoned on the seat. My father always hated that bike. He said a horse might step on it and break its leg.

When the day of my driving test came, I was more than ready. I'd been driving myself around illegally for years, and I was excited to shed the anxiety I felt every time I drove off the Hill. A woman named Karen Oliver ran the DMV. She was the epitome of a country girl, with no filter. If you were her friend, she'd love you forever. If she didn't like you, good luck. Fortunately, she liked the Freys.

My driving test began with her taking the passenger seat and saying, "I can smoke in your car, right?"

What would you have answered? "Fire it up!" I said with a big smile.

I passed.

Once I was a legal driver, I knew I could make real money and become truly independent. For a while, I'd been thinking of ways that I could improve on the one thing that I'd seen be truly successful on the farm: my mother's now-abandoned melon route.

While I was renovating my little house, I realized I was good at project management, and began to turn my attention to using those same skills to start my own small business. I'd always believed that the melon route had the potential to become so much bigger. Now

I had the freedom to put my plans into action, with bigger equipment and more stores.

Technology was changing in my favor. I could have a phone in the truck, letting me conduct business while the wheels turned beneath me. I knew that the faster I drove and the more melons I put in the truck, the more profit I would make. I also knew that I wouldn't turn the money back over to my dad for hay and grain for the horses like my mother had.

I went to the bank to ask for a $10,000 vehicle loan to buy my own delivery truck. The banker, John Dorsey, offered me two years to pay it off.

"No," I said. "I only want three months."

John said, "I'm going to give you two years."

I said, "No, I only want three months. The melon route makes good money, and it will make more if I have this truck. I'll make it back by the end of the summer."

He said, "I'm still going to give you two years."

"Give me whatever you want," I said. "I'm going to be back here in three months with the full amount." I didn't want to be in debt any longer than I had to be.

I went to a used car dealer in Orchardville and negotiated for a used 1989 red three-quarter-ton long-bed Chevy Silverado with a stick shift. The Ford club cab from the farm I'd started the business with was a beater—I had tires in the back because I knew there would be blowouts. This was progress. My Chevy wasn't covered in rust, it usually ran, and I didn't have to haul around a bunch of spare tires.

Sixty days later, after a long day driving and hauling but before the bank closed, I strode into the bank and walked toward John Dorsey's office. I hadn't changed out of my daily work uniform of jeans, T-shirt, cap, boots, and ponytail. The smartly dressed ladies at the counter looked over at me with curiosity. I just smiled at them. This was a big day for me. I knocked on John's door and entered when he called back to come in. Without a word, I handed him a thick envelope. It contained $10,000 plus interest in cash—dusty, in a wide array of denominations, but the whole value of the loan, every penny.

John Dorsey looked at me with wonder and amusement. Then he sat back down and started to count the money. As he did so, the look of surprise on his face grew, and he kept muttering, "Now I've seen it all."

I couldn't stop smiling as I shook his hand and made my way back through the bank's parking lot to my truck—*my* truck.

I loved my melon route. I loved seeing how different stores merchandised their products. I was fascinated by food. The colors of the packaging. The convenience of it—all right there in one temperature-controlled building. You could pick berries out of the produce department without getting chiggers, mushrooms without getting poison ivy. They had meat that you didn't have to skin first. Many of the farmers and the store buyers had seen me coming for a number of years with my mother. They wanted me to succeed, and they cheered me on as I added more and more stores to my route.

Well, most of them did. In the evenings, I used to take the Poseyville exit off the Indiana highway between there and Orchardville. In seven or eight miles I could round up 150 cantaloupes or so from each farm along the road until I had a full load. Then I'd drive home, sleep a few hours, and wake up before the sun rose to get them to market while the air was still cool.

One evening I was on George Dillon's farm in Poseyville, loading up my truck as usual. I sometimes brought someone to help me with the deliveries, but when I loaded the melons, my helper was usually the farmer who grew them. I'd pull my truck up alongside his wagon. The farmer would climb into the wagon and toss them to me. I stood in the back of the pickup truck catching and stacking them two at a time.

The trick to loading a truck with melons is you don't even really catch them. That's how you can stack twenty-pound watermelons without wearing out; you just keep them in the air and guide them gently into the pile. There's a real art to tossing melons. It usually takes about an hour, an hour and a half to fill up a truck bed with five to six hundred of them. On my truck I raised the sideboards by two feet so I could fit more. Later, I bought cattle racks that went even higher, way up over the cab of the truck. With those high racks, the truck looked ridiculous, but with cattle racks I could carry more than a thousand cantaloupes. Come to think of it, that's probably another reason I was always blowing out tires.

On that one day, George Dillon, his face leathery from the sun, told me he wanted to say something to me. He fidgeted with his toothpick until he finally found his words. He said every time he saw me coming down the road it was bittersweet. He liked to sell me his seventy-five acres of melons. I moved a lot of his crop. That pleased him. But it made him sad, too. He didn't like seeing me come back for another load. "Every time you leave here with a load of melons, I imagine that you sell them all and just keep driving with the money," he said. "I hope that one day you get in that truck and you keep going. I hope you drive far, far away."

"What do you mean? That sort of hurts my feelings!" I said, laughing. "You should like it when I come back because I pay you." George sold me each load of melons on credit and in good faith that I would come back for more and pay him for the previous load.

Then he turned serious.

"No," George said, "I mean it. I hope you get in the truck and you keep going all the way to California. You're special. You don't belong here, driving that truck alone and working like this. There is more for you, Sarah Frey. You are special."

"Aw, thanks, George," I said. *That's sweet. And you're right. One day, I will do more. There's a big life waiting for me. But I need your melons to help me get there.*

George gave me the nickname "Hollywood."

I was a teenage girl, strong and healthy, with blondish hair and green eyes. I may have been covered in dust most of the time, but it wasn't hard to imagine that I'd clean up nice. I didn't mind the nickname. I'd be lying if I said I couldn't see what George saw. I'd had dreams of stardom once. In fourth grade, I'd written a Christmas play. I cast it. I even tracked down the costumes. There was a time when I dreamed of being an actress, writer, or director. Of course, there wasn't much opportunity on that front in Orchardville. We had music class once a month, and that was it for the arts.

But for the moment I was content—more than content—to continue in my starring role as the hardworking melon delivery girl. The next week, that farmer saw me back on his farm, picking up produce. He saw me the next week, too, and the week after that.

Come fall, the melons had all been harvested, the air was turning cooler, and the school year began, reminding me that I was still a high school student. I was living on my own, though, so I had to have a winter job, too. I applied to Tractor Supply Company, the franchise that sells everything from farm supplies and Carhartt clothes to toys and candy and dog food. I wasn't shy about asking for a job and didn't go through the normal application process. I surveyed the store. *Lots of busy worker bees. Where is the leader? Ahhh, that guy is nice-looking, tight haircut, professional. He has a leader's aura, and his shirt is clean. It's gotta be him.*

"Hello, Rick," I said. "Are you the store manager?"

"Yes, I am," he said.

"I would like to work here."

He was mildly amused by my confidence. "Do we know each other?"

Nope, but your name is right there on your shirt.

"Look, the reason I want to work here is that I have knowledge of virtually every product in this store."

He stared at me. He seemed amused. "We aren't hiring, but I'm curious what job you think you want here?"

"Well, yours," I said. "I want *your* job."

He laughed out loud and started shaking his head like I was a child wearing him down by asking the same question over and over again. "Let me get this straight. You actually want *my* job?"

"Yes. Your job." I said it with a smile, but I didn't break eye contact.

"Huh," he said, as if he was going to call my bluff. "Okay. You're hired."

I was indignant that I still had to finish high school. I was ready to get on with my life. I negotiated with the principal to allow me to leave school early each day to be able to go to work and then to community college at night.

I'd been a good student most of my life until high school. The first couple of years I did pretty well, but by the time my junior year rolled around, I was checked out. Most of the teachers knew how busy I was working and turned a blind eye to unexcused absences.

I also negotiated with my former teacher Ms. Leyva. After the little country school in Orchardville closed for consolidation she took a job teaching kindergarten in Wayne City, on the same campus where I was attending high school. She allowed me to say that, for credit, I was helping her as a teacher's aide. She knew full well that I would rarely show up at the elementary school. She covered for me. It let me get away with my triple life of high school, college, and work. Looking back, there were so many people who helped me make that work—most of them probably didn't even know just how much.

Those were sleepless years. During the school term, I would go to high school in the morning, until about eleven. I liked leaving before lunch, because I was still a free-lunch kid, and handing over that yellow punch card hadn't gotten any easier.

From there, I would go to Tractor Supply, where I worked from noon to six. At six I would leave and drive to Frontier Community College, where I attended night classes like "Fundamentals of Effective Speaking," taught by Mary Lou Miller. I chose that class because I thought I might be good at it, given my prior speech contest win.

One assignment we had was to give a talk in front of the class while describing the activity we were doing. I decided I'd make snickerdoodle cookies. There I was in front of the class making the dough, and I forgot one of my ingredients. My dough didn't come together. I kept talking, as if the dough was supposed to be 90 percent flour. *What the hell is happening to this dough? Stay cool. Keep talking. Nothing to see here.*

I looked over at Mary Lou. She was looking back at me, smiling. She knew something was wrong and was watching to see how I handled it.

I set the dough aside and said, "If we had time for that, then we would bake those for thirty minutes at three hundred fifty degrees! But of course we don't, and so . . ." I moved on.

After the class, she told me that I did the right thing: "All that matters is that when something doesn't go right, you keep moving forward." She gave me an A.

Frontier is one of the noble community colleges in this country that offer special help to kids like me who are the first generation in their families to go to college. Not everyone can afford four-year college or take that much time away from work. Community colleges change lives.

My boss at Tractor Supply thought I was in college full-time. They didn't realize that I was still going to high school until Rick asked me if I could open the store one day.

"I can't," I said. "I have school."

"We thought you took night classes!" he said.

"I do, but I have to go to high school in the morning."

He didn't believe that I was only sixteen. He called Wayne City High School to make sure that I was actually enrolled there and not just trying to get out of opening the store. He also learned that I had not lied about my birthday on the application. He'd just overlooked it during my hasty hiring. I was very mature for my age, so no one ever questioned it. Everyone just assumed that I had to be an adult.

Even though most hours of most days were spoken for, I did manage to go to my prom, and I did date. I met my first crush in one of my college classes. His name was Scott, and I remember looking at him and thinking that he was one of the most beautiful men I had ever seen. He was twenty-four, with a head full of wavy blond hair.

He was tan, six-one, super fit. I'd never been interested in boys before Scott. Then I took one look at him and thought, *This, I'm interested in.*

Scott also assumed I was older. We'd been hanging out after class for a few weeks when he asked me on a date. I told him I couldn't that weekend, because I had to go to the prom.

"What college student goes to prom?" he said. "Why would you do that?"

I told him that it was my prom. I was a high school senior. He was shocked by this revelation.

"You didn't tell me how old you were!" he said.

"You didn't ask," I replied.

There was someone I liked more anyway—a college boy in one of my writing classes who reminded me a lot of Scott but was closer to my age. He asked me if I wanted to come over and have pizza at his place and study. I agreed and followed him to his apartment. As we pulled into the parking lot, I grew nervous. I realized he lived in the same apartment complex as Scott.

Ugh, small towns were the worst. It was inevitable that Scott would see my car and know I was there with someone else. *No big deal,* I reasoned. *We're just classmates. Pizza and study time can be explained away.* Everything was going great until he asked if I wanted to walk over to his brother's place and see what he was up to.

His brother, it turned out, was Scott.

It wasn't hard to decide that my love life needed to be put on hold until I left Wayne County. I didn't have time for dating anyway. I knew I didn't want to end up in southern Illinois long-term and so serious boyfriends were out of the question. Everything I did was geared toward giving myself greater independence. And yet my brothers and I needed one another desperately, especially when we were visited by what seemed to be increasingly frequent catastrophes.

One morning Ted dropped me at Tractor Supply as usual and then drove to work at a nearby farm where he was helping out.

After that, he doesn't know what happened. He veered into the other lane and collided with a truck head-on. The other driver was killed.

The mother of a mutual friend of ours called me at Tractor Supply and said that Ted had been in an accident and that he was being airlifted to Evansville, Indiana. Since Ted had dropped me off, I was stuck with no vehicle there and no way to get to him until a friend was able to pick me up and take me to the hospital. Hours had passed by the time I walked in. I saw Ted, but he didn't look like Ted. Bloodied and broken, he looked like a monster with a face swollen to the size of a basketball. Tubes were everywhere, to relieve the pressure from the head trauma.

As the days passed, the nurses would have to wake Ted up every hour. He wasn't responding to voice commands, so they would use an electrical shock device, like a tiny Taser, to shock Ted's foot. Ted would yell curse words and then fall back asleep. I apologized to the nurses and told them that it wasn't like him to cuss. For the first nine days, Harley stayed by Ted's side, sleeping in a chair next to his bed at night.

I was so happy when Ted was finally back in our little house with me. I took care of what I could while he was away, but I really missed having him around. After three months in the hospital, he wasn't the same person, and his head wasn't fully healed. But he was home. He'd had some facial reconstructive surgery but would need much more. At one point, he had to have his jaw rebroken and wired shut; he lived on protein shakes and painkillers. He had to carry a pair of wirecutters with him so that if he ever choked you could cut the wires and clear his airway.

With almost no fiber in his diet, Ted wound up getting hemorrhoids. I had no idea what they even were and I stopped him when he tried to explain. Reporting on hemorrhoid progress became the highlight of his day. One morning I woke up late and was rushing to get ready when I started gagging. *What is this creamy, awful-tasting toothpaste?* It turned out I'd started brushing my teeth with his hemorrhoid cream. *Who puts butt cream in a drawer with tooth-brushes?*

"I'm going to break your jaw a third time!" I hollered from the bathroom.

Ted was never the same after the accident. After they took the jaw wires out and his mouth was free again, the voice coming out of him was new. He was more thoughtful, a deeper person, probably because he felt such guilt about the driver who'd died. But he was also, strangely enough, funnier. His head injury had given him a whole new sense of humor. Since that tragedy, he's been our family's comedian.

The pressure of working and studying long hours while worrying about my parents' tanking marriage and Ted's and Harley's recoveries started to get to me. My temper became shorter than usual and I had very little tolerance for immaturity. Not long after Ted's accident my brother John, who was in college in Louisville, bought a small house in our neighborhood, not far from the Hill, to have a place of his own to stay in when he visited. I was happy that I would see him more, but he always showed up with his friend Binky.

Binky looked like a clean-shaven Seth Rogan. He grew up in the hills of Kentucky and was my brother John's college roommate for years, thus becoming an extended member of the Frey family. He was a great guy, but we were like oil and water. He didn't have a serious bone in his body. I was an eyes-on-the-prize girl. He was fun. I was always working. He drank. I didn't. He smoked pot constantly. I didn't like it. He was able to cut loose. I was not. He was lovable but reckless, and that scared me. I didn't need more people to worry about, and now I had this honorary new brother. I shook my head when I saw the types of shenanigans he and John would pull. His visits to the farm had become more frequent, and I suspected there was more growing in John's new basement than black mold.

One morning I was getting ready for work when I heard a gunshot echo down the hallway. *Okay, who's the idiot cleaning their gun in my kitchen?* I found Binky standing there in shock, holding a rifle. He'd shot a hole through my kitchen floor.

"Binky, what in the hell do you think you're doing?" Even though he was a few years older than me, I shouted as if he were a naughty child and I his exasperated mother. "Put down the gun!"

He started to explain, but I didn't care to hear the story. I had to get to work and didn't have time to give him the scolding he deserved. "No more guns for you in my house, Binky. Ever. Got it?"

I was John's little sister, but Binky was terrified of me. I could scare him with just a look.

"Yes, Sarah," he said, looking down in shame.

If only everyone in my life were so easy to manage. On the Hill, the tensions between my parents were about to reach a crisis.

Chapter 8

Taking the Hill

One sunny afternoon in southeastern Illinois, my mother was driving her Ford Country Squire station wagon with the wood-grain body trim down a narrow country road when she saw my father's girlfriend driving toward her in a little green Ford Taurus. My mother would later tell me that she came very close to cutting the wheel and plowing into the woman's car, but she restrained herself—until she caught sight of my father's truck in front of John's house, a field's distance from her home on the Hill.

When she came closer, she saw that my father was actually sitting in his truck in the driveway—most likely having just seen off his girlfriend, she figured. Without another thought, she drove her car at full speed directly into his Ford. She hit the truck with such force that my father was ejected out the open passenger-side door. Without even assessing the damage, my mother turned her car around—her station wagon somehow still in almost perfect shape—drove it to the neighbors' house, and called me at my little house.

"Sarah," she said, "there has been a little bit of an accident. By mistake I slid into your father's truck. Could you please go over there and help? The police might be coming."

Her voice sounded odd. She spoke in a soft, measured tone that I had never heard her use before.

"Mom," I said, "can you not talk because the neighbors might overhear you?"

"That's right," she said.

"Mom," I said, "you did this on purpose, right? You hit Dad's truck?"

"Um-hmmm."

"Is he dead?"

"I don't think so," she said. "But I left rather quickly. Can you go over there?"

I drove to John's house. When I arrived, I found my father's truck in the driveway, totaled. The whole driver's side was caved in. My father was sitting in the yard on a five-gallon bucket with an ice pack on his head. His nurse-girlfriend showed up and began hopping around like a wet hen. She must have witnessed the collision in her rearview mirror. She certainly must have heard it! She flipped her sunglasses up and marched toward me as I approached my father.

"Your mother needs psychological help!" she said indignantly, sounding annoyingly self-righteous. "I've called the police and they're on their way!" She went on a rant about how crazy my mother was, how my father could have been killed.

As I listened to her, I thought: *Oh, good, one more adult who needs to be parented.*

My voice never gets loud when I am angry. It usually gets quieter. My blood pressure didn't rise a point. I just looked her dead in the eye and said, "Stop. Talking." She could tell that what had just happened to my father was nothing compared to what I was capable of doing to her.

"And you," I said, turning now to my father, yet another unruly child, "if you say one word to the cops when they come, I will never speak to you again."

He looked pitiful sitting there on that bucket. I was so angry, but I continued speaking calmly. "I'm going to clean up your mess now," I told my father. "You're all an embarrassment!" I added as I turned toward the road and tried to think of what I would say to the police officer.

I muttered, mostly to myself, *You let her call the police . . . really? Is that what we do now—call the police? New one on me. Has everyone gone completely mad around here?*

The clock was ticking. I surveyed the situation and tried to imagine how I could cover it up in time. I quickly calculated how many minutes it would take before the cop would arrive. *It would be a Wayne City officer. She called about five minutes ago. I have less than ten minutes to get rid of my injured father, his fuming girlfriend, and the destroyed truck.* It was doable as long as nothing else went wrong.

Something did.

John's roommate, Binky, stumbled out of the house high as a kite, engulfed in a cloud of marijuana smoke. Binky had been smoking so much pot that he missed the excitement happening just outside the house.

Remain calm. Breathe. Just breathe. I gagged from the powerful stench of pot. *No! Wait! Don't breathe!*

I was trying to build a business and earn a college degree while supporting myself. I had no time or tolerance for unnecessary drama. If my parents wanted to fight to the death, that was on them, but now I was involved—and my brother John was squarely caught in the crossfire as well, because he owned the property. The last thing I needed was for the officer to say, "Let's go talk about this inside." How many members of my family would be in handcuffs before the day was out? That would be another, even bigger mess to clean up.

"*Whoaaaa.* What's going *onnnnn?*" Binky asked in drug-induced wonderment.

The scene was a lot to take in straight sober, let alone in Binky's state. He became energetically childlike and bounced over to the truck to inspect the damage. Then he asked my dad why his head was hurting.

"Harold, you gotta get that looked at!" Binky said. "Hey, isn't that Donna, your nurse? *Heyyyyy*, Donna, how you doin'? Hold on now, you mean Liz did this? Damn, Liz went all kind of crazy on all y'all."

He noticed my stare and shouted, "Now Sarah's got them green eyes out lookin' all mad like she goin' to light somethin' on fire. Now that's what I'm talkin'' bout!"

I snapped. "Shut up! Everyone. Just. Shut. The. F. Up. Binky, the cops are coming. Go back into the house and hide. Please, Binky. Get it together."

"Nawwwww. Nooo wayyy. The police?" Even stoned, he was amazed that anyone in my family would ever allow the cops to be called.

"Yes, Binky. The police. Like the put-you-in-handcuffs-and-take-you-away police. Now go back in the house!"

He wasn't processing a word I was saying and couldn't grasp the urgency of the matter. He started to ask me if I was okay, as though I had been the one in the truck. Then he couldn't remember why the police were coming in the first place.

"Binky, I'm done now," I said. "Go back in the house. I swear to God, Binky, if you come back out, I am going to kill you. Okay? Kill you. Do you understand?"

Now he understood. He started walking toward the house. One down.

Okay, now, where was I? Injured philandering father. Gold-digging nurse. Police on the way. Primary mission: keep Mom out of jail.

After closing the door on Binky, I heard the sound of tires rolling over the gravel. A patrol car slowly pulled up. *Oh, boy. Here we go.*

So many thoughts raced through my mind as I approached the car. I recognized the officer, Deputy Atwood, and greeted him cordially as he pulled up. He was the father of one of my former classmates, an authority figure, but from the wrinkles around his eyes I could see that he was tired and not looking forward to dealing with this mess. I saw him taking in the scene. He registered my father sitting there on the bucket, head in hand, his girlfriend blustering around her Taurus. And then he saw me, this little slip of a girl, marching urgently toward him, waving. I caught him before he exited the car. I leaned down, resting my forearms on the driver's-side door. *Be calm. Be cool. Be casual. Everything is under control. Trust. Gain his trust.*

"Can we sit in your car and talk for a second before you get out?" I asked him with a smile. *I can't believe I'm actually volunteering to get into a cop car.* I summoned every drop of "These are not the droids you're looking for" Jedi magic.

The man knew me. He knew that my brothers and I worked hard and that no one ever had an issue with any of us. We'd been raised so strictly that we were never the kids getting in trouble. We never drank on a tailgate. We didn't throw parties in the woods. We never left the Hill. I knew that gave us some credit in his book.

"Sure," he said.

I climbed into the passenger seat.

"You know," I said, as we both stared out the front window at the scene of adults in crisis, "this is very embarrassing for me. This is a complicated family situation. The woman over there is someone that my father may or may not be involved with. I have a feeling my mom probably just *slid accidentally* into that truck and wasn't *necessarily* thinking about the repercussions. I'm not even sure if these farm vehicles have insurance, to be honest. You know, I should probably just go ahead and take care of this situation myself. I've got this. I'm not sure it's worth your time. I'm sorry that you've had to drive all the way out here for this misunderstanding. If we could just maybe forget this ever happened, that would probably be good." Then I tried to change the subject to my old friend, the sheriff's son.

The sheriff's deputy sat in silence.

I could almost see the wheels turning in his head. On one hand, it was his job to get out of the car and start writing things down in his little book. There had been an accident. Maybe even an attempted murder. Property had been damaged. There was an injured man in-volved.

And on the other hand, he had . . . me. A teenage girl, saying it was a family matter and I had it under control. He'd seen me plenty of times rolling through town with a rickety truck overloaded with melons. I'm sure I must have looked ridiculous, but no one could question my ambition. Now he could see what that Frey girl was working so hard to escape. The Frey girl was trying to save her own life.

"Yeah, okay," he said, finally, looking over at me. "Good talk. I'll see you around."

I'll never forget how I felt stepping out of Deputy Atwood's car. I didn't watch him drive away. I just stood motionless there in the driveway, relief washing over me, staring at my father until the sound of the engine faded into the countryside. I steadily approached this man who had raised me, who had taught me everything he knew. He was still on the bucket, staring up at me with wide eyes and an open mouth. I could read his thoughts: *Who is this girl who just handled this situation? What kind of daughter have I raised? Who's in charge here?* He was flustered and annoyed that the deputy hadn't even checked on him or asked for his point of view.

The nurse, too, was in shock. Everything she had just witnessed was too much for her. She became manic. "Your father has a concussion!" she yelled at me, gesticulating wildly. "What is wrong with you? Why did that officer just leave?!"

As I walked away, I just shrugged and said, "Maybe you should watch him better."

I could see that my mother was working hard to build a better life for herself. But after years of being controlled by Dad, she clearly held a lot of pent-up resentment that was beginning to show itself in ways that could turn tragic. I sure didn't blame her for having those feelings. With my brothers gone, I knew Mom needed my help, but when I told her she should meet with a lawyer to talk about a divorce, she seemed hesitant. I insisted. I drove her to the office of a friend of mine, a lawyer in private practice a half hour away in Fairfield, Illinois.

In the lawyer's office, she and I sat side by side as I introduced her, then got right down to business: "Mom," I said, "tell him why you want a divorce."

She didn't say anything.

My friend, the lawyer, looked over his glasses at her and said, in his Foghorn Leghorn voice, "Elizabeth, do you want to get a divorce from Sarah's father?"

She turned to look at me and then back at him. "Well," she told him, "you see, I never actually married the kids' dad."

Wait. Did I hear that right? I fell back into my chair. The attorney lowered his glasses and looked at her cautiously. I gripped the armrest of the leather chair, then slowly rolled my hands back and forth over the smooth leather.

"Wait," I said, "so you never had a religious ceremony? You just went to a justice of the peace . . . or what?"

"Well, you know what I mean," she said.

"No, Mom," I said. "I don't know what you mean."

"We have a common-law marriage," she said. "We've been together enough years."

"That's not a thing in the state of Illinois. I don't know if that applies anywhere anymore. You are not married, Mom."

"Well," she said, seeming nowhere near as embarrassed as I thought she should be, "it has certainly been *like* we were married."

So much went through my mind. Now it made sense why there were no wedding pictures around and they never celebrated an anniversary. I wondered how they had gotten away with pretending. She did have a point. It was *like* they were married.

What bothered me most about this revelation was that she had waited to tell me until I was in the chair in front of someone else. She hadn't said anything when we were in the parking lot about to go in, or five minutes prior, or five years prior. Selfishly, I wondered what this meant for me socially. I worried my brothers would take this revelation much harder. Then I wondered what else I didn't know. I felt foolish. Finally, I felt guilty for wasting everyone's day. I had no spare time and here we had driven all the way to Fairfield for no reason.

I was embarrassed, too, that once again I was in the middle of a mess. I started to rise from my chair to walk out on my mother and the attorney.

Wait, I thought. *No marriage also means no messy divorce. I'm going to go ahead and put this one in the win column. This is good. I'll worry about how I feel about this later.*

When we'd left the office together, I turned to her before starting the car and said, "Mom, did it ever cross your mind that maybe you should have had that conversation with me before we were in front of a lawyer? You knew I was bringing you here so you could start the process of getting a divorce. That's the thing that people do when they're married and they don't want to be married anymore. That's called divorce. But you had to wait until this moment to enlighten me that there was no divorce needed."

"Well, I just figured I needed to talk to an attorney anyway," she replied.

In that moment I realized she needed that trip to the attorney's office to be part of her process. In her mind and to the world she was his wife. For nearly thirty years they had represented themselves to the world as Harold and Elizabeth Frey. One unnecessary meeting with an attorney was the necessary step she needed to get closure. Never mind the fact that I'd been blindsided. Up until that point her whole life had been about him. What he wanted. What he needed. His dreams. His wins. And, more often than not, his losses. It was the beginning of a new season for her.

In spite of all my efforts to settle my parents' affairs before the bank took the farm away, the final notice arrived. My father's charm wouldn't work anymore. They couldn't press their luck for another year, or even another month. The bank was taking the Hill.

It had been coming for so long that I wasn't even sad. So many small farms around the country were dissolving. What was one more? I viewed shutting it all down as one more job to be done. I found homes for animals. I sold off old equipment. After years of strategizing and working and sacrificing, all I had to do was settle my parents' affairs and I would finally be free.

And then, one day at sunset, as I led the last horse off the farm to the trailer that would take it to its new home, I froze. The land around me started glowing like gold. My arm holding the lead shank fell at my side. The horse stopped walking.

This is it, I thought. *This is the end of the farm. Right now. I'm going to sell this horse. Then all that's left is the old house and the land itself, and the bank will take that. My parents will go their separate ways and live God knows where. I will move away to a big city. My brothers will live in other cities and towns. We will be thrown to the four winds. And we will never come back here again.*

Where were these feelings coming from? I'd always wanted to leave. Now that I had the chance, the finality of it devastated me. The prospect of having no tether, no anchor, no *home.* I felt responsible for my family, and I felt responsible for that farm and for the future. Eventually some of us might have children, and how could I live with myself if children of mine or my future nieces and nephews never climbed these trees or ate these blackberries?

My mind flashed back to all the memories of growing up there— some glorious and some tragic. I looked at the pond and saw myself learning to swim. I looked at the trees and saw myself learning to hunt. I saw myself at three, at seven, at twelve. I saw my brothers at all ages, too—as little boys, as teenagers, as men.

I saw us hauling water for the horses, playing hide-and-seek, watching mares birthing foals, huddling by a woodstove, growing our food, hunting our food, hanging meat in the smokehouse, laughing, crying, bleeding. All of it happened here.

The saddest part for me was remembering all our effort and all our worries about the farm for so many years. There was so much work to do every day—seeding, feeding, growing, raising, harvesting. The life was so simple and so hard, but it was building toward something: making this land ours. We worked every day to survive and to prosper, to take care of our land and one another. How could we just walk away from all that now?

Before this moment, I'd dreamed of killing off the main character of my story—the Frey girl, the melon girl, the girl in the ball cap and work boots—and starting over anywhere else in the world. I dreamed of California, and of Chicago, and of Europe—anywhere but the Hill, and as anyone but the girl I was. Now, faced with the finality of that decision, something changed. It wasn't just this failing piece of land that I wanted to save. It was my family.

By this point, the others were losing sentimentality about the farm. When my mother looked at it, she saw the money and labor she'd poured into it over the years—her inheritance, every cent she'd made selling melons, all the money she had given to my father. My brothers saw all the work and money they had contributed over the years, wasted. Everyone had tried their best, and for what? It was over now. But it wasn't over. I could still take a stand.

Without this land, I thought, *where will we be? More important:* who *will we be?* How could I ever make sense of myself if I let this place go? If I walked away, my brothers and I would never have anything to come home to. It would be my fault because I was the last one.

For years I'd longed to leave. My dreams just weren't strong enough to pull me away from all these memories. This land—it was the cover on our family's book. Everything we did and said and experienced was our story. If you don't have the cover, the pages scatter in the wind. I needed the binding to keep us together.

With perfect clarity, I knew I had to save the farm. I also knew that I couldn't just bail my parents out. I had watched as my brothers took out student loans and then, instead of using the money to live in the dorms or enjoy the college experience, given the money to our father.

No, if I was going to do this, it would have to be my land. I would manage it how I saw fit. I wouldn't let my father be in control. No more watching Dad take out mortgages. No more watching Mom do whatever he said. I would do what *I* believed was right. The deed would be in my name.

The horse was staring at me now. The sun dipped behind the hills as I stood there on the golden earth, thinking, *I must do this . . . I will do this. Because I'm the only one who can.*

I looked back at the horse. We stared at each other for a moment. I ran my hand down his face one last time and led him to the horse trailer. I would find a way to save the farm, and it would not involve horses. That was my father's dream. My way would be different. Still, I walked the horse the rest of the way with a heavy tread. It felt as if the earth was pulling me down into it. My dreams of being a lawyer in Chicago, or anything at all except the Frey girl, were dead. Now I was never getting off the Hill.

Chapter 9

Frey Farms

Not long after I had my epiphany, I floated the idea of buying the farm to my banker, John Dorsey. He'd seen how quickly I'd paid off the loan for my first truck. He respected me. Still, I couldn't really share with him the emotional aspects of why I wanted to buy the farm. Speaking to him, I kept it all business. I described how I was going to try to put the land to use growing fruits and vegetables. In reality, I had no idea what I was going to do with it, or even if the former horse pastures would be suitable for growing anything but weeds. He had faith in me regardless, and agreed to loan me the money and to help me work with my parents' bank to buy the land from them.

My father, in spite of his ill health and lack of resources, struggled to face reality. He wanted to keep control of the farm even though he had used up every last chance with his bank. I tried to reason with him.

"Dad, look around. It's over," I said. "Are you really okay with letting this place end up on an auction block for all of the neighbors to see?"

He still wanted to be in charge. There was nothing left to be in charge of beyond dilapidated barns and pastures full of pigweed. There were no more horses or any livestock—not even a stray dog. We'd tried it his way for a long, long time. I hoped he would see that I could make real money and perhaps change our family's luck. Wouldn't he somewhere deep down find comfort in knowing that at least someone had the will and ability to step forward and shoulder the responsibly?

I wanted to push it. To convince him. I realized this was how Harley must have felt a few weeks earlier when he tried to confront our father. Home from college, Harley told him that he wouldn't send home any more money because our father was misspending it, and not even paying insurance on the land. He also said that he wasn't treating our mother right, flaunting his nurse girlfriend the way he was.

Dad told him he had some nerve, and insisted that Mom was the one having an affair. He had always hated it when she left the Hill for any reason, even to work. Every move she made toward independence, whether volunteering at the school or taking college night classes, he saw as a threat. He berated her until she quit or he told anyone who would listen that she was sleeping around.

Harley was not having it. "Mom is not doing anything but working at a radio station," he said. "You're the cheater."

Our father had been clenching a coffee cup in his hand. As soon as Harley said that last line, Harold lifted the cup in the air and bashed it into Harley's head. It split open his face.

Harley could have killed his father that very minute. He was strong enough. Instead, he glared at him for a minute, blood gushing down his face and neck and soaking into his white T-shirt, and then he drove himself to the hospital.

Harley was supposed to graduate that day. He had a 4.0. Instead of walking with his classmates and being honored for making the dean's list, he spent hours at the ER, having his face stitched back together.

Some weeks later, as the afternoon sun shone through the kitchen window, it was my turn to try to make our father see that it was inevitable; soon I would be in charge. Things would change. And yet, with the very first mention of this reality, I felt the tension in the room rise, and I saw the anger in Dad's eyes. He accused me of siding with my mother against him. I checked the room for weapons he might grab. I had never felt at risk of violence from him before. Now I wasn't so sure. He was rapidly losing control over his children and my mother, and the loss of power was making him come unhinged. Rather than continue trying to make my point, I walked out of the room.

Did he really expect that after all those years my brothers and I would turn our backs on our mother? Maybe, but I was old enough now to see behind the curtain. I knew truths that couldn't be buried. I was faced with a choice. The facts at hand forced me to be the judge, jury, and executioner. I resolved to do what had to be done, and to do it without anger. To me, holding on to hate was like dragging a dead horse. (I've actually had to drag a dead horse. They're heavy.)

I took no pleasure in it. This was, after all, my dad—the man who had taught and groomed me, who had told me he loved me, who since I was small had spoken to me like an adult, like his equal. I had worshiped him when I was younger. But now I loved him and I hated him. And there was only one way this was going to go. My way.

Not long after our confrontation about buying the farm, I ran into my father in the parking lot of one of the grocery stores along my melon route. He was there alone, wearing filthy clothes, struggling to unload cantaloupes into a grocery cart by himself.

I had hot cantaloupes in the back of my truck, too. He was at my store. The produce manager was waiting for me to deliver my melons. Somehow my father had found out and had beaten me there with his own small truckload. I couldn't believe what I was seeing. I was furious. He was trying to steal business from me. This was the last straw.

He noticed me and stopped loading the cart. He steadied himself against the side of the truck. As I walked toward him through the parking lot, I could see in his eyes that he thought I was about to let him have it.

In the time it took me to walk across the parking lot, something shifted inside me. Watching him standing there, frail but determined, his green eyes, so like mine, still flickering with fire, mixed with a little fear, my rage melted into pity. Trying to sell melons at my store wasn't an act of aggression so much as desperation. Without a word, I climbed into the back of his truck like I had done a thousand times as a child. He stared up at me as I handed him down the cantaloupes so he could make his delivery. Then I watched as he awkwardly pushed his grocery cart into the store. I left before he came outside with the money from the sale.

It took some time, but finally the sale went through and the day came to take over the farm outright. I would pay $50,000 for a hundred acres, in two parcels—eighty acres and twenty acres.

My dad had to go to the title company to sign over the deed to me. I would like to think he'd come around to believing it was the right thing and that he wished me well, but the truth was, he realized he had no other option. You could see it in the slump of his shoulders as he sat at the title company's table. He felt defeat. His youngest child was taking over the land he'd been managing since before she was born. His big, strong body was starting to betray him. His life was winding down.

My brothers were a little confused by my decision to buy the Hill. I drove up to the University of Illinois to get Leonard's signature on the transfer of the twenty-acre title, which had his name on it, too. He was in graduate school and everyone had always thought that I'd follow him there. Now it suddenly looked like I would never get a real education. I didn't want to pull Leonard down into the darkness that had been unfolding back at home. It seemed as if he was doing great at school. He had nice friends and a high-paying part-time job, and he was on the way to earning his doctorate. He didn't need any distractions. If I told him about the realization I'd had when I walked the last horse off the farm, he might have staged an intervention. I just needed his signature. We met up at a coffee shop. He looked good—happy and clean-cut.

"Why the hell do you want to do this?" he asked.

"I don't," I said. "I just can't stand to see it go away. Don't you care?"

"No," he said. "We all sacrificed so much. And for what? I want to get as far away from it as I can. How can you care so much?"

"I'm not sure," I said. "Everything would be a lot easier if I didn't."

I thought but did not say that I could see how even though his life seemed better and he was off the Hill, Leonard was still carrying the emotional equivalent of those heavy water buckets we hauled, year after year. We all were. They needed to be dumped. He couldn't understand why I was adding more water to mine. But his indifference was exactly what I was afraid of. If we ever decided we needed each other, where would we go? We were all so close growing up. We needed to stick together no matter what. That is what family does. Right or wrong doesn't matter. Blood is blood. Alone in the world we could be broken. Together we could withstand anything. Right?

Leonard and I sat in the coffee shop looking at each other without another word. He saw the resignation in my eyes, shrugged, and signed the paperwork.

Once I bought the farm, I had to figure out what to do with it. The good news about a failing farm is that it can't get much worse. I'd learned what not to do. Meanwhile, I had to continue to make money any way I could to keep up my payments on the land.

. . .

One source of income was scrap iron. My father had instilled in us kids a respect for steel because of his early job as a steelworker in Granite City, Illinois. He taught me so much about metal that I could look at an old plow or combine in a farmer's fields, rusting away, and know just how much it was worth. I began to pick up any equipment that farmers wanted to get rid of. Then I'd haul it to a scrapyard in Evansville, Indiana. The farmer would get a third of the weight ticket and I would get two-thirds. Sometimes they would just give me the old broken-down equipment to get it out of the way.

John was living in Louisville, going to college and working in the racing secretary's office at Churchill Downs and at a nightclub. He knew what I was working toward and knew that in the winter my income was much less, the opportunities fewer. John loved the entertainment business. After being trapped on the Hill, he let loose in Louisville. He came home one weekend with a bright idea that led to one of our more colorful moneymaking ventures: hosting fight nights. In the mid-1990s, a bar in a warehouse in Junction City went out of business and John said, "Let's turn it around and start booking bands and having concerts. Come on, Sis, we can do this! We'll make money."

For a short period of time, we did. We even hooked up with some sleazy promoters to bring in fighters and a boxing ring. It was a seven-week deal, and we called it Friday Night Fight Nights. I hired the beer tub girls and bartenders and booked the bands. I handled the cash and the booze, and the advertising and promotional money from the local beverage distributors. About eight hundred patrons came to the bar every Friday night to drink and watch amateur boxers clobber each other into submission. Sometimes the door would be $10,000 or $12,000 a night. That didn't stop us from picking up the cans in the parking lot to make another $150.

By that point, my job was pretty much just to make sure we didn't get ripped off. So I watched all the money. In my experience, nearly everyone was skimming, and the beer tub girls stole the most.

You could almost hear them singing, "One for you, two for me . . ." You had to make sure they weren't comping their boyfriend and their boyfriend's buddy a bunch of beers. I never drank, just ran around counting the cash.

When we were nearing the end of the fight nights, the fight promoters tried to change the deal on us. They saw we were making a lot of money, and they thought, *These kids, they've stumbled onto something*. They told my brother John, "You have to give us more money—80 percent of the door." John came to me and said, "Well, I guess we have to give them 80 percent."

"Nah, the deal was 50 percent of the door," I said.

"Well, you know they're not happy with the returns they're making," said John. "And quite honestly, Sis, they're really big goons. Never mind the fact that they all carry guns."

"John, that's bullshit," I said. "We're not giving them 80 percent of the door. We have to pay the lease, the fighters, and the overhead. We can't afford a shakedown. Let's go get this straight right now."

John was a super-skinny computer geek. Neither one of us wanted to go, but I made him drive us over to their office, which was inside a gym in a strip mall.

As we parked in the large lot, before we went in, I noticed that John was literally sweating. It was the dead of winter.

"Listen, John," I said, "I don't want to go in there either, but we're going to face this head-on. We had an agreement. A deal's a deal, right?"

John said, "Yeah, yep, you're right."

"Good," I said. "Here's the plan. We go in there and pretend we don't need the money. You tell the guys it's fifty-fifty. If they don't like it, they can break the contract and take down their ring and we'll cancel the remaining fights. They won't want to give up their take of the door."

"Okay," John finally said, "we're going in."

I let him get out of the truck first. When he wasn't looking, I took our gun out of the console and put it in my deep coat pocket.

In the office, we found the three hulks we were in business with.

They were indeed humongous, with veins popping in their temples and their necks vanishing into mountains of shoulder muscles. We nervously sat down across from them.

Strong out of the gate, John said, "Okay. We can't give you 80 percent of the door. It's 50–50, a deal's a deal."

The guy became instantly angry. He was not used to hearing no, especially not from a scrawny kid. Standing up from his seat and walking toward us, he said, "Where do you think these fighters are coming from? We're sending people in there to fight so there's a show. Your customers are only there because of the fight nights. We deserve more of the take."

"Excuse me," I said, standing up myself. "That's why we hired you—to attract fighters. You set up the ring, you run the fighters, and we split the door. Maybe you have contacts in this town to set up your boxing ring, but last time I checked, we have the only venue with enough room for twelve hundred people to come in and watch a fight. The way I see it, you need us. But if you want to take the ring down, I understand."

As I spoke, the guy kept getting madder. His face turned red. He seemed to grow even bigger and he began to lurch closer to where we sat. Rather than continue to negotiate, he wanted to fight John. *Yeah, this is what I was afraid of.* I scanned the room in anticipation of someone reaching for a weapon. Even unarmed, they could have broken John in half with one punch.

My father always said, "Don't ever pull a gun unless you intend to use it." I thought about the handgun in my coat. I knew that if this guy tried to hurt John, I would have no choice. *Confront the bad guys. Whose terrible idea was this anyway? Oh, wait, it was mine.* Now John's life was on the line.

The guy got right up into John's face. *The gun was a bad idea. I might actually have to shoot this idiot.* I stood and stepped in between them in the little office. My eyes were on fire. My body filled with fury.

"Back off," I said. "A deal's a deal. It's half the door. Or I'll take down the ring myself and burn it in the parking lot. You lay one hand on my brother and this doesn't end well for you or anyone in this room."

Our eyes were locked. He didn't move. He was smarter than I thought. Something told him to listen to me and let us leave.

We walked outside and hopped back in the truck. John was shaking. I pulled the gun out and laid it on the console between us.

"Oh my God!" John yelled. "You had a gun?! You took a gun in there? You had the gun on you the whole time. Oh my God. I'm going to be sick."

"Yeah, John, you're damn right I had a gun," I said. "What was I supposed to do? Let them kill you? Every meathead in that gym carries a gun. I'm out now. We'll finish the scheduled fights and then I'm out of this business for good. I don't care if I have to scrap iron the rest of my life. I'm done. And so are you. We're better than this. Nothing good can come from slinging booze and working with these lowlifes. I never want to feel like I have to carry a gun into a business meeting again. Understood?"

"You're right," he said. "There are plenty of ways to make money in the light."

The rest of the fight nights went smoothly for the most part, though those guys grumbled the whole time. The only glitch came after the last fight night, when we made the most money.

The final night was cause for celebration. This was it. My limited time in the bar business was up and during my entire tenure I hadn't consumed one drop of alcohol and had never gone to an afterparty. Everything had been business, all business. John and I were going to pay the lease, pay the promoters, and never step foot back into that world again. We decided since it was our last night we would stay in town and celebrate for the first time ever. We put nearly $15,000 cash in a briefcase and sent it back to the farm with Binky—yes, that Binky.

John and I danced for hours and stepped out of the after-hours club as the sun was coming up. John looked down at his pager. "We have to get to the hospital!" he yelled. "Binky was in an accident."

Binky had promised me he would drive straight back to the

farm. No stops. He didn't tell me he was taking a girl back to the farm with him. Apparently they started fooling around while he was driving, and he must have gotten excited because he drove the car off the road and rolled it. They were both taken to the hospital. The car was impounded along with all of our money.

I stood at the foot of the hospital bed clenching the footboard in my hands while Binky gave a detailed account of why he'd run off the road. It was hard to listen to. *Unbelievable! One simple task. Just one.*

"Binky, I don't need to know this," I said. "Where is the car now?"

"I'm real sorry, Sarah," he said with his drawl, part southern and part pothead.

"Binky, where is the car?" I said.

I left John at the hospital with Binky and headed to the impound lot. I snuck in past the guard office and found the car. I looked inside. There was no briefcase. *Morons!* I looked up to the sun and just screamed. I was sure the money was gone for good. We needed it to settle up with the meatheads and pay the lease. How could I have been so stupid as to trust Binky, of all people? Defeated, I drove back to my house and walked in to find my mother sitting at the kitchen table. *Oh, not now. This is really not a good time.*

"What's wrong?" she asked with a smirk.

Well, let's see, Mom. I am wearing the same clothes that I had on yesterday, I smell like a brewery, and I'm missing fifteen grand. Oh, yeah, I almost forgot—any minute now I will have a carload of armed, steroid-addled ogres in my driveway looking for their cut of the cash. What could possibly be wrong?

"Nothing, Mom. Everything is fine." I paced around the kitchen. *I have to call John. This is bad. This is so bad.*

"Are you looking for something?" my mother asked.

I turned around and there was the briefcase. Right there on the kitchen table. She opened it and smiled. *Unbelievable!*

She'd heard about the wreck. The night before, while everyone else was going to the hospital or dancing, she went straight to the impound lot. She told the worker there, "That's my car. I need my briefcase." And he'd let her have it.

With that, our time in the bar business ended and it was time to focus on the farm. When Ted left for college, I started using his old bedroom in our little house as my office. I had two chairs, a computer, and a printer. As the ice thawed outside, I sat there and plotted my next move.

I had some idea of what crops could turn things around. The profit margin was much bigger on fruits and vegetables than on, for example, hay. The risk was greater but the required number of acres fewer. I could do more with less. Trying to follow the traditional midwestern grain-farming model was a recipe for disaster. From my years on the melon route, I knew that I was good at selling. I decided to focus on expanding my old melon route until I found the right use for my own land.

My second office was in my pickup truck. There I kept my bag phone, receipt book, and notepad. I kept getting bigger and bigger orders from the independent grocery stores, and I filled the orders using my own produce supplemented with that of a large network of loyal farmers I'd cultivated.

As the orders grew bigger, I often had to go around to multiple farms, buying from fifty to three hundred melons at a time to get a load of twelve hundred melons on my pickup truck and trailer. These melons were not boxed or in bins. They were in bulk. That meant they had to be lifted one by one out of my vehicles and put into whatever containers the stores had. If anyone bought one of the melons I sold, no question it had my fingerprints on it. Loading and unloading took all my strength and then some. My arms were always sore. My back felt like I played for the NFL.

When I bought up all the local farmers' melons but still had demand from stores, I started to travel more. I began buying from the fruit and vegetable markets, too—great big wholesale fairs where the leading produce companies would offer huge quantities of whatever they had in season. Once I started going to the markets, I was able to move a lot more volume in far fewer trips.

It was at these markets that I started to learn about produce brokers. While some of the fruit or vegetables you saw could be bought directly from the farming company, other loads were represented by brokers who had taken the crops on commission from farmers, marked them up, and were now selling them to people like me.

The way I saw it, this was cheating. These middlemen would sit in their air-conditioned offices, fiddling with their gold chains, and broker fruit and vegetables without ever stepping foot on a farm. I thought some of them were shady, with their carnivalesque patter and their pinkie rings. They hadn't worked on farms like I had. They just worked the phones all day. They never got in a truck. They never went out to a field. They'd just buy and sell, buy and sell, book the trucks, get a piece of the action with every deal. Then they'd show up and they'd take their store buyers out golfing or to clubs.

I thought maybe I could work with them to get the volume I needed, but they didn't want to play ball with me. They didn't like me coming into their territory because they sensed I preferred dealing with the farmers directly, which meant I threatened the good thing they had going. They could work from six in the morning until noon and then go play golf all afternoon. The brokers were old. I was young. I was an unknown. And when it was clear that I was helping farmers and retailers connect directly, I unwittingly made enemies.

One day I was in Immokalee, Florida, home of the famous Immokalee fruit market, when a broker decided to put me in my place in front of a group of his cronies. This guy was the epitome of what I thought was wrong in the produce industry. Farmers grow the crops and they work really hard. Retailers buy and sell the crop, and they work hard, too. The problem was these in-between brokers, this melon mafia. A broker named Howard hated me because he knew I was endangering his phony job. *He's insecure,* I thought. *He's vulnerable.*

"What are you doing here?" Howard said, loud enough for everyone to hear. "This is no place for a young girl. You think you know what you're doing?"

I didn't respond, but I was sure he could read my thoughts. *Well, no, not exactly, but if* you're *doing it, it can't be that hard.*

"You think you can just come down here and take these growers?"

Just the good ones.

"Well, you've got another thing coming. You're going to fail."

Never heard that before.

"You can't keep up with us, and you never will. Why don't you just run on home?"

Well, when you put it like that, I really like it here. I think I'll find a nice little farm here in Florida to call my own someday. This place is starting to feel like home.

I smiled. I kept my cool.

There is something to be said for being underestimated. Maybe I would have felt differently about the situation if my life to that point had been more comfortable. But, frankly, I had been bullied at school far worse. By girls. Big girls who were way more spiteful and crueler than Howard.

Maybe dealing with those girls on the bus and at school helped. Maybe the time I stood in the girls' bathroom during my freshman year in high school and took three slaps in the face without hitting back prepared me for this moment. Maybe if I'd had it easy his words would have hurt more. Maybe I would have questioned my abilities.

My mind flashed back to something my dad had always said: "Don't ever let them know they're getting to you."

I'd pleaded with my father, "But Dad, it hurts. Those girls are so mean. They make fun of my clothes. They make fun of my house. They make fun of everything. They threaten to beat me up every day. You don't understand how awful they are. I have to stand up to them! Just one good pop in the nose."

I'd learned from him that if I wanted to go hunting and fishing with my brothers, I couldn't let a snapping turtle upset me when I met one in the road. You have to know inside what you're capable of. He made me believe I could do anything. But he wouldn't let me handle the bullies the way I handled the turtle.

"And then what? You get a demerit at school. Suspended for fighting. There are records now. You'll have that on your record for life. It might feel good at first, but you'll regret it. Because you will have wasted your energy on trash. You'll be no better than they are. Use your head."

What did Howard know about what I could or couldn't do? It's not that I didn't want to pop Howard in the nose or tell him where he could stick his produce. I just didn't want to give him that power over me. Instead, I just kept the smile plastered on my face as I calmly walked away. I didn't have time for him. I had work to do.

The St. Louis produce market, known as Produce Row, has never been the safest place for a girl to show up at two in the morning with $10,000 in cash. But when I needed to fill out a load fast, that's where I went. The giant fruit and vegetable market on the Mississippi, in business since 1953, was my kind of place.

Opening before dawn, the bustling market has a hundred stalls filled with every fruit and vegetable you can imagine—some sold by wholesalers, others by brokers. With mountains of perishable goods to unload, they're all motivated to make a deal. In no time, I could usually get as much as I needed of anything at a good price. But one morning I arrived to find that my usual guy was out of cantaloupes, and I needed thousands. I asked him who might have what I needed.

"They have fruit over at United," my guy said. "But . . ."

"But what? They're cutthroat at United?" I said. "I've heard that. I don't care."

Everyone was afraid of the guy who ran United: Stanley Greenspan. He was crass and ruled with an iron fist and a filthy mouth. Still, I walked over to United's part of the market and saw big bins overflowing with cantaloupes. The containers weren't tagged, so they were available. Bingo. I told the guy working the docks that I would take them all.

"It's all spoken for," he said, looking me up and down. He seemed amused that a young woman would even talk to him, much less think she could buy from him. There wasn't one other woman anywhere on Produce Row; at least I never saw one.

"Oh, yeah?" I said.

All right, buddy. Watch this.

Looking behind him, I saw that there was a staircase leading up to United's offices. My business wasn't big enough to work with the guys up there. I had to deal with the guys on the docks—but I was over it. I walked right past the rep and up the big flight of stairs. With each step, the higher I climbed, the more nervous I grew. By the time I got to the top and opened the door, I'd begun to doubt the wisdom of my rash plan. I opened the door onto rows of desks. This was the bullpen. When I walked in, a dozen well-dressed men looked up at me in shock. It was like they'd never seen a woman before in their lives. At least not in the bullpen. I was wearing a white T-shirt, jeans, boots, and a ball cap. No one asked me what I was there for. No one said anything. They just stared at me as if a comet had crashed into the middle of the room.

Well, this is awkward. Act like you belong. Yeah, no, I definitely can't just blend in and disappear. Act like you have an appointment. Do something.

I looked past them and saw that there was a door at the end of the row of desks. *You can't just stand here like an idiot. What did you think you were going to do when you busted into this room like the DEA? Move. March toward that door. Act like you know where you're going.*

I took off for the door, scared to death inside but walking with purpose. Maybe it was the infamous Stanley's office. I didn't knock. I opened the door. And then I shut the door behind me. *Thank God I didn't just walk straight into a broom closet. That would have been embarrassing.*

Stanley was a large, balding man with heavy jowls and dark eyes. Before he even looked up, I started talking at full throttle: "I need cantaloupes to fill out my load. This guy down there says they're spoken for. I don't believe him. I need three hundred cases. I have cash. Are you going to sell them to me?"

He stared at me for a moment without saying a word. Then he walked past me as if I weren't even there. *Oh, no,* I thought. *How mortifying. I'm getting kicked out. Maybe I should have knocked.*

He stepped through the doorway, pointed back to where I stood in the middle of his office, and screamed at the reps: "You see this girl? I bet she's not even eighteen and she has more balls than all you fucking rejects put together! Get this girl her fucking cantaloupes!"

Well, that was a little harsh, Stanley. But, hey, we all have our own leadership style.

From that day forward, I went upstairs to buy my produce from Stanley.

Chapter 10

Seeds of Hope

With my summer melon route going so well, I decided to extend the selling season by adding a fall crop to my route. Furthermore, I thought I might be able to raise some of this new crop myself, which meant I could keep far more of the profit. When it came to what to grow, I didn't have a lot of options. In grain farming you need a thousand tillable acres to make a decent living. I had a little less than eighty tillable acres—a relatively small rolling plot of clay dirt. What high-value fall crop was it possible to grow a lot of in a small space?

The answer was pumpkins.

I knew I loved pumpkins. They made people happy. They made me happy. And after slinging fruits and vegetables out of the back of a hot pickup truck all summer long, I loved the cozy feeling of walking through a pumpkin patch wearing a jacket and gloves.

When I decided to grow pumpkins, not everything went quite as planned. Actually, nothing went remotely as planned. My neighbors thought the Frey girl had really lost her mind. They didn't understand my world outside Orchardville and had no idea that I had the ability to sell all that I planned to grow. I was the talk of the local coffee shop, where all of the old farmers would gather at one big table. Some rooted for me to fail. Others said, "If you get into financial trouble, I'll buy that land of yours."

But just like so many other unexpected angels who helped me along the way, one farmer in the community stood up for me. One crazy farmer. That was okay. I needed crazy.

I had met Mark Donoho a few years back when I was sixteen and my car needed a jump in the driveway. He was driving by and noticed that my hood was up. I hopped in his truck without knowing who he was to head to the shop for jumper cables. As I pulled the truck door shut, he proceeded to lecture me about the dangers of getting into a vehicle with a strange man. *Good point. How do I get out of here? Oh, joy, the door handle is broken. I can't get out! I'm going to die today.*

"You shouldn't be so trusting."

Yeah, I'm gathering that. I could feel the blood draining from my face.

"You don't know me. I could be a bad man."

My eyes widened in shock. *Really hoping you're not.* He had a great big wooly beard and a front tooth missing, and he was covered in dirt and grease from head to toe. He had loose tools all over the cab of his pickup. The dash was covered with an inch of field dust.

"Do you live here alone?" he asked.

"No, sir, I live with my brothers. All of them." My voice was fast and nervous. "I have a bunch. In fact, they're probably wondering where I am." Ted was the only brother staying in the house at the time.

I tried to keep my eyes on him while I surveyed the tools for a suitable weapon to defend myself with. The best I could do was an Allen wrench. My heart began to race. *This is it. This is how I die.*

All of a sudden, he began to chuckle. "I'm just messing with you." *Good . . . I think?* "I just wanted to scare you." *Who does that, man?* "I have daughters your age, and I would be so upset if they did something so stupid. Now promise me you'll never be so trusting again. There are bad people in the world, and just because you live out here in the country doesn't mean that you won't run into one. Say, you might know my daughter Amber?"

Oh, thank God. I did remember her. She'd gone to Orchardville grade school with me. She was about three years younger. She seemed very normal. Smart, cute clothes, great hair, sparkly backpack.

He had a point. That little conversation with a great big burly guy three times my size scared me. Really scared me. I went out the next day and bought a Rottweiler.

I would come to know Mark as a kind, caring man—a great big teddy bear with a heart of gold. He would also come to know my dog, Bruno. I would actually go on to introduce him to his wife, Karen, one of my college professors. Karen had just gone through a really tough divorce. I would visit with her after night class and just listen. I was only sixteen but, as I often did with people I cared for, I wanted to fix her problem. She also let slide my frequent absences from her classes as long as I did the work and showed up for the tests. She was a wonderful woman who deserved someone worthy of her love, loyalty, and cooking abilities. I owed her one. So I gave her a farmer. Eventually I would stand up for Mark at their wedding as the "best person." I'm glad to report they are still happily married today.

But back to pumpkins. Mark loaned us some of the equipment that I needed to plant my first crop. He studied up on pumpkins and believed that I was on to something. He never doubted my ability to sell whatever I grew. I became obsessed with all of the different varieties of pumpkin—the sizes, the shapes, the colors. Pumpkins brought joy to the faces of little children, and selling them made me feel like a kid myself. They reminded me of the good childhood memories, the pure and simple pleasures of life on the farm. They tickled my heart with the kind of happiness that could make worries disappear for a moment. A symbol of harvest and bounty, a reward for hard work and perseverance. Every time I looked at a pumpkin, I felt gratitude.

Illinois has long been the top pumpkin-producing state. Traditionally, most of the pumpkins grown were canned, but the types of pumpkin I was growing were meant to be harvested and sold fresh. I wanted to educate myself about what I was getting into, so I invited a University of Illinois professor of crop science named Mohammad Babadoost to tour my fields. He taught me about potential plant diseases and recommended prevention strategies.

I took his advice seriously but I don't know how serious he considered me. While Mark Donoho and I drove the professor through the fields in the pickup, I had my arm out the window and a bumblebee flew up my sleeve. I was too embarrassed to say anything as I tried to stealthily remove the bee, but it kept buzzing against my body. Finally, I pulled over, jumped out, and ripped my shirt off in the middle of the pumpkin patch in front of the professor and the farmer. I hadn't said anything, so they thought I'd lost my mind, stopping the car to strip down. I just really wanted the bee out of my shirt. Mark still laughs about how confused they were by my spontaneous, frantic display.

The sight of the first field of pumpkins I grew took my breath away. It was the most beautiful thing that I had ever seen. The bright blossoming flowers welcoming the bees. The crunching of the vines under my feet. The brightly colored dots of joy in the brown dirt. Running, skipping over them, laughing, brought the greatest joy I had ever experienced. I wanted the world to see what I saw and to feel what I felt that day. Pumpkins were my salvation.

Ted and John helped with that first beautiful harvest. My brother Leonard and his girlfriend came home from college for a couple of days, too. Before they left, John reached into his pocket and handed Leonard cash. That was a big moment. It felt good that something I'd started was letting us give my big brother money. There were never any family loans. You just gave it if you had it. And, increasingly, we had it.

"Hey," Leonard's girlfriend said, "where's my cut?"

"You don't understand," Leonard told her. "We don't get money for helping. We just give each other money when we can."

I'm sure it sounded made up, but that was the truth. That's just how we handled money back then.

My brothers and I didn't see as much of one another as we wanted to. They were all making their way in the world away from the Hill, but they'd come back for visits now and then, or back for a season. My dream was that at some point we would all end up back there together full-time, but we needed a lot more money before that day might arrive.

Every dollar I made I put back into the business. During melon and pumpkin season, I was working every minute of every day. Even though I was succeeding in business, my mother encouraged me to finish college. When I was in grade school, she'd taken some night classes herself. She told me I should try that, just get it done. Although I was college age, returning to night school for a few electives felt like cruel punishment. Thanks to my growing business I was making real money. Why did I need a piece of paper? Still, under protest, I added night classes back into my schedule to satisfy my mother and watched the clock tick in those classrooms each evening until I completed my degree.

A few years later, I was honored as a celebrated Frontier alumna. When I spoke at graduation, I felt proud of the fact that that institution and the people of Wayne County were part of my journey. When the college president, Dr. Mike Dreith, introduced me, he joked that I'd made good even though they basically threw a diploma through the driver's window of my truck as I drove through the Frontier parking lot.

I was proud of what I was accomplishing in business, but I was also exhausted. There had to be an easier way. And certainly a more cost-effective one. I opened the First Cellular phone bill for the month of July and discovered that I had racked up $1,200 in charges. For weeks I'd been pulling out my big old bag phone while I was out running my route. I'd call every store ahead of time to give them a heads-up: "Hey, I'll be there in five minutes! How many do you need? Where do you want me to unload?"

I managed everything from the cab of my truck, thousands of items of produce a day, dozens of stops. I did everything using paper invoices and I timed everything out to the second, so I wouldn't waste any time. I was in grubby farm clothes, my hair pulled up under my baseball cap, which helped hide my age. If my eyes started to blur, I would pull off the road and catnap.

When I was delivering produce and it grew late, I was too cheap—and too young—to get a $50 hotel room for the night. I would just sleep in the truck with the seat leaned back. But mostly I just drove and loaded and unloaded melons, all day and all night. Farm to customer. Farm to customer. Repeat. I knew I'd rather have that cash in the winter than spend it on a hotel in the summer.

I didn't have time for boyfriends, but there was one guy I actually attempted to make room for. He was a young entrepreneur who through hard work had built a business of his own. We dated for a couple of years. He was perfect for me at the time because we understood each other's priorities.

Most of his friends liked me. But their girlfriends? Not so much. They called me "the truck driver," as in "Oh, are you still dating the truck driver?"

I tried not to let it hurt my feelings. It was clear to me that they put me down to feel better about themselves. One time I became upset when Ed told me how he had explained to the girlfriends that I was an entrepreneur, not just a truck driver.

"Hold on," I said to Ed. "Wait a minute. You mean to tell me that you actually dignified their snide comments with an explanation? That means you care what they think. Even if I was 'just a truck driver,' would that matter to you?" I didn't think he should have felt the need to explain anything. A simple "Shut the front door" would have sufficed.

I loved what I was doing. I didn't mind that the weight of the whole business was on my shoulders. Sure, it was a lot of responsibility. But it felt so good to go to the farms, buy the produce, and be my own distributor. If I hustled, I could get fresh produce from the soil to the retail shelves in just a day or two. It was literally fresh off the farm—it doesn't get any better than that. I was bringing pumpkins and melons to a network of grocery stores all over the region, including a dozen of what they called Division One Walmart stores.

I'd been noticing that Walmart was starting to convert some of their small brick-and-mortar stores to Supercenters. That meant that they would be expanding their food offerings. They would still be primarily selling general merchandise, but now in addition to stocking shelf-stable items, like canned goods and cereal, they would offer more perishables.

The Walmart stores became my favorite delivery destination, mainly because of the people. The store associates were hardworking folks. When I delivered to Walmart stores, a dozen associates would come running out to help unload. They were good people, eager to be useful. That was the culture there; enthusiasm was rewarded. Even if all you had was a high school diploma, if you worked hard at Walmart, you could become a manager or go on to corporate. Walmart made it a habit of hiring ordinary people who went on to do extraordinary things.

I also loved selling to Walmart because they would take so much more from me than anyone else. Where I might have to go to four grocery stores and sell each one fifty cantaloupes at a time, Walmart could take and sell two hundred cantaloupes in a matter of forty-eight hours.

On one of my runs I was driving along Route 50, just about an hour from home, when I saw construction beginning on something big. For about a year and a half I watched as the earthmoving equipment moved in and out and this site came together. I'd driven by at least thirty or forty times before I saw that they'd finally put a sign out front: "Walmart DC 6059."

DC. Distribution Center.

Wouldn't that be nice? I thought. *I could make one stop instead of a dozen.*

I pulled in there the first day I saw cars in the parking lot. I had no appointment. I just went through the front door. I had gotten pretty good at crashing through doors by this point. They didn't even have a security person yet, so I started meandering down the hallways, peeking into offices.

Finally a man came up to me and asked if he could help me find something.

"I deliver fresh produce to your Walmart stores directly," I said. "I was just curious if you're going to have fresh produce coming through this distribution center."

"As a matter of fact," he said, "we are going to have a fresh produce buying officer here. The woman's name is Laura, and she's moving into her office right now. I'll take you back there to meet her."

There's preparation and there's luck. When the two meet, it can be life-changing.

We knocked. Inside, I saw a woman setting up her computer. She was wearing pants and a blouse. She was a pretty woman with shoulder-length blond hair. Right away, she reminded me of Donna Leyva, my role model growing up.

"Sarah Frey," I said, holding out my hand. "I own Frey Farms. I deliver cantaloupes, watermelons, pumpkins, and other fresh produce items to your stores directly. It would sure make my life a lot easier if I could just bring it all to a DC instead of making all those stops. Will you be receiving fresh produce here?"

She looked me up and down. I think she could tell I was young, but I don't think she knew I was only nineteen. She seemed incredibly busy, and I think she sensed I had saved her some work showing up like this, coming to her with an enthusiastic offer.

"As a matter of fact, yes," she said. "Here's what I need: two loads of cantaloupes and five loads of watermelons a week. Can you take care of that when the DC opens in a couple of months?"

"Of course. No problem," I said. "It's what I do."

We shook hands and had a nice visit. As we were talking, she said this was the calm before the storm, before all the semis started coming in, needing to be unloaded . . .

I smiled and nodded. But when she said the word "semis," my heart skipped a beat. In that moment, I realized something: By "loads," she hadn't meant pickup truck loads. She meant semi truck-loads. Thousands upon thousands of melons. Every week. I had no semi truck. What I had was a pickup truck and open-air trailer. I had no commercial driver's license. With my brothers away, I had absolutely no help. And I didn't have anywhere near enough melons.

And yet, I believed that I could do anything, no matter how absurd or impossible it seemed from the outside. I'm sure my little vagabond melon business probably looked silly to most people but I was too busy to care. The greatest gift I had was my unfailing confidence in myself and my ability to deliver. If I'd taken the time to think, I would have missed my chance. But the second the words had left my mouth, I knew I would have to deliver, even if at that moment I had no idea how.

Soon the reality of the situation sank in. This was a multimillion-dollar deal—the difference between a one-woman operation and a company. I was beyond excited. This was the opportunity I'd been waiting for—the chance to give my brothers something to come home to.

People have said to me my whole life, "You're so lucky." Was it luck that I walked into that place like I owned it? Everybody who stays in business does so because they've gotten a break at one time or another. And I knew that day in the Walmart DC that I was getting mine. I never thought for a minute that I wouldn't take it. That was the moment my life changed.

In the parking lot, my elation gave way to a single thought: *Call John.* He answered before I even climbed back in my truck. He immediately started unloading on me about how bad things were in Louisville. He was still attending the university there, living in a basement apartment, and working in software sales. Some guys he was working with were cutting him out of the commission on a deal he'd orchestrated. He was so frustrated and he kept prattling on as I tried to get his attention: "John. John. John!" (I usually have to say his name three times before he hears me.) "Pack your bags. Come home now. I need you."

Then I called Ted, who was going to Kaskaskia College and working part-time in a veterinary clinic in Highland, Illinois. "Good news," I said. "I just made a deal that's going to allow you to come home. It's a real business now. I can pay you. I need your help."

They both said yes.

Within twenty-four hours of my meeting with Laura in the distribution center, John showed up back at the farm with everything he owned in a primer-gray 1969 Firebird ragtop convertible. I looked in the backseat and saw he'd brought some great computer equipment. We would start using it immediately to keep professional records for the new business. No more receipt books strewn around the cab of my truck—our new business was growing. Then I looked in the front window and saw a huge smile on John's face.

Chapter 11

Every Which Way

One thing we needed right away was more product. I found willing farmers all over the region, but I also wanted to grow as much of my own produce as possible. My farm was suitable for pumpkins, but for watermelons I needed sandy land. I found some in Indiana, in the Wabash River Valley, and snapped it up. I planted seeds on every bit of land I owned in both states.

In Poseyville, Indiana, that summer, I was once again a prime source of gossip: *That Frey girl has lost her mind. Did you see how many acres she's planted? Who's going to buy all those melons? How's she going to fit them in her little truck? It's all going to rot in the fields!*

When I walked into the diner, people would fall quiet and just stare at me like I was from outer space. I began to envision my tombstone: "Here lies That Frey Girl. What was she thinking?"

I chose to treat these naysayers with patience and sympathy. People live in different-sized worlds. Sometimes their minds can only comprehend the place they live in and not what might lie beyond. You can't hold it against somebody if they live in a small world.

That said, you don't necessarily have an obligation to explain your potential-filled universe to them.

To make it work, I knew that I had to keep going, keep planting more and more melons and pumpkins. For me, it never felt like an option to say "I can't deliver on this order." There was an "act of God" clause in every contract, but I was going to do everything in my power to deliver even if the weather was bad or my growers failed or a million other things went wrong. I never wanted to be scrambling, so I had a thousand contingency plans. A big agribusiness could say they ran out of something and they'd still be there selling the following year. If I blew it, that would be it. I was a nineteen-year-old girl with no track record. Every load mattered. One wrong load could be our last. I needed a plan B, but also plans C, D, and E.

On one hand, it was good that I had control over some of my own produce. But the problem was that much of the land that I farmed was my father's old horse pasture. Year after year, when weeds grow in a pasture, every fall those weeds turn to seed. That seed can lie dormant in the ground for years. When you turn that ground over without herbicide, you bring up all of the seed that's populating the field for years, just waiting for light and moisture. When you plow a field that used to be pasture, it's a wonderful gift to those weeds. It makes them very, very happy. I couldn't use herbicide because a pumpkin is what's called a broadleaf; you can't kill the weeds without killing the pumpkin plant. I would weed for hours by hand every evening, trying to eradicate the pigweed. It was the worst job ever—dirty, sweaty, and itchy. Still, it seemed like the weeds would grow two feet overnight.

One time when I was out there weeding, a friend of Ted's whom I'd later hire, Mike Shelton, asked me why my brothers weren't out there helping.

"Oh, Ted's just gone to town to pick up some hoes," I said.

Mike was puzzled. "And left you here alone to do all this?"

"Well, Mike, it's going to go much quicker when he gets back with the hoes."

He walked away shaking his head, under the impression that Ted was in town picking up women, not farm equipment.

None of us was taking a salary at that point. We had about $25,000 in the bank. I kept buying bigger and better equipment and trying to figure out newer and cheaper ways to do things. Tractors cost a lot of money. Instead, we bought school buses. You could buy an old school bus for $2,000 versus a $25,000 tractor— and the bus went faster. All we had to do was take a cutting torch and cut out all the seats in the bus and remove the sides. Then you'd have the tractor and wagon combined in one unit. We would drive the buses through the field, weather permitting, and that's how we would harvest. Buses hold more than tractors, too. The only downside was that when the fields were muddy, we'd have to use the bus as a wagon and pull it through the field with a tractor rather than driving it alone.

You have to learn to think a different way when you're struggling. Out of necessity, we were scrappy and nimble. Now everybody uses buses in the industry, but back then it was a pretty novel concept. Of course, when the neighbors saw me chopping up school buses with a cutting torch, it didn't help my reputation.

The school buses were a simple and effective innovation, but I did make plenty of big mistakes in those early days. In one of our fields in southern Indiana, there was a row of trees and a series of massive concrete watering structures for livestock that looked like a row of pyramids. I wanted to tear them all out so the equipment could move through the fields in straight lines, and so I could use those bits of land now buried under the pyramids for irrigation and planting. The tree line looked silly, too. Who needed a line of trees separating their fields into pieces?

We ripped the trees out, and then I called my neighbor to ask him to bring over his backhoe, track loader, and front-end loader, along with some workmen, so we could take out the concrete.

The neighbor and his men come over.

"We're taking this out," I told him, standing there in my coveralls and pointing at all of the concrete structures. "Get rid of all of it!"

I climbed up on top of one of the pyramids and said, "Why would anyone even build this? I want this gone. Everything that you see on this land, take it out. We are starting new! Progress!"

Everyone shrugged and shook their heads like, *Okay, whatever you say.*

Just then the wind whipped up and the sky went dark. It was a brownout dust storm, similar to a haboob. The wind spins the soil around like a mini tornado.

There I was standing on top of this pyramid, which I now realized was part of the same windbreak the trees had until so recently provided. The sand showered my face and the old men started laughing at me as they retreated to their pickups. They knew that the trees I'd torn out were wind guards, and very necessary this time of year.

"Look at you—Cleopatra standing up there on her pyramid," my neighbor said in between chuckles. "You might want to keep these pyramids. Mighty fitting, if you ask me. You can probably expect more of this blowin' sand since you took those trees out. I reckon 'bout another month or so of it."

Half of that farm blew away the first year. We replaced the trees and learned a valuable lesson about the importance of wind breaks and cover crops. You don't know what you don't know.

O ur deadline to deliver on the Walmart deal was approaching. By the time summer came, we would need some semis. We also needed to get John his commercial driver's license so he could drive them.

My brother Garrett, who is my mother's oldest son from her first marriage, worked for a trucking company in Chicago. He told

John to come up for a job driving a semi. John, who is a devout Christian, worried that he would get corrupted in the big city. He was not joking. When we were little and the preacher warned the congregation about hellfire and damnation, John believed. He often woke up screaming at night that the Devil was going to get him. The dancing shadows cast on the wall by the fire in the stove were enough to send him into a panic. Surely in the big city temptation and sin lurked around every corner.

On John's first day in Chicago, the trucking company paired him with a tough trucker to learn from. John climbed into the milk truck's passenger seat.

The trainer turned to John and said, "You mind if I listen to some tapes?"

"Sure," John said. He braced himself for ungodly heavy metal music or something equally distressing.

From the speakers came the voice of T. D. Jakes, the pastor of a nondenominational megachurch called the Potter's House. John was delighted. Soon he and the trainer were attending church together. They became good friends.

On the second day, the trainer put John in the driver's seat. They were driving a semi on Cicero Avenue, that chaotic major road running north-south through Chicago, during lunch hour. John says you could have dumped a ton of metal shavings out of that transmission after he was done, he ground the gears so bad. He learned quick, though, and within the week he was able to move the biggest trucks in and out of tight spots on the streets of Chicago.

John worked for the Chicago trucking company for three months. He was a great driver and they were sad he had to go home to southern Illinois. John wasn't sad, though; he couldn't wait to leave the city behind. Back with us, John went for his CDL test. He was used to driving a fifty-three-foot trailer through Chicago. For the CDL test, they gave him a little old box truck and all he had to do was take it around our county. He smoked that test.

· · ·

The weather was growing warmer. The crops were coming in strong. The quality was good that season, and we were always out there looking for more to supply to stores. We just couldn't say no. If someone ordered from us, we did whatever it took to make that delivery, even if we broke even or lost a little. I'd gotten a hold of multiple trucks, a few flatbed gooseneck trailers for hauling, and a thirty-six-foot box truck that I painted navy blue to conceal its former life as a yellow Penske rental truck. Now it was time to bring in the semis.

John and I went to see Frank Riley, who had a trucking company in Poseyville, Indiana. Frank was harsh, but he knew a good opportunity when he saw one. He wanted to give us both trucks and drivers. I told him that I would pay him more for his trucks if he would let my brothers drive them rather than putting his own drivers in there. I needed access to big trucks, and I wasn't old enough to rent them myself from a major rental company. He said that letting me use his trucks would cost $1,200 a week per truck. I knew that was far more than the $400 a week he was usually paid, but Frank had me over a barrel. I agreed, and he took John and me to see the giant trucks he had available.

When we saw that fleet, John and I looked at each other with big eyes.

"Are you sure you can really drive this thing?" I asked John, gesturing toward the biggest truck of all.

"Oh, yeah," John said, puffing up with pride.

Frank seemed dubious, because he said, "I need to take you out on a drive before I let you rent this."

I couldn't blame him. We were still basically kids and Frank was worried John would crash it. They were on the road five minutes before Frank was convinced that John was a gifted driver.

John taught Ted how to drive, so once he, too, had his CDL we went back to Frank and rented another truck. And I kept driving my navy-blue box truck. I'd find produce at one farmer and ask that farmer where other farmers were, and I'd keep going like that, farm to farm, on farmers' recommendations, until I had enough of what I needed. That year I sent my brothers all over the country to get enough produce for all of our retail customers.

One day I said to John and Ted, "You get in that truck, drive to Missouri, and don't come back until it's full of watermelons!" I gave them three thousand dollars cash. They drove down and asked where the watermelons were.

My brothers were sensitive to how I responded whenever someone told me that something couldn't be done. Ted and John both were smart, hardworking guys who figured things out on their own. They went around and asked farm to farm until they found farmers who would sell. There was never a single farm where we'd get a full load of melons. No one had enough volume. They'd have to work hard to find a hundred here, a hundred there. On those infrequent occasions when my brothers had to call me to say they were having trouble filling out a load, there was a great debate between the two of them about who would actually have to speak to me.

One farm down there always put us at the back of the line. They wouldn't load our truck until all the other customers were taken care of. They gave John and Ted the scraps. But the Frey boys worked hard to load their own trucks. They waited patiently in line. The farmers would watch and notice these things. They knew the Freys had pockets full of cash. We never argued. We were farmers ourselves and good customers. The farmers finally agreed to move us up toward the front of the line. Eventually we became the first ones in line. Then we started moving so much volume that we became their only customer.

Eventually the farmers stopped wanting cash and started to say, "Just write me a check!" And then they started to say, "I'll just send you a bill!"

Another time I told John and Ted, "Go to Georgia and don't come back without watermelons!"

Ted and John had never been that far south before. They stopped at a roadside joint to eat burgers and fries. When the waitress repeated their order back to them, her Georgia accent was so strong that they didn't understand a word of what she said. They called me saying, "Where did you send us, Sarah? It's like a foreign country down here!"

I like to say we've had to learn at least five foreign languages while running this business: Florida, Georgia, Missouri, Indiana, and West Virginia.

By flagging down a truck he saw on the interstate hauling melons, Ted found a farmer down there nicknamed Big Foot. Big Foot then hooked them up with thousands of melons, and they were happily heading back home when the truck's engine started overheating. The only thing to help cool it down was to turn on the heat in the cab, because as the water runs through the heater coil it helps the motor cool off. They drove the rest of the way back to Illinois with bandanas around their foreheads and no shirts, smoking and sweating, the heat turned all the way up. The heater vents melted and fell out. Still, they delivered the load on time.

Back then, my brothers were unloading the trucks themselves. The produce in those days was transported literally piled loose in the belly of the trailer. Once you arrived at the distribution center, you'd have to take all those melons, anywhere between 2,700 and 3,000, out of the truck one by one and put them into the DC's shipping containers. If you didn't do it yourself, for $75 you could hire a worker called a lumper who would do it for you. I was too frugal to pay the lumpers, so my brothers and I would unload all the melons by ourselves. It was harder work for us, but it was faster if we did it ourselves.

When it became clear that we could more than live up to our giant Walmart commitment, Laura was pleased, and I was ecstatic. From there on out, large retailers kept giving us more and more business. We were making money hand over fist. We just never slept. We spent three years like that, hot and heavy, with me directing the farm operations and my brothers doing the long-haul driving.

One time John and Ted were driving a giant load of melons when they found out that the melons hadn't been stickered for the supermarket checkout. To avoid rejection by the customer, a minimum of 70 percent of the product had to be stickered. They didn't have a second to waste, so John kept driving while Ted climbed into the back of the loaded trailer and put the stickers on in the dark, climbing over bin after bin of melons, stickering as many of the thousands of pieces of fruit as he could reach with our Frey Farms sticker, all as the truck barreled down the interstate at 70 mph. Usually we had enough of our Frey Farms stickers to cover us, but a few times we had to hand-write thousands of those little neon dot stickers from Staples to get the PLU (product lookup number) on the fruit.

One time Ted climbed into the truck's sleeper and told John, "We're in Missouri. It's your turn to drive." The next morning they woke up in the sleeper together, still in Missouri. Somehow John hadn't made it up to the driver's seat and Ted had fallen asleep too quickly to notice.

We were just tired. People outside the business don't realize what you risk when you have millions of dollars' worth of crops in the ground while facing uncertainty in the weather and your workers. Agriculture is full of unknowns. To make it work, Ted and John had to go from Illinois to Missouri and back, over and over again, seven hundred miles a day. The two of them were doing the work of a ten-person crew. We needed more help. We called Harley and Leonard, and they both came home soon after.

Leonard returned after he graduated from the University of Illinois with his doctorate. In spite of the initials after his name, Leonard went out on the road as a delivery driver, too. On one of his first runs he took a load of cantaloupes to a distribution center in New York. His load was rejected because he'd had the refrigeration on too high and had frozen the entire $20,000 worth of cargo. For a while after that we called Leonard "Ice Man."

Another time, he drove to Arkansas with an expensive load of watermelons, $12,000 worth. It was rejected for some bureaucratic reason. Leonard called me to complain and I said, "Keep driving to Oklahoma. I'll make sure they'll take it." He arrived in Oklahoma the next morning after hours and hours of driving. The quality control person there told Leonard he'd have to reject it.

"Oh my God!" Leonard said, falling to his knees, about to cry into the Oklahoma dirt.

"Nah, just messing with you," said the quality control guy, who happened to be a friend of mine. "Sarah told me to tell you that before I told you we were taking it."

The margin for error was so slim. The truth is, even if you do everything right in farming, you often lose your shirt.

One day when I was twenty-two I was out in my field feeling proud of the crops, walking around looking at my weed-free, gorgeous field. I had the most beautiful acres of pumpkins. Bright orange globes as far as the eye could see. I pushed a vine back to marvel at my perfect fruit. On the pumpkin I saw spots. Leaning in, I smelled rot. That one was no good. I turned another vine over. Same thing. I went from row to row. More spots. More rot. I ran many rows over and did the same thing. The whole field. It was all gone.

I fell on my knees into the dirt and bawled.

Every last pumpkin in my field was rotten. They'd contracted a disease called bacterial spot. It rots them from the inside out. When the pumpkins are growing, the leaves form a protective canopy. That year it rained a ton. The moisture was trapped under the pumpkin leaves and became one big humidifier, a breeding ground for bacteria. We were spraying a copper-based fungicide, which should have killed the bacteria, but we didn't have an air-blast sprayer to move the vines around to really get under there.

Meanwhile, I couldn't call my customers to tell them we wouldn't have pumpkins that year. I sent Ted to New Mexico. I ate every penny of that freight cost and lost money getting the customers what they needed. To our buyers, the crop loss remained invisible, but it hit us hard.

During that transitional period, there was a persona, a mask I put out there for the world. Nobody realized how we were bootstrapping it. I stayed professional, pulled-together, on top of it, no matter what. I always acted cheerful with the buyers. I let people assume what they wanted to, which was that Frey was a multigenerational, well-funded agribusiness. I think my customers back then might have been scared as hell if they knew that it was really just a girl and her big brothers winging it.

We spent the 1990s doing that—trying to figure it out and make it happen. I was an unqualified leader, but my brothers and the people I hired were willing to follow. We were so scrappy in those days that some of us ended up taking dumb chances, like overloading trucks—a crime that is far back in our past and for which I very much hope there is a statute of limitations. The semi and its combined cargo can only weigh 80,000 pounds max. That means you're only allowed to put 40,000 pounds on a semi that already weighs 40,000 pounds. Every pound over that is a 50-cent fine, and you can get your license revoked if you go too far over.

One night John's truck was nearly 23,000 pounds over the limit. The melons were double-stacked from front to back. If caught, he'd be facing a fine of more than $10,000 and probably jail time. To avoid the scales, he drove on back roads. As he passed the Ohio River, he was listening to gospel with the volume turned up loud, hoping the Holy Spirit would help keep him awake. He looked into his mirror and saw police lights. He was being pulled over. Then he saw fire coming out from behind his trailer. It took a while for him to get the truck stopped and to pull out the air brakes. By the time he had stopped fully, the cop was up on the steps to his cab, staring at him.

"Can I help you, Officer?" John asked.

"Don't you have your CB radio on?" the cop asked.

"No," said John. "I was listening to gospel music."

"Semi drivers have been yelling at you for ten miles! You have flames flying out of the back of your trailer!"

"I'm sorry. I wasn't looking back, Officer," John said. "I was looking forward."

John climbed out of the cab to see where the fire had been coming from. Both tires were blown. The axle had fallen and been dragging. There were no tires and no rims, just a tiny ring spinning on the axle. Then the cop asked John if he had a logbook. John did have one, but it was empty. He'd been neglecting his paperwork.

"You fill that out while I make some calls!" the policeman said.

From the cab, while he scrawled in his logbook, John called me and said, "I just got pulled over! We're doomed! I'm going to jail!" He sounded exhausted and delirious.

While we were on the phone, John told me that another cop car had pulled in front of him. Then another one pulled up alongside. Soon, he was surrounded by five patrol cars flashing their lights.

The officer asked John to get out of the cab again. They walked to the back of the truck and the officer said, "Open the truck doors."

The cops clearly thought that John had something terrible in that truck. They were standing in a semicircle around the back of the truck waiting for it to come open and unleash some apocalypse.

John opened the door slowly. It was so packed with watermelons that he wanted to make sure none fell out. The doors opened and the police realized they had drawn their weapons on thousands of pieces of fruit.

One officer climbed up to the top of the bins, eight feet up, and shined his flashlight all the way back to make sure there weren't people or something back there.

"Yep!" he called down. "Just watermelons as far as the eye can see!"

The first officer could tell John was overloaded and dodging scales. He said, "I don't know if you were going to go around Crab Orchard National Wildlife Refuge or State Route 37, but you're going to cross those weight scales before you leave my county."

The truck had two flat tires, so no one could scale it yet. Until we made those repairs, the truck was detained on the side of the road. The cops told John he had to call a guy named Dr. Diesel and then go to the scale house. They called the scale house in front of him and said, "This guy Frey is coming by with an O'Reilly truck as soon as he gets his tires fixed. Look out for him."

I drove straight to the site to see if I could help John. By the time I arrived, the cops had left. I was sad to see the sorry state John was in. He looked like he hadn't slept in a month. His hair was standing on end. Still, there was no time to mess around.

"Quick!" I said. "Let's throw half the watermelons in this ditch!"

"No!" John said. "Let's make a pile in a field and come pick it up later!"

Then salvation arrived in the form of Dr. Diesel, the mechanic who showed up to repair the tires. He looked like Kevin Costner, with floppy blond hair, blue eyes, and an appealing five o'clock shadow. Fortunately, he was amused by the predicament we had created for ourselves. He had a plan for us. He said, "You come with me. You can be 'detained' at my place. Until you pay your tire bill, no one can make you move off my property. I have a forklift. Before you leave, I'll help you get your load right."

That night I made John crawl back into the sleeper of the truck while Doc and I unloaded and restacked the melons. We were trying to make our six a.m. drop-off time, and it looked like we still had a chance.

John was fast asleep. Dr. Diesel and I used his forklift to unload the entire truck. It took hours. By the time we were done, the sun was starting to rise. Once we were legal, I woke John up. He drove to the scale. He was so scared driving over that scale. The way it works is that if you drive over it and you're overloaded a red light will light up. As he drove, the light stayed green and it stayed green and it stayed green . . . We were in the clear.

"Thank you, Jesus!" John yelled as he cruised out of that scale house. He made it to his appointment.

I called Ted. That same day, he went with my box truck to pick up the remaining bins of watermelons. He left some melons with Dr. Diesel as a thank-you.

Having learned from the scale house that no overloaded truck had passed that way, the cops went out looking for John. They went to Dr. Diesel, who said he'd left hours earlier. The police noticed our thank-you present, a pile of watermelons in his yard.

"Where did these watermelons come from?" the cops asked.

"What watermelons?" Dr. Diesel said.

We're still friends with Dr. Diesel.

Chapter 12

Serious Business

Year over year, we began to grow and diversify. Having a big family with so many brothers gave us the ability to grow the business in many parts of the country at the same time. We could spread out and farm in different states simultaneously. We began growing more vegetables—sweet corn, tomatoes, peppers, and hard squash like acorn, butternut, and spaghetti. I leveraged a lot of relationships I had with other small farm families that my brothers and I had met throughout our travels, even some we'd worked with when we were kids. Their businesses grew with ours. We helped them financially, operationally, and with a route to market for their crops. It wasn't just Frey Farms that was growing; it was a lot of small farms in multiple states. They were the forty- to two-hundred-acre farms that farmers like my friend George Dillon ran, and they helped us grow the volume we needed for major accounts.

When our business started, it was fresh and local. We knew we couldn't just grow our business to be a national supplier and lose what was our most important core value—delivering fresh, in-season produce. We were able to buy our small growers things like seeds, fertilizer, and packing materials in large enough quantities to receive big discounts we could share with our little suppliers, allowing them to compete with large farms when it came to the cost of doing business. And we kept buying our own land, too, until we were growing about 60 percent of the produce we were selling.

Every growing season is different. One summer it rained so hard and so often that the melons took on too much water; thousands of cantaloupes literally exploded. I stood there in the field looking at hundreds of thousands of pieces of fruit rotting. I felt sick. I felt so *sad*. No one had died. But it was such a waste. As a farmer, you need to have the stomach to stand there and look at your labor literally rotting in front of your eyes. Then you have to plow it under and forget about it, plant new seeds, and try again.

Frankly, there is nothing simple about a farmer. They're the most complicated people you'll ever meet. Farmers were also the first scientists. You can't farm if you don't understand science. A lot of farmers are also very spiritual people, because they have to be. To me, they are the deepest, most centered people on the planet. In many ways, they resemble Buddhist monks. They have to struggle and fight and understand that it might all come to nothing. Sometimes, through no fault of your own, you have a catastrophic year. And then you have to go out and do it again as soon as the weather tells you to.

Farmers are the ultimate optimists, but you'll never hear a farmer say, "I had the most fantastic year ever! We knocked it out of the park!" Even if they did. There is a reserve to their optimism. If a farmer says, "We had a pretty good year," it means she had an *incredible* year. If you hear her say, "It was a really bad year," it might mean breaking even. If she says it was disastrous, it means she lost a bunch of money.

The farmer's rule of thumb is you need three out of five years to be good ones. If you have worse luck than that, then your business might be in serious danger. Worse, the government isn't likely to help you out if you're a fruit or vegetable grower. Corn and soybeans are heavily subsidized, but not fruit.

On our land in Indiana, we built a packing shed with a little apartment over the loading dock. There was always at least one Frey sleeping in that apartment. Leonard would work on the farm by day and drive a truck by night. When he returned from a delivery, he'd take a shower and a nap before heading out again. We had the Weather Channel on up there all the time and no other entertainment. I'd crash there some nights at three a.m. after loading a truck. Below me, in the coolness of the night, the work of the warehouse would continue. In my little apartment upstairs, I would fall asleep to the hum of forklifts and the drumbeat of pallet forks hitting the concrete floor.

One morning after I'd been up almost all that night loading trucks, the phone rang downstairs. My warehouse manager answered it gruffly.

"Frey's," he said.

"Hello," the man on the other end said, "this is Steve and I'd like to talk about placing an order. May I please speak to Sarah?"

"Not now!" my manager yelled. "She was up loading trucks until three in the morning and I ain't gonna wake her up!" He said he'd have me call back. Then, after hanging up, he thought better of it.

I heard steps up the stairs and then a knock at the door.

Through the door, my manager said, "Sarah, sorry to wake you up, but this guy Steve just called and—"

Steve? He was the buyer for a big company. Before my manager was done speaking, I was down the stairs and calling Steve back.

"We'd like to give you five more regions," Steve said. "Can you get them all watermelons?"

"Yes!" I said, looking around at the packing shed and realizing we'd have to put on an addition.

That summer, our Indiana packing shed smelled like cantaloupes and watermelons. As summer gave way to autumn, we left the doors open so we could enjoy the smell of the crisp fall air. I spent about half my time out in the field with the workers and half running the packing house. Then I'd sit myself behind a computer. I did every single job we had. I harvested, drove trucks, cleaned the floors, brokered trucks, handled sales, balanced the books, and served as our business analyst. I learned how to use GPS tracking units on our tractors to help us lay the rows out in perfectly straight grids that optimized the number of plants we could grow on each acre.

Since at some point or other I'd done the entire range of tasks that take place within our company today, I have a unique appreciation for everybody's job, and can usually offer helpful tips. I bristle when someone tells me that a task I've asked them to do can't be done. I only ask my employees to do things that I know can be done—because I've done them.

When people joined the business, they had to be a Swiss army knife. There were very few roles in the company with a specific job description. You have to be willing to do anything. You can't pay people big salaries in operations and have them only do one thing. I became devoted to anyone who made my life easier. And I had no patience for anyone who stood in my way.

We hired seasonal guest workers from Mexico who had work visas to help harvest our crop. They worked so hard. I saw how eager they were to make money for their families, and I saw myself in them. One Thursday they returned from their lunch break looking dejected. Usually on Thursdays, everyone was cheerful because it was payday. Not this time.

"You guys get your checks cashed okay?" I asked.

"We didn't have time," Arturo said, not making eye contact with me. He looked embarrassed.

"What do you mean? You always have time. What changed?"

"They would only let us into the bank two at a time," he said, staring at the ground. "We didn't all get to cash our checks."

"What?" I said. "I'm sure there's been some sort of mistake."

I had Jan, my office manager, call over to the bank, and I went out to the fields to work. We were harvesting melons in the hot Indiana sun. It was a hundred-degree day and I was drenched in sweat. After a little while my cellphone rang. It was Jan. She said the guys were right. The bank wasn't comfortable with that number of Hispanic workers coming in. They'd instituted a policy: the workers had to wait outside and enter the bank in pairs. I thanked Jan for the report and I walked straight out of the fields, hopped in my truck, and drove to the bank.

Heading over there, I had smoke coming out of my ears. Those guys worked so hard. They never even went out drinking. They loved their families. These were good people. What's more, they were good for the community. They were making $800–1,200 a week. They sent most of it home, but they spent a lot of it in the local community—mostly at Dollar General and the supermarket.

When I reached Main Street, I pulled up right in front of the bank and left the truck running. I shoved the swinging doors hard and ran in, hair flying, dust clinging, sweat dripping, with the knocking sound of the diesel engine behind me. I first saw the bank teller behind the window, and almost walked over to her to let her have it. Then to my left I spotted an office with the bank president sitting inside. I figured that he must have approved the policy, so I made a hard left into his office. He was wearing a suit and fussy little spectacles. I noted with some satisfaction that the sound of my truck parked just outside was rattling his window. With my dirty leather gloves clutched in one hand, I put both my hands on the desk and leaned over. He tilted his leather chair back, his eyes wide as he cleared his throat.

"I understand that you folks are a little uncomfortable with our workers coming in to cash their checks," I said, keeping my voice steady. "You're making them wait out in the heat because you're not comfortable with them all here? Well, you know what? Now I'm uncomfortable, too. I'm uncomfortable having my money here. Close out all of my accounts. Now.

"There," I called on my way out. "Now no one has to feel uncomfortable."

I jumped back into my truck, still running, and drove my business over to a bank that was more accommodating, then returned to the field.

It wasn't the only time I'd face local opposition to my workers. Once at an auction I bought an abandoned old school, very much like the one I'd attended in Orchardville. It was out by the interstate between my Illinois and Indiana farms and I knew I could fix it up nicely as temporary housing for my workers for those few weeks of pumpkin season.

As I was leaving the auction, a fiftysomething man in a plaid shirt and jeans and a ball cap grabbed my arm and said, "I want you to know what you've done." Standing behind him, his wife was in tears. "You're going to put these Mexicans in this community. They're going to ruin everything."

"These men are here working hard for me on the official agricultural visa program," I said, staring at his hand on my arm. "They are legal workers. They've all had background checks. They've been vetted more thoroughly than anyone else living in this community. I actually feel safer with them around. Could every one of your current neighbors pass a background check? I'm trying to be compassionate about your concern about having these thirty or so guys here working for a few weeks. But at the end of the day, they're too tired from work to want to even go out. They will be here to harvest our crop. You'll hardly see them and in a few weeks they will return to their home country."

"Easy for you to say!" the man said. "You won't be living next to them!"

"You know what? I do," I said. "I've lived alongside these guys and I work with them every single day, all day. We work together and we eat together and they are family to me." I could feel the blood getting hot under my skin. I again looked down at the man's hand holding my arm until he removed it. I said goodbye and got in my truck and drove away.

Since then I'm proud to say that that community has become very welcoming to seasonal workers. It took a while, but now the economic benefit of their work is undeniable. It's not that Americans won't do the jobs, but rather that there simply aren't enough Americans in rural areas to do them. Even if you could attract enough domestic workers to a particular part of the country to do the job, the season for it would be over before they got their moving trucks unloaded. The more guest workers we hire for those harvest weeks, the more year-round domestic jobs we create in the area—opportunities for forklift drivers, office workers, mechanics, packers, and more. Ultimately, those guest workers allow us to expand our business, which in turn creates more employment opportunities for U.S. citizens.

Meanwhile, with the help of those workers and others, my brothers and I were building and creating a great company—literally digging a new life for ourselves out of the dirt. *When you have nothing, you have nothing to lose.* I had something now, and so I had something to lose. That overloaded truck experience was a wake-up call. We had built up a good reputation for being reliable and no-drama, and we wanted to keep it that way. My and John's mottos had been "Make it happen. Whatever it takes" and "You have to want it more than you want to breathe." We decided we needed a new motto. At the ripe old age of twentysomething, we would now be dedicated to taking it to the next level.

We acquired suppliers in multiple states and hired new truck drivers. We soon had our own trucks on the road. There was more paperwork than I could handle alone, so John went behind a desk to coordinate and dispatch and invoice.

One day in Poseyville I was at a warehouse when one of our new drivers said to me, "Just when I'm tired and ready to stop, you get on the phone and make me think if this load of cantaloupes doesn't get there exactly on time, the whole damn world's going to fall apart." It took me a minute to see that it wasn't a complaint; he meant it as a compliment. I could make him believe it because I felt like that was the truth.

So much of our business was focused on getting produce where it was supposed to go exactly on time. It was our obsession. On the Night of Dr. Diesel, John thought we'd get a huge fine and go to jail, but he was much more worried about missing that six a.m. appointment. No one was going to call the buyer and say we weren't going to get the melons there. That was non-negotiable for us. The appointment would be kept, come hell or high water. I could bail out John later.

Professionalizing our business happened in fits and starts. Every day was different, and problems could come out of nowhere at any hour.

One year, one of our farmers trying to save on seed costs took every old melon seed he had in his freezer and mixed them all together. Some of the seeds were more than forty years old. We went to his field expecting to pick up traditional Starbrites and instead were met with Crimson Sweets with dark stripes, pale green Dixie Queens, Black Diamonds, and all sorts of rare varieties in different shapes and sizes and colors. They were almost impossible to stack.

"What are you doing to me?" John yelled at the farmer while he tried to wedge these weird melons into the bins. At the distribution center, the quality control guy made so much fun of John. But the melons were unique, and they tasted good even if they looked bizarre, so the buyer decided to just go with it. He put together a funky-looking floor display at the store and pretended it was a deliberate choice to offer a wide selection of colors and shapes. Customers loved them, and so did I, which made me expand my thinking around the possibilities of heirloom varieties.

One year, twenty-one years ago, our Indiana harvest had wound down. Everything left out in the melon field was too small to pick. I was delivering fresh produce at the state fair when I got a call from a buyer asking for watermelons.

"We're done picking for the season," I said. "All we have out there are little ones. They won't meet your size specs."

I hung up the phone and got myself a corn dog. As I walked through the fair I thought, *Wait a minute, who says we have to ship to that spec if we call it something different? The melons taste good. They're just little.*

I called the buyer back. "Here's the deal. I don't have watermelons that meet your spec, but I have watermelons that are so unique that they're better. Let's say I grew small melons for a specific market—people living alone, especially women who don't want to put a twenty-pound watermelon into their shopping cart. Here's what I need you to do: write a specification for a personal-size watermelon of four to six pounds. I can get you eighteen semi loads of them."

I called my label maker and asked for a run of stickers. I asked for it to read "Melon Babies by Frey Farms," and to feature a little cartoon melon with big eyes, blowing bubbles.

People loved them. Now we plant smaller varieties on purpose and sell hundreds of semis of them every year.

The more I learned, the more inspired I became. There are thousands of different pumpkin varieties. I discovered that pumpkins are consumed year-round in other parts of the world. They are part of daily life. It seemed as though we were missing out in America by just carving them up once a year and then tossing them to the squirrels. Uncut, a pumpkin will last a long time. They have astonishingly high nutritional value, and you can cook them in so many ways. You can make soup, mashed pumpkin, twice-baked pumpkin. In Australia, they eat pumpkin as much as we do potatoes. What if we mixed varieties of pumpkin seeds together? We could take seeds sourced from around the world and make a colorful mixed bin! And we could give people recipes so they could cook them all year round!

Inspired by one of the French varieties, I branded my eccentric pumpkin medleys "Autumn Couleur." Retailers bought them by the semi load because they were so pretty, but I kept encouraging folks to cook them, too. "Sure, decorate with them," I told everyone, "but then please eat them!" It made me crazy that you could only get pumpkin during Halloween season or in canned form. I started dreaming of packaging it frozen, and I started promoting the use of pumpkin in savory dishes.

Around this time, we started growing mini-pumpkins. To harvest these millions of little things, we needed to hire extra help. Finding enough workers to harvest was always our greatest challenge. It was the last thing I would think about at night and the first thing I would think of in the morning. I was desperate and would hire anyone willing to work. Anyone with a heartbeat—teeth were optional. I found a contract crew manager named Vivian, a big, strong woman from south Georgia who had good credentials and references. She assured me that her crew consisted of documented U.S. citizens. I was excited to work with her and hired her on the spot. I thought, *Well, this should satisfy anyone who might have had an issue with the foreign guest workers in the fields! I should call the guy who grabbed my arm and let him know he can relax now.* On Vivian's crew's first day on the job, I reviewed her insurance and her workers' IDs. Every one of the IDs had been issued in prison.

Sitting beside me that day in the office was Gearry Davenport, my new CFO. He was a classically trained accountant with an MBA who had worked at major corporations. I'd brought him on to help me professionalize my company, and he was gutting it out with me on this scrappy farm. He was my battle buddy. He had made peace with my flights of fancy. He had come to terms with how involved in the business my brothers were. But he had not bargained for Miss Vivian and her crew of convicts. He looked nervous. *"Criminals?"* he whispered. "Don't go out there and work alongside them anymore!"

As I copied over the ID information, I came across a woman's ID in the stack. I hadn't seen a woman out there picking, so I asked if that was there by mistake.

In a thick southern Georgia accent, Vivian said, "Oh, she's the *hookah!*"

The look on my face: *You have to be kidding me.* The look on Gearry's: *How fast can I get to the airport and return to civilization?*

"How you think I get a crew to stay around?" Vivian said. "Ya gotta have a *hookah*! She's a real happy hookah. Been with me over twenty years."

Nope. Not kidding me.

She said it as if we were idiots not to know that "ya gotta have a hookah." Poor Gearry. But what were we going to do, fire Vivian's gang and let my crop rot in the field? They were citizens. They'd paid their debt to society. I was grateful they were willing to do the job. And I also believed in redemption. I handed Vivian back the IDs. I told her that I would under no circumstances be employing any "hookahs," but I hoped that the farmers she'd brought could start work as soon as possible. Then I waved her out of my office.

The farmers wound up doing a good job for us. The last image I had of Vivian was of my brother John's face smashed into her voluptuous chest as she hugged him goodbye, yelling, "I love you, John Frey!"

Miraculously, Gearry still works full-time for me. He's retired several times, but I keep pulling him back in. Everyone needs a wartime consigliere, and he is mine. Labor is still our biggest challenge. Some years, we still struggle to find enough help. At these moments, I can always lighten the mood by saying, "You know who we should call? Vivian."

Buyers were always changing at the retailers I sold to. Walmart was no exception. They moved their buyers around. After Laura, my buyer became Robin, whom I've now known for more than twenty years. I admired her style. She was in her early thirties when we first met, but she had the swagger of someone who'd been in the business for decades. Every day, Robin put on her makeup and did her hair and went to her job, where she bought hundreds of millions of dollars' worth of produce. The way she always came across as classy and unruffled while wielding massive power made her my hero. I would've done anything for her—and as time went on, I did do anything for her.

It turned out Walmart needed even more product than they originally thought when they converted those smaller stores into Supercenters. We were all learning together just how big that grocery business could be. For Robin and every other buyer, the cardinal sin was to be out of stock. You could not run out of *anything*. The pressure was on.

Staying in stock when you can't fully anticipate demand is harder with produce than it is with canned goods or with non-food items. With a crop like pumpkins, either they're growing or they're not. You can't just ramp up production in the pumpkin factory. If you need more to feed your market, you have to scrounge up what you can find in little patches in the backwoods.

One time I was told about some new Amish growers. They had no way of delivering their pumpkins to major retailers, because they couldn't drive trucks and no truck for hire would go there to load. I would soon find out why. Calling ahead was out. They were completely off the grid. Even once I was there, it wasn't easy to communicate because they saw the world so differently than I did. I had to invest the time with the Amish families personally, to learn their ways and win their trust. The group I dealt with wouldn't have a phone inside their house and didn't allow rubber on their tractor wheels (because fully functional tires might have tempted them out of the fields and onto the roads). Trying to do everything on metal rims made me crazy, especially when the ground was wet.

It was a cultural exchange. A gaggle of Amish teenage girls once cooed over everything I was wearing. "Ooh, look!" one squealed. "She has *sunglasses!*"

One day we ran into a problem and I had to call Walmart. I needed a phone.

"We do have one phone," a little boy told me. He was nine or ten, wearing a white dress shirt and dark breeches with suspenders, but he talked like someone much younger. There was something off with his speech.

"Where is the phone?" I asked.

The boy pointed into the woods.

"There's a phone in the forest?" I said.

The boy nodded. *Horror movies start like this,* I thought. But I saw there was an opening among the trees, a walking path that led into the woods.

He couldn't speak clearly, but he kept pointing into the woods.

Whatever. Here goes nothing. I started walking into the woods. While I walked, I thought, *Here I am, by myself, in the middle of central-northern Indiana. It's hilly and it's wooded and no one would have any idea where to search for my body.*

Finally, in the darkest part of the woods, I found a wooden box attached to a tree. I opened the box, and sure enough, inside was a phone. And the phone had a dial tone.

I dialed Walmart. Robin answered from her office at the distribution center.

"You're never, ever, ever going to believe where I'm calling you from," I said. "I'm calling you from a tree. You don't pay me nearly enough for this, Robin. But listen, how badly do you need the product? They have pumpkins but it's raining here and it's muddy. They have horses pulling this tractor that has no rubber on the wheels. And did I mention I'm calling you from a tree?"

Robin laughed. "Yes, I need all of the pumpkins you can get," she said. "We need them for other DCs. I'm sure you'll figure it out." *Other DCs, huh? If I make it out of here alive, I'm going to find a way to get those other DCs' business.*

"Okay, thanks," I said. "I hate you, by the way."

From the comfort of her climate-controlled office, she just laughed again.

For me, it was easy to grow my business as long as I never forgot that most major retailers just wanted to know two things: *What's your price? Do you have the volume?* That's what it came down to. If you delivered, if you did what you said you were going to do, you were rewarded with more business. It was a simple formula, and I loved it. So it surprised me when one day I had a call from a business contact of mine: "Sarah, are you a registered WBEC member?"

"What is WBEC?" I asked.

"The Women's Business Economic Council," he said. "You get your company certified, and then we can account for those retail dollars and show our leadership and our customers how we do business with women-owned businesses."

I was offended by it at first. *Just my luck someone's noticed I'm a girl. Eye roll.* I didn't think it should matter whether I was a man or a woman, whether I was black, white, whatever. I thought this request minimized what I was accomplishing. "It didn't matter when

I started and it shouldn't matter now," I said. It was the first time I told a customer no. I didn't want to be "branded" as a woman.

But then, over time, I realized that there were few women with leading roles in the industry. I was so used to being around boys and men that I guess I just didn't notice that there weren't other women doing it, too. Eventually I started to realize that I, like most women in this country, did most of the shopping for the family. I could tell when a brand seemed to know what women like me wanted, and when some other brand didn't seem to have a clue. If companies had more women in the rooms where the decisions were made, wouldn't that benefit the consumers as well as the companies? It just made good business sense. I agreed to participate in the program.

After all, how many times have I had a man show up at my farm or at one of my facilities and ask me if they could speak to the "man in charge"? Probably a million. Every time I politely smile and say, "Sure, I'll go get him." Then I go find one of my brothers and say, "Hey, he wants to speak to the man in charge. Maybe you should go have a conversation with him."

My brother goes to speak with the guy. And as soon as the guy asks a question, my brother says, "You know what? I don't have any idea. I'm going to have to talk to my sister. She's the boss. You had the opportunity to talk to her directly, but now she's gone. Don't worry, though. I'll pass along your question and I'm sure she'll make it a priority to get back to you right away."

Sometimes it's better to let people find out after the fact that they've been rude, rather than depleting your energy educating them.

As my business grew so did my customers' curiosity. Walmart was no exception. One day Robin and her boss, Kevin, came up from Bentonville, Arkansas, to ride along with me on my farm. Robin had prepared me: "Listen, my boss wants to see where I'm getting the melons from. Whatever you do, do not tell Kevin how old you are."

I was worried. I was getting it all done, meeting our deadlines, and we were working hard to get things to run more professionally, but behind the scenes it was constant hair-on-fire chaos. I didn't have a super-sophisticated packing house or swank equipment. I had a brand-new one-ton power-stroke Ford diesel truck that I thought Kevin might like. The rest of our equipment was less impressive. Robin didn't care about that. She just knew that I was barely old enough to drink. At this point, I was probably doing $10–12 million a year with Walmart. Robin was terrified Kevin would say, "Robin, your produce supplier is a child."

When Kevin and Robin arrived, they breathed in the fresh air and looked around. He was wearing slacks and a button-down shirt. She was in black pants, a silk shirt, and sensible closed-toe shoes. Kevin had worked in retail produce for a long time and Robin was a horse girl, so they seemed at home on the farm. I took them on a crop tour in my new red truck. They got up close and personal with the melon vines. Everything looked good. I showed Kevin our packing shed and talked about what we were building next. It was a nice visit. We got along well.

Then, as we were driving back through the fields, with me in the driver's seat, Kevin in the passenger seat, and Robin in the back, I caught Kevin looking hard at my profile. He had daughters around my age.

"Say, how old are you, Sarah?" he said.

I looked in the rearview mirror. Robin winced.

I can't lie.

"Don't you know you're never supposed to ask a lady her age, Kevin?" I said, trying to affect a coy smile.

Kevin laughed, and that was that. I kept the contract.

Chapter 13

On the Road

The business had me traveling constantly. In so many ways, it was terrific. Finally, I was able to enjoy all that city life had to offer while still returning home to life in nature. Every few weeks I'd get to put on heels and explore new places. Then I'd change into boots back at the farm, a place where I could focus and stay grounded. I had the perfect mix of town and country.

I also had a lot of devoted people backing me up—chief among them my four brothers. I would often get asked about the challenges of working with family. Granted, we had plenty of little sibling squabbles, but working with my brothers felt natural to me. And, frankly, they were accustomed to me setting the agenda and communicating the plan. We didn't get to travel together often, but we made it a point to take at least one annual business trip together. One year that took the form of a trade show in Los Angeles.

I rented a space big enough for all of us to stay under the same roof not far from the convention center where the trade show would be. Our first day there, my brothers had already taken showers and put on suits when I realized we didn't have to attend the show until the following day. We only had one vehicle, so we had to agree about where we wanted to go. I voted for Rodeo Drive. They wanted to go to the racetrack.

"Okay, here's the compromise," I said. "If you let me go to Rodeo Drive first, I will go to Santa Anita with you after that."

It was a deal.

We piled into the green Chrysler minivan and headed into downtown L.A. It was my first time shopping in Beverly Hills, and I was in awe of the beautiful clothes but also shocked by the high prices. My brothers mostly refused to go into the stores. They stood outside and waited for me, bored to tears but never complaining. When I walked into Versace, John decided to join me. Right away we spotted an incredible dress.

"Sarah, you have to have that dress!" John said. "It's perfect for you."

There was a formal event coming up at the conference that Friday night. We were making money. I could justify the purchase easily, whatever it cost.

I turned the tag over. The price was $3,600.

"I don't like the color," I told John.

"It's totally your color!" he said.

"No, John," I said. "I don't. Like. The. Color." Without letting the sales associate see, I flipped the tag over and showed it to him.

He nodded and said, "Oh, yeah, really bad color."

I just couldn't spend that amount of money on an article of clothing. To me, that dress meant 3,600 pumpkins, a semi load full. I imagined all the work that went into growing, harvesting, and hauling all of those pumpkins. I just couldn't make the purchase.

When I stepped back out on the street, I told my brothers I was almost ready to leave for the track. But something had changed. Now my brothers seemed to be having fun.

"Hey, Sis, when you and John walked into that store, a woman took our picture."

"Yeah, I think she thinks I'm Tom Cruise!" Leonard said.

Then another woman took our picture.

Harley looked around and said, "Wait a minute, lots of people are taking our picture! They don't think you're Tom Cruise, you idiot. They think she's famous." He pointed at me. "We look like her security detail."

I looked at the four of them standing there scattered around me and realized Harley was right. They did look like security. When the paparazzi saw little ol' me going into stores surrounded by these burly guys dressed in suits, they decided I must be famous. *Oh, this is going to be fun,* I thought.

From then on, every store that I went into, I made sure I kept my big sunglasses on and didn't make eye contact. I acted aloof. I turned my head away from people as I walked, flanked by two brothers on either side of me. They were totally into their new roles. I could care less about shopping at this point. The entertainment factor alone was worth the trip. My brothers started saying things like, "Secure the premises. She's walking into Gucci." "No photos, please," and pretending they were wearing security earpieces. By the time we reached the end of the street, traffic was backing up and tourists were asking me for autographs.

The paparazzi seemed to be enjoying themselves, too. One tourist couple chased us into the store, filming us. By now I was acting extra haughty as I flipped through the clothes. As we walked into one of the fanciest stores, a man with a giant professional camera jumped right out in front of us, his shutter clicking as he took hundreds of pictures in seconds.

Harley stuck his hand out in front of the man's camera and yelled, "No pictures! No pictures!"

We ran back to the green minivan, laughing hysterically. We kept imagining all those people getting their pictures developed and wondering: "Who'd we get?" And I couldn't help but think, *Will you look at that? Farmer George would be proud. I made it to Hollywood after all.*

. . .

My brothers were so protective that the world guessed they were my bodyguards. And yet even they couldn't keep me safe all the time. One evening I was on a work trip with my brothers when I found myself on the elevator at the Orlando Marriott. We stopped at a floor and all these sunburned people stepped out, leaving just me and one man. Suddenly I felt a pair of eyes on me. I moved away to give the man space.

"I liked it when you were standing closer," he said, his leering eyes traveling up and down my body.

I moved farther away.

We arrived at his floor. Just before he left, he pushed me up against the wall and grabbed me. I threw a hard, boxing-with-my-brothers right hook that hit only air—he was already gone. The whole thing was over so quickly that I never even made contact.

Stepping off the elevator, I didn't know what floor I was on. I looked frantically for my purse, then realized I was holding it. I felt mad at myself because my punch never landed and the man had such an evil smirk on his face.

As soon as I arrived for my meeting with a colleague, I told him what had happened. He immediately called hotel security with the man's description and poured me a drink. The hotel investigated, but they never did catch the guy.

I didn't tell my brothers. We were doing everything together and we were close as could be, but there were limits. If I'd shared this with them, they would have burned down the hotel to make sure they caught the guy who assaulted me or gone room to room dragging everyone out into the hallway. I also knew that if I told them, every time I traveled alone they would worry about me. No, better to keep them focused on our business and on having a good time together.

The following March my brothers and I decided to throw a party on the farm. It was a slow winter in Wayne County. Our friends and neighbors were glad to have something fun to do. In fact, more than a thousand people showed up. We charged just enough at the door to cover the band.

That year, we booked Johnny Lee and Doug Supernaw. As the show was about to start, I noticed a girl who was a high school acquaintance of mine arrive with what appeared to be a handsome new boyfriend. I caught John trying to upsell them on folding chairs, but I intervened. "You just can't help yourself, can you?" I said to him, then shook my head and smiled. "Stop trying to get more money out of them! This is my friend!"

She introduced me to the man with her. He was gorgeous. I thought, *Good for Amy.* I kept my distance for the first part of the night, but then I noticed Amy's boyfriend was staring at me. It was making me uncomfortable. *What if Amy thinks I'm encouraging this?* I thought. *She's going to let me have it.*

Then I saw Amy marching in my direction.

Uh-oh, I thought. *I so don't deserve this. I haven't even smiled at the guy.*

"Do you know who that guy is?" she asked me.

No, but I'm sure you're going to let me know.

"Your boyfriend . . . ?" I said.

She looked confused. "Oh, no, we're not together! He's the new executive director of the Farm Service Agency. You should go over there and suck up to him. He's a good person for you to know."

Okay, I wasn't expecting that. But wait—me suck up? Yeah, no. That isn't happening.

"Oh, thanks. I'll say hi when I get a minute," I said.

I was relieved she wasn't going to kill me, but I wasn't exactly on the friendliest terms with the state FSA office. And this guy—Justin, she said his name was—may have been handsome, but he'd also just replaced Sam, a man I respected who had retired early because of a dispute I was having with the state of Illinois. The state director at the time claimed that there was no way a "girl" was growing that many fruits and vegetables on her own.

Illinois is a traditional grain-farming state. There aren't many fruit and vegetable farmers—certainly not many who are participating in the types of programs that help fruit and vegetable farmers. I was a thorn in the FSA office's side because, thanks to me, the local agencies had to train staff on how to administer these programs. I had also had a crop loss the prior year that they were refusing to compensate me for even though by law they had to. Sam told me that part of the reason he'd chosen to retire a little early was that he was offended by how he was being asked to "handle" me.

But before the night was out, I saw Justin standing alone and decided I needed to put my ego in check and be hospitable, at the very least. The truth was, I was intrigued by him. His eyes were kind. He had broad shoulders and dark, wavy hair.

I went over and started a conversation. We chatted for five minutes, then I told him to stay right where he was, I'd be right back. I found my family and closest friends gathered in my office overlooking the show and announced to them that I had just met my future husband.

Justin asked me to marry him a few months later. We met on March 15, 2002, the ides of March, and were married one year to the day later. I was twenty-five.

To be honest, I was terrified of getting married. I was afraid of losing my independence and freedom. I couldn't even go a day back then without knowing that I had a vehicle in my driveway and that it had gas in it. It would not matter if I didn't need to go anywhere. If there was no clear means of escape, I panicked. I love the ocean and the beach, but even island vacations proved troublesome. After a day or two of enjoying the beauty, I'd get island fever and want to get back to a larger landmass.

Still, my whole life, every time I'd tackled something I was scared of, it had worked out for the best, so when Justin proposed I said yes.

Justin checked all the boxes for me. He was the perfect man— intelligent, hardworking, straightforward, kind, and incredibly handsome. I loved that his parents were still together. I liked that he was in my kind of work, so he knew what he was signing up for, how hard agribusiness could be. We were going to be able to grow together; he could be just as curious about life and its opportunities as I was. What's more, by settling down I could set the example for the rest of the family and show them that having a stable life was possible. Justin's life was so different from the way that we had grown up. It seemed so *normal. He* was so normal.

My business was growing. I had incredible friends and business associates across the country. I had money. I had nice clothes. I had a beautiful home. My past was nearly invisible. Anyone who met me at this point would assume that my brothers and I had never known hunger or strife. There was just one problem—we were mostly all still single. I figured if I married and had children, I would have the final piece of the puzzle for a traditionally happy life. Even though I was a lifelong commitment-phobe, I took our engagement seriously.

Our wedding was in a small Episcopal church from the late 1800s in a tiny, beautiful, historic old town called New Harmony, located right where Illinois and Indiana are separated by the Wabash River. We had a very small ceremony, just the family, followed by a four-hundred-person reception. It was important to me to make the ceremony private. Pledging eternal devotion at age twenty-six made me uneasy. My brothers knew this well. Ted left his Dodge Ram running outside the church in case I wanted to take off at the last minute. I found that amusing, but I told him that he should've known that when I make up my mind, I make up my mind. And I loved Justin. I wanted us to start our own family. I hoped it would be happier and calmer than my own had been when I was growing up.

Soon after we married, Justin came home, walked into the kitchen where I was sitting, and told me he'd quit his job at the Farm Service Agency. He said it matter-of-factly, the way he said everything. He looked calm, as if a burden had been lifted. I swallowed hard. In a rush, I felt even more responsibility. Emotionally, I'd been leaning on him. I made so much more money than he did, but I also had to take far more risks. The fact that he had a job outside the business gave me a sense of security. That was gone now.

"Really?" I said. "You didn't want to talk about this first?"

"I was just fed up."

"What are you going to do now for work?"

"Oh, I just assume I'll work with you," he said.

"Well, it's not just up to me," I said. "I work with my brothers."

My brothers and I had always had a rule that we would never allow significant others to join the company. Nobody ever thought about it potentially applying to me, though, because I was the one who created the no-spouse rule in the first place. I had to explain that to Justin, and then my brothers and I had to take a vote about whether to amend it to let Justin in.

So the five of us voted on whether to let Justin in. It was split. Two of my brothers voted for, two voted against.

It was up to me to break the tie. I had to live with the man. How do you think I voted?

Justin joined the team. And he contributed. He was an incredible asset. He got along great with my brothers. The downside was that work came home. And because he was in my daily life and in my business, people saw him as a conduit to me. They would use him as a way to have conversations with me that they couldn't get during the day. They went to him with their issues, and then he would bring up those issues at night. I hated it. By the time I arrived home, I was smoked and didn't want to hear it anymore. But I chalked these squabbles up to a newlywed adjustment, and we worked through it.

A year after we were married, Justin and I had our first son, William.

When I gave birth, there was a massive family gathering at the hospital. Everyone was there. John had recently married his girlfriend Andrea, the best sister-in-law I could ever ask for, and to this day I think she's everyone's favorite Frey spouse. There in the waiting room, fifteen Freys gathered to whoop it up while they waited for my first child.

I was in the delivery room trying to get a giant baby out of my body and I could hear the entire family through the walls. I was in labor for so long that the epidural wore off. I started screaming toward the end and then I heard the nurse yell, "Lady! Who are you?"

"I'm her mother!" my mother shouted. She'd pushed the nurse out of the way and come into the room to check on me.

"I wish I could do it for you," she said. "My babies were so easy."

Finally, though, he was out in the world—a beautiful baby, strong and healthy. I felt love like I had never known before. We were so proud of him. Still, I fell into a terrible postpartum depression. I had no trouble bonding with my baby, but I didn't feel great about myself. I was sleep-deprived, overweight, and leaking milk. But I was still the head of the business and happened to have a baby during the busiest growing season of the year.

Watermelons are to the fourth of July what turkeys are to Thanksgiving. We had millions to sell and ship, so I had to keep it together and answer work calls and take meetings from home. My sadness and all the hard work put a strain on our marriage. I kept my feelings to myself, but inside I was keeping a checklist. My exhaustion could make me unforgiving.

When William was two weeks old, Justin was invited to his high school's ten-year reunion. He'd been voted "Most Handsome" in high school and been incredibly popular, so he wanted to go. (Meanwhile, in high school I had been christened "Rowdiest Girl," presumably because I was rarely there.) We thought maybe it would do me good to get out of the house and go with him. His parents said they would watch William. When we got to their house it was so hot there. My body was ridding itself of all of the pregnancy hormones, and as I was getting ready to go, I soaked my dress with sweat. And yet I had nothing else with me to wear to this reunion. I felt gross, my body still reeling from producing an 8-pound 5-ounce human. I fed the baby and then went along, against my better judgment.

As soon as we walked in, I realized it had been a mistake to go. Justin's friends were thrilled to see him. They all looked great. I felt terrible. My boobs already felt like they were going to explode. I felt insecure. I imagined all of Justin's normal friends thinking, *How did she catch him?*

I had to leave after about an hour to get back to feed the baby again. Justin said he wanted to stay, so he gave me the car keys. I went back to his parents' place and nursed William, then fell asleep. I woke up in the middle of the night and Justin still wasn't back. I couldn't sleep, so I lay there watching the clock. *I wonder if he's hanging out with the twin sisters he used to date. I wonder if he regrets getting married. Did he even want to have a baby as much as I did?*

Finally he rolled in at four in the morning. I didn't say anything to him, but I stewed. We'd had this baby, but his life wasn't different. Only mine was.

For weeks afterward, the postpartum depression endured. That whole time, I didn't want to eat. I had to force myself. My mother-in-law would cut up fresh strawberries, my favorite snack. I would look at them with apathy and push the bowl away. I would think, *You are a stable person. This isn't you. These feelings do not define the real you. They will go away. This is a temporary hell. You will be free eventually.*

After about six weeks, I began to feel like myself again.

What brought me back to the world, in the end, was work. Determined to build a business worthy of my growing family, I set about meeting new retailers, hiring more people, diversifying our offerings, and adding value to Frey Farms. One of the large retailers that we supplied recommended that I complete an executive education program at Dartmouth's Tuck School of Business.

That week in New Hampshire felt like boot camp. It was fifteen below there that winter. I wasn't used to the weather. It could get cold in southern Illinois, but it was nothing next to the damp, bone-chilling New England winds. We had a working breakfast, working lunch, and working dinner. Homework lasted until midnight and then you were due back in class at six a.m. A lot of us felt we'd earned the right to a leisurely evening here or there. At this point we had reached a level of success. We were making money. The thing about owning your own business is that yes, it's all-consuming, but you create certain comforts and flexibility for yourself that you take for granted until you no longer have them. No one cared at Dartmouth. They broke you down and built you back up.

One of our professors put me on the spot. She asked, "What makes your melons so special?"

I told her it's difficult to brand fresh produce because it's a commodity. She wasn't having it. "You're telling me there is no way to make a watermelon different? You go back and put a sticker on your melons that says 'Eat me.'"

The class erupted in laughter. I loved that woman.

Slowly Justin and I were figuring out how to be a team at home. William grew bigger and brought us so much joy. In 2005, we found out we had a new baby on the way. Justin and I always knew we wanted William to have a sibling, and now we learned we were to have another son in January.

Then a big scare: a few months into the pregnancy, we received a call from the doctor telling us that there was a problem. A test had come back with a strong likelihood for a genetic defect. They thought he would die either inside me or shortly after birth.

But I knew, as a mom, that it would be okay. I just had a feeling that there was nothing wrong with this child. And I felt so strongly that he was *my* child, no matter what. We were sent to St. Louis for more genetic testing, counseling, and amniocentesis. That helped rule out trisomy 18, but the marker they saw on the test indicated that he could have one of 350 other issues, including a skin disease known as ichthyosis in which the skin resembles fish scales. My heart was breaking. They wanted to do further testing and to find out more. The counselor told me it wasn't too late to do something.

"Too late to do what?" I asked.

"You can still get a late-term abortion in Kansas City," she said.

"I've felt him *kick*," I said. "We're done with the testing."

I went on bed rest. While I was lying there, working in bed, the phone rang. It was a professor named James Sebenius at Harvard who said, "I'd like to interview you for a case study."

"Okay," I said. *Do case studies come with food?* I was starving throughout that entire pregnancy. "What kind of case study?"

"You do business with Walmart, right? Could you give us some examples of your negotiations with them?"

From bed, I did the interview with Sebenius and his research associate Ellen. I had plenty of time to reflect on my business while waiting for my new baby to arrive. But I realized that it was hard to answer the man's questions about how I had accomplished so much in such a short period of time. *I don't know how I did it. I just made it happen. I don't even consider myself successful. I don't even think about it. I'm on a wheel and I can't stop running.*

They were looking for a negotiation case study that had a successful outcome. It was eventually published, and it compared me to David, of David and Goliath. It was about how a small company like Frey Farms could negotiate with a large global company and beat out the competition.

I certainly didn't mind being compared to David. I've always respected David because he didn't play the giant's game—he played his own. To me, that may be the secret of both business and life: playing your game, not theirs.

Luke was born three months after we were told we might need to consider an abortion. They induced me on the early side.

Again the Frey family moved into the old county hospital's waiting room for the hours of my labor. But the party was more subdued this time. At one point Luke's heart rate dropped dangerously because he'd become tangled in the umbilical cord. They rushed me in for an emergency C-section. When I heard him crying, I started crying myself, and thanking God that he was okay.

When he was born, he was perfect. He had a beautiful, full head of blond hair; it looked as if it had been styled. I was too wobbly to hold the baby right away. After they sewed me back up, they wheeled me out on a gurney, still in a hospital gown with a surgical cap on my head. The hospital was so small that patients on gurneys rode the same elevators as civilians. So much for taking time to pull yourself together in private just after giving birth. As the nurses pushed my gurney through the waiting room, I saw nearly every one of my family members lean over and stare down at me, teary-eyed and smiling in relief.

Partly because they'd taken him out early, Luke was in just the 5th percentile for height and weight. But otherwise he was healthy. Justin and I joked that since William was in the 95th percentile, together they made a perfect score. And this time I didn't have postpartum depression. We'd beaten the odds. Now our family was complete and we could focus on growing the business and raising these beautiful little boys.

During the holidays, I threw big Christmas parties. I invited all my employees and their families. It was always so much fun for me to go out and buy special Christmas presents for all the little kids, to make sure they had their names on their presents. I'd try hard to figure out what they wanted most. Christmas is for little children, and I love seeing the look on their faces when Santa hands them the exact present that they wished for.

As I've said, when we were growing up, our parents only rarely gave us birthday cakes or holiday gifts. My sister Angela made me a cake once when I was a very little girl, but I only remember it because of a photograph. When I was driving my route on my birthday one year in my teens, a produce manager who had a crush on me gave me flowers and a balloon, and that's the only true birthday gift I remember getting during those years. So I made sure my children and my employees' children always had a Christmas party and presents. Giving brought the kind of joy that had been missing from my early life.

The business grew. I explored and fell in love with unfamiliar rural areas across the country, and reinvested our profits into more land. There was not a second of the day that I wasn't fully en-gaged with my children, with my company, or both at the same time. I kept taking on more and more.

Becoming a mother changed the way that I thought about so many things. My creativity began to center around figuring out ways to make my life at home easier. Time or lack thereof was the central focus around creating family-friendly packaged goods.

I wanted my children to grow up enjoying foods that were pure, simple, and fresh from the farm. I found that nearly everything con-venient was full of ingredients that required a food scientist or chemist to explain their purpose. And yet I couldn't step away from my business and be a full-time homemaker. I developed a love of cooking and a passion for food. Real food. But too many people depended on me in the business. I also knew that if I just embraced that one part of myself, I wouldn't be happy, either. My kids were the reason for everything that I did, but I was still a professional. There was no way I could sacrifice either part of my identity, the mother or the entrepreneur.

I began developing clean packaged foods that were made with ingredients from my farms. Because I was so excited by this idea of bringing fresh food to families, I managed to eke out the time to write and self-publish a book called *For the Love of Pumpkins*. The book was a tribute to the joy that pumpkins brought to my life. I wanted the world to share the magic that I saw when looking at pumpkins, and to inspire creativity. It was a visual book. We shot the photographs in New Harmony.

That was such a chaotic but inspiring time. Every season I was coming up with a new value-added product. I started selling pump-kin decoration kits, pumpkin puree, and canned pumpkin. My life became pumpkin-focused! Each night I cooked dinner, tucked the kids into bed, and then hopped back on my laptop.

When business associates visited the farm, I often invited them into my home and kitchen for family dinners. Meetings took place wherever I needed to be. There were no clear lines of separation between the different things I was doing, and that was fine with me.

I wanted my children to grow up unsheltered from business discussions. New employees who joined me in the efforts to build Frey Farms were welcomed as part of my family. I don't care if you sweep the floors at Frey Farms—you're going to sit at my table for dinner. The food safety supervisor has a job that is equally as or more important than mine. If that person doesn't do a good job, terrible things could happen. Everyone deserves a seat at the table and an opportunity to be heard.

In those early days, I was proud that I'd found my own way of taking care of both my home and my business. I was happy just throwing it all together in one bucket. Kids in the boardroom. Employees over for dinner. My boys coming along on work trips. The whole work team hanging out in my backyard. Everyone was pulling together like one big family. Whatever works, right?

William and Luke have traveled several times internationally and they've been to all but about seven states. I took William everywhere, even to buyers' meetings. William was a baby the first time he went to a buyer's corporate headquarters with me. I brought him in his car seat carrier to a meeting. To their credit, no one complained. It was pretty funny to me that they weren't shocked to see a baby, only to see that *I* had a baby. Until I became a mother, they thought I was going to be a career woman who would never have children.

The best thing I did for my children and my business was to send the boys to our local rural school. I knew and liked every one of the sixty kids there, as well as their families. I could go out and do what I had to do in the world and never worry about my boys back home. If it weren't for that school, I think I would have had so much more anxiety about traveling and working long hours.

I had to be in Washington, D.C., on the day of William's kindergarten graduation. At school drop-off, I went in to talk to the teacher, Mrs. Hales, also known as Aunt Gug, also known as Karen, who happened to be my brother John's aunt-in-law. I said I was struggling with leaving that day and was going to bag the trip. I didn't want to miss the ceremony. She sprang into action.

"You're not going to miss anything," she said, and she immediately had the kids put on their graduation caps. Mrs. Hales told the tiny group of kindergarteners that they were going to have a dress rehearsal. She staged the whole ceremony in front of me so I could see William graduate and get his certificate. William doesn't remember his kindergarten graduation, but I do. And I remember how that wonderful teacher and kind soul helped make things work for another woman.

Chapter 14

Hunting Grounds

As my business grew, so did my village. I found that, as workers, people fit into either the hunter category or the gatherer category. In my company, the gatherers are the ones who keep the tires full of air and make sure the paperwork is in order. In the wild, they'd be cleaning and cooking the wild game. They are there every day, the most solid team members that you can have. They are extremely important—as important as, if not more important than, the hunters.

The hunters are the ones who are always thinking ahead to the next deal, the next kill. I'm a hunter. If there is a bird in a tree, I have to get from here to there to kill the bird. I will do whatever it takes to get there, even if I die between here and the tree. It becomes an obsession. Nothing else matters. I fight to win.

When I started my business, it was easier to take risks and gamble knowing that the worst thing that could happen was still better than the hardest thing I'd survived. I'd been poor. If I was poor again, I could handle it. But as my team grew, I increasingly felt responsible for making sound business decisions. I had a multimillion-dollar company now, with hundreds of employees I cared about, and I had kids.

More motivated than ever to make the business all it could be, I now spent more effort than ever tracking and closing deals. I'd been negotiating with major players for a while, and now Frey Farms was one of them. If I ever thought of giving up on something, I would tell myself, *If you can't beat them . . . Wait, all these folks are depending on me. Yeah, no, to hell with that. Beat them.* To me, the word "no" just meant "not today."

I was really good at hunting retailers and becoming their supplier partner. We were doing business with every one of the top twenty retail chains in the country: Walmart, Target, Whole Foods, Kroger, Safeway, Publix . . . all of them. Any big retailer in the country you can think of, anywhere, we had a vendor agreement with them and could sell them anything. But there was one store that eluded me for years: Lowe's. Every time I spent money there, which was often and a lot—I bought plants, grilling equipment, cleaning supplies, tools for the farm—I would lament the fact that I wasn't *selling* them anything.

Just driving by a Lowe's would make my body tense. I wanted that business so badly. I made a few cold calls to the company. I know a lot of people, yet for some reason I couldn't get anybody on the phone who worked for the Lowe's corporation. Tracking that bird was taking me a very long time. But I finally picked up its scent one autumn afternoon in Virginia.

I was in D.C. for meetings on Capitol Hill for the fresh produce industry. I naively thought I could just explain the issues facing our industry and tell them what the commonsense solutions were. Surely these bright folks serving our country would act as soon as I let them know what had to be fixed and how to fix it cheaply and easily. Not so, it turned out. By the end of the day, I felt that trying to explain to lawmakers about the impact of immigration law on farmers was just taking another day of my life that I would never get back.

Well, while I was there in D.C. being disabused of my illusions about the political system, my phone rang. It was John, haltingly saying: "Hey, so, I sold pumpkins to this guy . . ."

Here we go! John's bad stories always start with "a guy."

"Okay, John," I said. "You sold pumpkins to a guy."

"Yeah," said John. "I just figured since you were in D.C. . . . Maybe you want to swing by, go visit him? Maybe get our money?"

"How much is he into us for?" I asked, and braced myself. What was it this time—five, ten grand?

There was a pause. Then, quietly, John said, "Fifteen thousand dollars."

I scolded him for giving an individual so much credit, but secretly I was thrilled. After the frustration of seeing all that political inaction, I was looking forward to stepping back into a world where I could make things happen quickly. I could feel as if I had accomplished something real that day. A simple shakedown on my way out of town was just what I needed: get the money, feel a sense of accomplishment. A thankless task for some, but fun for me.

Once my meetings were over, I took off my camel-colored coat and heels, put on my fleece, and drove to Alexandria, Virginia. Soon I pulled up to this guy's farm, a little two- or three-acre plot, clearly a family farm, surrounded by high-rises and hovering on the edge of a very busy highway. Right away I noticed the abundance of wealthy women swarming the place. The farmer had a picturesque fresh-vegetable stand. There were chickens and even a pig that ate peanuts out of your hand. Like moths to a flame, the place appeared to have drawn every yoga mom in the D.C. suburban area. I marveled at all the toned women loading pumpkins into their Land Rovers. My pumpkins.

Looking out over the bright field of orange, I felt pride. Also, joy. How can you look at piles of pumpkins and not smile? They're pretty special. They bring people so much happiness. If all I ever end up being known as is the Pumpkin Queen, I'm down with that.

I climbed out of my SUV and started looking around until I found a guy on a forklift. He was a good-looking older man wearing a plaid shirt. I figured this must be John's guy.

"Cary Nalls?" I asked.

"Yes, ma'am," he said in the thickest southern Virginia accent I had ever heard.

"Quite a place you have here, Mr. Nalls," I said, and it came out in a full-blown southern twang. *Oh, great, now* I'm *doing it. What the hell is wrong with me? One southern voice and I go full Miranda Lambert.* "Your pumpkins are quite lovely," I added, smiling at him a little mischievously.

"Yeah, we had us a real nice crop this here year."

Oh, this is so fun. He pretends he grows them, marks them up astronomically, and sells the experience of coming to his little farm. I'd just spent the day trying to convince politicians that I needed more farm workers to pick my fruits and vegetables. This guy had figured out how to get rich people to *pay him* to walk around his fields and then haul their chosen produce to their cars. *I wonder if that accent is even real. I like him already.*

"My name is Sarah Frey," I said. "These pumpkins—I hear you bought them from my brother John. Looks like you're charging twelve, fifteen dollars each and they're selling pretty well. John tells me that we need to get caught up on a couple of invoices. I happened to be in the neighborhood, so why don't you just go ahead and cut me a check?"

"I was wonderin' when you were goin' to get down to it and ask for the money," he said with a laugh. "Not sure who you thought you were foolin' in them there pretty pink tennis shoes."

I was shocked. *Could he see through me that easily?* I had driven into his place in a black Cadillac Escalade. I thought I looked like every other customer on the lot.

"Don't you worry now," he said smiling. "I'm gonna get ya your money, but first I want to know a little more 'bout Sarah Frey." His ear-to-ear grin said, *You can't hustle a hustler.* We shared the same win-at-all-costs spirit.

He asked me a few questions about myself and my business. Then he pulled out his checkbook and wrote me out a check for the full amount. Just like that. I wish it were always so easy.

I stuck around and chatted for a while. Cary, as it would turn out, had long been a traveling produce salesman himself. He routinely headed into the Deep South to buy and sell watermelons and tomatoes for markets on the Eastern Seaboard. I met his daughter Valerie, who ran a CSA—community-supported agriculture— program bringing produce straight from the farm to families. I learned that his parents' farm had been shrinking and shrinking, but that he wanted to save what was left of it. He created an agribusiness that let him hold on to a few acres, to keep it alive. This was where he'd grown up, and he didn't want to let the place go—we sure connected on that one—so when all these high-rises erupted around him, he refused to sell. Instead, he created a retail farm, and he made a killing. He knew more about my industry than I did. Much more. He also had a guy for everything, just like I do.

I became friends with Cary Nalls. He reminded me of the good side of my father. From then on, every time I would go to Washington, I would stay at the Mandarin Oriental, in the lap of luxury, and then at the end of my trip I would plan for an extra day so I could spend an afternoon visiting farms with Cary. He would pick me up at the Mandarin and we would go to Pennsylvania or Maryland, where he'd show me a new farm or a new agritourism business.

"You know, most of the Christmas trees in America come from North Carolina and Pennsylvania," said Cary on one of our educational farm jaunts. "I know that because I know the man who sells Christmas trees to Lowe's."

"Lowe's!" I said. An alarm began ringing in my brain. "I sure would like to be able to sell my products there, but I can't find the buyer."

"The man I know would help you out," said Cary. "Let me talk to him and see if I can set up a call."

There is so much serendipity in business. You just never know which meeting or connection will be the one that changes your life. Angels show up in many different guises. They become unexpected characters in your story. For example, the head of diversity for a major company was taking a Delta flight. His snack pack was so good that he looked up the supplier—who, it turned out, was a small businesswoman. Before that day, Delta was her only client. Now she also does big business with stores all over the country.

I went home to Illinois. Cary called me a couple of days later. "All right," he said, "I set up a call for you. I gave him your home phone number. He's going to call you tomorrow at five a.m. Eastern time, four a.m. your time."

This seemed a little weird, but hey, I'm a farmer. I can do early. I set my alarm so I could wake up ten minutes before the guy called me.

At four a.m. sharp, the phone rang.

"All right," said the man, whose name was Cubby. "Cary told me to call you. I'm really busy." In the background, I heard saws and shouting.

I chatted with this guy for twenty minutes. I learned that Cubby sells the majority of the live Christmas trees in the country. What I didn't learn is the name of the person at Lowe's I was supposed to call.

As the call seemed to be wrapping up, I said, "So, who do I call at Lowe's?"

"Well," he said, "you should talk to Mike. He's my merchandiser. I'll have him call you."

I was thinking, *Why did I just wake up at four in the morning and spend twenty minutes on the phone when I could have been sleeping?* But I said, "Thank you. I look forward to talking with Mike."

Three days later, Mike called. We talked for thirty minutes. He did not give me the name or number of anyone at Lowe's.

"Okay," I said, at last, "are you the guy that's going to give me the name and the number of the person I need to call at Lowe's?"

"Well, you know," he said. "I think you should come down to Orlando, Florida, and meet a merchandise manager for Lowe's first."

"Okay, so is this the guy who buys?" I said.

"Well, no, not really. But I need to introduce you to him before we get you to the next step." I began to feel like a private detective, wearily tracking down one lead after another, the rubber on the bottom of my shoes wearing thin.

A couple of days later I took a plane to Orlando and drove to the appointed Lowe's store. In a lawn-and-garden aisle, I found the guy I was supposed to talk to. His name was Jeremy, and I knew that right away because he was wearing a name tag.

We toured the store together. I told him a little bit about the farms and what we did. He suggested we go for sushi. Why not?

Sitting there in a Florida strip mall having sushi with Jeremy, I was thinking about how hard I was working for this phone number: I went to shake down a guy for money in Virginia. He gave me the name of a Christmas tree dealer in Pennsylvania, who might as well have been a character in a Coen brothers movie. He put me in touch with his merchandiser, who now had me meeting with a Florida worker in a Lowe's apron.

"Do you ever sell your products to BJ's?" Jeremy asked.

When I said yes, he asked for the name of my contact there.

"Patrick Morris," I said.

"Patrick?" he said. "We grew up together in New Orleans!"

If I'd only known that I could have saved myself at least three steps, I thought. *More wasabi, please.*

"So," I asked Jeremy, "who do I call in Lowe's corporate?"

"Well, you know what," said Jeremy, "I need to probably call up there and try to arrange the meeting."

Are you kidding me? I thought. *I just want a telephone number and a name! Please, for the love of God and all that is good, give me a number! I don't even care if it's a working number at this point. Just give me something.*

But I was committed. I went back to Illinois and waited.

While I was waiting, I kept thinking of alternative routes. *I could call on someone in my network, maybe another CEO who knows the CEO of Lowe's. Then I could call the CEO and get the buyer's number from him.* But I've learned in my life that it's actually better to do things from the grassroots level up than to try to push a new deal from the top down. I've always been a believer in this bottom-up approach. But nothing had tested this conviction as intensely as my Lowe's quest.

A week later Jeremy called and said, "Okay, I have the meeting for you."

I headed to Lowe's HQ in Mooresville, North Carolina. Walking in, I found it to be just about the most beautiful corporate office campus I'd ever seen in my life—there were waterfalls, lakes, beautiful buildings. *Of course it's perfect,* I thought. *It's Lowe's. Their motto is "Never stop improving."*

A young assistant took me into a conference room alone to wait for the buyer. The conference table was mahogany and shiny. I threw my bag underneath it and sat in the head chair. I looked around. Then I broke into a wide smile. I started laughing like a child. I actually started spinning in the swivel chair, I was so giddy with joy. I felt elated. If I had landed that meeting any other way, it wouldn't have felt nearly as good as this did. *It doesn't matter if I sell these folks a thing,* I thought, *because I have won. I've bagged the bird. I've won the hunt.*

The buyer, a guy several years older than me in a white shirt and dress pants, entered the room with a swagger. When he sat down, I went to give him my card, and he said, "I'm not going to give you one of my cards, because I don't like emails."

Well, aren't you just a sunshine-dipped lollipop?

I laughed out loud. I respected his honesty. I also realized that he had absolutely no idea what I had done to get inside that room. I did not care at all about whether he took my card, whether we ever emailed each other. This was my rabbit. I'd already shot it. Without taking my eyes off him, I cupped my hand over my business card and slid it back to my side of the table.

"I don't like emails either," I said with a big smile. "And I probably wouldn't respond to you if you wrote me. Honestly, I don't care if I sell you anything. Because I went through a lot to get here. And I did it. It was weird, but actually pretty fun. So. Here's the deal: I sell my produce to the largest retailers in the world. I have some of the nicest farms in the country. We ship more volume than anybody else of these commodities you need. If you want to carry a high-quality product and reduce your costs, that would be great. If you don't, that's fine. But personally? I'm just really happy to be here. Oh, and by the way, I spend a lot of time and money in your stores."

Clearly no one had ever spoken to him like that, ever. He just stared at me. He knew that I meant every word. He smiled and shook his head. In that moment I knew we were going to be friends, and I suspected we'd be able to do some business together, too.

By the time I walked out of that room, I had the Lowe's pumpkin business, and more besides. I wound up creating new home décor items for them, and selling them scented pinecones.

What I realized in that meeting was that in the course of the adventure, I had learned Lowe's culture, from the bottom to the top. By the time I found myself in that meeting room, I was already familiar with their business in ways that I wouldn't have been had I just called their CEO. I was thankful that I hadn't discovered a shortcut into that room. An academic friend of mine calls what I learned on my odyssey through the ranks of Lowe's "campaign-style negotiation." It's served me well many times since then.

That meeting resulted in millions of dollars' worth of business for Frey Farms annually. And, as unlikely as it may sound, that anti-business-card guy became one of my biggest champions in the industry. But even if he'd said, "No, thanks. We're satisfied with our suppliers. Who the hell are you?" I still would have whistled all the way back to Orchardville like I did with my first rabbit. Because who the hell was I? A hunter, that's who.

Those trips with Cary yielded bounty in so many ways. On one of our drives, I fell in love with a little area of West Virginia in the Shenandoah Valley. I was particularly drawn to the land around Shepherdstown. It's the oldest town in West Virginia and close to the Civil War battlefield of Antietam. Now that I had to ship to Lowe's, I was in the market for farmland that would let me transport my products more easily to their distribution center in the Northeast.

I was traveling in the Carolinas one day when Martha, a friend

Cary and I had made in West Virginia, called to tell me that a woman who owned a farm down the road from her had died and two of her relatives, a father and son, both preachers living in Oklahoma, were planning to sell it. The land had been in their family for years, so I knew this would be an emotional decision for them as much as a financial one. I drove straight to Martha's place in West Virginia. She invited over the preachers and they took me to see the farm. I spent the whole day with them.

As we walked the land, I listened to their stories. They were sweet men and I enjoyed our time together, but as the shadows began to get long and they said they should be heading back to Oklahoma, I grew anxious. I knew that the fate of this land was a sensitive subject, but I also knew how eager I was to buy it. I didn't want to be pushy, but I also couldn't let them drive away without making it known that I longed to buy it.

Finally, as they were about to get back in the car, I said, "So, do you think maybe you want to sell me the farm?" I promised them I wouldn't put in cookie-cutter suburban houses like other developers were building around there for D.C. commuters. I told them I would grow pumpkins that first year and then see what else I could do with the soil.

They told me they would have to wait to see if God gave them a sign that they should sell me the farm.

They left to go back to Oklahoma and I headed farther south in West Virginia to Berkeley Springs. Our founding fathers, including George Washington, took vacations there to enjoy the mineral springs, and I was interested in having a look around. I changed into clean clothes and went to a restaurant called the Earth Dog Cafe, where I ordered dinner and a drink.

There weren't a lot of people in the place that night. As I sipped my drink, I reflected on my day with the preachers. I wondered what kind of sign God would send them if I was the one. And I thought about my own relationship with God. I believed in God, but I wasn't sure he spoke to me. Or, if he did, I wasn't sure I knew how to listen.

I considered what he might say to me if he were to speak about something like this plot of land, and how he would say it.

While I was seated at the bar, a text came in from one of the preachers. It was a sweet note about how nice our day had been, accompanied by a photo of the beautiful sunset they had just seen while driving home. He said this was how God talked to them. He seemed to approve of our connection. It sounded promising.

Around me, the Earth Dog Cafe began to fill up. Several women of varying ages came in wearing strappy heels, tight cashmere sweaters, flowers in their hair, and short shorts. I learned that they were there for a 1950s pinup girl contest. A band began tuning up. The restaurant transformed into a honky-tonk. As more and more women in sexy fifties-style outfits arrived, I felt like the whole place was traveling back in time. It was a little weird, but then the whole day had been pretty weird.

Just as I was finishing my meal, the band began to play. Not long after the music started, I heard a gasp. I turned and looked and saw that a three-hundred-pound man on the dance floor had dropped his pants and was mooning everyone. It appeared that he had something drawn on his body. I couldn't believe my eyes. On his butt, the man had giant tattoos, one covering each cheek. The tattoos were of—oh, sweet Jesus—pumpkins.

As their sign, God sent the preachers a beautiful sunset. That was how he talked to the kind, gentle father and son who were men of the cloth. And *this* was how he talked to me—by interrupting my dinner with the vision of a large, smiling man on a dance floor, his massive pumpkin-covered butt cheeks swaying to a rockabilly song.

The next day the preachers sold me the farm. I kept my word to the preachers. I used that glorious land to grow pumpkins for Lowe's. And I said a prayer of thanks for the golden sunset, and for the full harvest moon.

Chapter 15

Sunshine and Rain

As my fresh produce business expanded and the need for more farmworkers grew, we began to attract the government's attention. One day in 2012, five federal agencies showed up on my farms. I was getting ready to head to the office when the office called and said, "The Department of Labor is here." Before I was out the door, they said, "Department of Homeland Security is in Indiana." And, before we were off the phone, "OSHA is at your office in Missouri."

All in one day, agents from the Department of Homeland Security, Illinois Migratory Services, the Food and Drug Administration, the Occupational Safety and Health Administration, and the state and federal Departments of Labor all turned up to look into my business. It was the busiest time of year. It took all of my people to show them around and to handle the audits. Some of the audits lasted days, others weeks. In the end, they found nothing worth their time. I was relieved, of course, but I was also annoyed by how much dealing with their inquiries had slowed us down. That's the kind of thing that gets businesses frustrated with the government.

I've been asked several times to run for political office. Sometimes I'm tempted.

But our high profile earned Frey Farms the good kind of attention, too: I was asked to serve on the National Watermelon Promotion Board. Yes, there is such a board, and one for just about every other type of produce as well. For as long as I'd been in the watermelon business, I'd been complaining about how the NWPB took so many cents per ton of product to promote the consumption of watermelons nationwide. Yet for years I didn't see the value of what they did.

When I was asked, I thought, *If you don't serve, you can't complain.* I let them put my name forward. President Obama's Secretary of Agriculture, Tom Vilsack, approved my appointment.

My first NWPB meeting was in Savannah, Georgia, where I would also attend my first watermelon convention. In all of my years in the melon business I hadn't attended once. Don't get me wrong—I love melon farmers and I'm a confident woman. But I'd be lying if I said I felt up to the challenge of seed-spitting competitions. Yes, that is actually a thing.

The South Carolina Watermelon Queen took the stage to address us in her sash and million-watt smile. She began to talk to us about how great watermelon is for athletes like football players. *This is my life now,* I thought. I had such big plans and high hopes for my business, and here I was being lectured to about high school sports teams by a perky girl in a minidress and fake-diamond tiara. Why wasn't she at least wearing a watermelon-print cape or watermelon-shaped headpiece?

The watermelon queen went on to quote from some research the promotion board had done on the specific health benefits of watermelon for athletes, but I questioned the direction she was taking it in.

"Y'all, I think we should cut up watermelon and serve slices to football players at games!" she said, looking each of us in the eye as if she meant *right now.*

I had visions of us in our business attire slicing up watermelons and carrying trays to players with our sticky watermelon-juice-covered fingers. I saw the players trying to force a wedge of watermelon through the face mask on their helmets and getting watermelon juice all over their jerseys. I saw players getting the football all sticky, slipping on rinds, and getting injured. *Excellent intentions, Watermelon Queen,* I thought as I sat there.

When the meeting ended, I left thinking, *What the hell did I sign up for?* This being Georgia, I was enjoying a seventy-five-degree day in February, so I put on my tennis shoes to go for a run by the river. Before I started, I stretched on a bench and wound up just lying there in the sun. I reflected on the meeting and thought, *Actually, it's a good idea to give watermelon to athletes. But there has to be a better way.* With that, a lightbulb went off in my mind. *They need to* drink *it. I'll put it in a bottle! If I bottle it, then I won't have to volunteer my time handing out slices of watermelon at football games!*

No one was juicing watermelon at the time. I immediately started working on a plan to create a new sports beverage: cold-pressed watermelon juice. I'm a geek, so I decided to name it Tsamma (it's pronounced *sah-mah*), after the mother of all watermelons: the ancient Tsamma varietal from Africa. Three months after I had the idea, I was at a plant in Florida, having my melons pressed into juice. Less than thirty days after that first pressing, we were on the shelves of the high-end Fresh Market supermarkets nationwide. Within months, Tsamma was the chain's top-selling single-serve juice.

Making watermelon juice using fruit from my farms that would otherwise have been wasted inspired me to look at other fruits and vegetables that might be turned into beverages. We learned so much from producing Tsamma about how to make fresh beverage ingredients on the farm, and how to use new technology to press and process the juice so the quality stayed high.

The project—bringing natural, fresh juices into national restaurant chains—seemed so promising. When my brothers and I were growing up on the farm and wanted to drink something besides water, we would muddle freshly harvested fruit with a small amount of real cane sugar and water to create homemade refreshing beverages. These types of light fruit drinks, known as aguas frescas throughout Mexico and parts of Latin America, are deeply connected to my rural midwestern upbringing. My theory was that no adult or child in America could resist a cold, farm-fresh beverage on a hot day.

And finally, I believed that my company was the first one to crack the code on making high-quality juice from farm-fresh fruit. When a national chain approached me to develop beverages for its restaurants, I saw an opportunity to improve the country's diet in a real way, and also to bring more family farms into the beverage space, something I'd dreamed of doing for a long time. I could continue to create products that incorporated the mission of improving food quality and ending food waste, all while helping other families earn more profits from their small farms.

The more I learned about the beverage business, the more I became evangelical about the value of drinking natural beverages instead of sodas. What baffled me was how, even as people became more health conscious, fast-food restaurants had stayed stuck in the past, still offering mostly just soda or sweetened iced tea.

As I explored the industry, I learned why that is. Big beverage companies pay enormous amounts of money to control these dining spaces. If you keep low-margin, high-quality products out of the stores, you force consumers to choose from a narrow selection of high-margin carbonated sugar waters. It's strictly business. Your local franchisee may well want to offer a healthy beverage choice instead of or alongside the sodas, but they can't. The national soda contracts are attached to billions of dollars' worth of marketing dollars, which don't allow competing products into the space.

When I discovered this, I was in shock. All those years of walking into fast casual restaurants with my kids, I'd never even questioned the choices we had. I made do with diet sodas or overpriced plastic bottles of water and didn't think twice about it. I became consumed with questions about how we could find a balance between convenience and freshness. That's been a big struggle for me. I'm busy. I love a fresh fruit smoothie, for example, but I hate spending time to make it and dirtying a blender. The beverages we make solve that problem for me.

I love looking for answers to questions like this one. I love hanging out in supermarkets. I feel at home in all of them. Every chain grocery store has its own smell. Put me in any grocery store in America blindfolded and I'll tell you what store I'm in. The small independent grocery store smell might be my favorite. Walking into one, whether in New York City, the Midwest, or Rome, I'll sniff the air as though I'm in the mountains. I wish they had small-grocery-store perfume.

When I started getting Frey beverages into supermarket chains, I felt like my career was newly full of potential. The beverage industry was so exciting to me. It seemed like the sky was the limit for what I could accomplish.

Meanwhile, my marriage was in shambles.

Here's the thing—I get to a certain point with a problem and I just think, *Burn it down, break it up, start over, get a new one.* My brothers like to remind me of the Lawnmower Incident. We owned a great White-brand riding lawnmower. My brother John bought it. I used to love to mow. The task has a beginning and end. You complete the task and you look back on it and feel a sense of accomplishment.

One day I wanted to mow. It was therapy I'd come to count on. I went out there to get on this lawnmower and the thing wouldn't start. I know how to fix mowers, but I was so mad that it wouldn't start that I didn't even lift the hood.

"Nope," I said. "Not today." I drove to town and bought a brand-new John Deere riding lawnmower. When my brothers saw it, they almost fainted.

"Yeah, I bought a lawnmower," I said. "So what?"

"A *really expensive* lawnmower!" John said.

I would later find out that the battery cable on the first lawnmower had been loose. I could have fixed that in two seconds. I didn't even care. I was working so hard all the time that I just couldn't deal with a lawnmower that wouldn't start. When I hit a wall, that's it. It's time to move on.

At some point, my marriage became a lawnmower that wouldn't start.

Not everything I've ever done in business has worked. I've had many failures. I've won a lot, too, but it felt like it didn't matter how much I won, because Justin always focused on the losses. And even when I was winning, he'd bring up past losses—as if I couldn't remember them myself. It still seems to me that something good comes out of everything that fails. It's like going to a business school, learning hands-on every day. But at the Sarah Frey School of Business, I was learning with real money and affecting real people's lives.

Still, through it all, I managed to stay optimistic. Butterflies and rainbows. We will persevere. I could always make people believe, get them to rally around a cause. The thing was, I could never make my husband believe. By the end of the day, I didn't feel I should have to work so hard to get him to see what I saw. I stopped talking to him about things that I was passionate about.

I'm sure I was no picnic, either. I was conditioned at such an early age to be able to handle a huge amount of stress. The things that Justin fretted over seemed insignificant to me. And it turned out that even our ways of relaxing didn't mesh. I wanted to talk about what was going on in the world and new ideas. He wanted to watch reality TV to escape.

Justin started to say that he wished I weren't so ambitious. He wanted me to be happy with what I had accomplished, and he wanted me to work less. Maybe I could change careers and become something normal, like a teacher. When he said that, it knocked the wind out of me. Don't get me wrong. I'm a huge fan of teachers. I love children. Yet being in a classroom day after day wasn't exactly in my DNA. I'm impatient, driven, restless, and at times obsessive.

When Justin said he wanted me to be a teacher, it was almost as if you were tall and your husband told you he wished you were short, or if you were scared of the water and he said he wished you were an

Olympic swimmer. How could he say that he loved me when deep down he wished I was someone else?

Over the years, it became clear that we had grown too far apart. I resolved that I would handle our inevitable split in such a way that the boss would barely notice. Thank goodness Justin and I could agree on the most important thing—our children. We vowed to make sure that nothing about their lives changed except their parents sharing a bed. I also knew that I had to protect what I was working so hard to build. After all, I was the one who'd broken the rule and allowed my husband to work for the company. Now I had to handle whatever our breakup meant for the business. I could not let my emotions cloud the situation.

Looking back, I realize that I could have taken the time to get inside Justin's world and try to relate. I think if we both had worked harder at it, we could've saved our marriage. But we didn't work at it. I kept everything inside and so did he. We never fought. We never talked enough to fight. From the outside looking in, everything seemed nearly perfect. But it was far from that. We could have shared our feelings with each other about things that made us feel vulnerable. Instead, we'd let us grow apart until we couldn't see any way to come back together.

I prepared divorce paperwork and presented it to him as if it were just another deal. Justin and I didn't sit in the attorney's office longer than the thirty minutes it took for us to sign documents. I handled every detail fairly, and I went to great lengths to keep the divorce private. We would not speak of it to anyone. I wasn't ready for the world to find out our marriage was over.

I didn't want my children to have to deal with having divorced parents, especially not while they were still so young. I was embarrassed by my epic failure to be normal. We were divorced for nearly a year before I even told my brothers. I told them individually, one after another. How embarrassing that I, who was supposed to be a stable example, had failed. Still, they supported my decision and seemed relieved that I had handled it the way I did, with no disruption to the family or business.

In retrospect, I see the irony. I'd been so angry with my mother for having pretended to be married. Now here I was doing more or less the same thing. Justin and I continued to live in the same house, like roommates. It was amicable. We never fought. But we were both in purgatory.

Finally a day of reckoning came. We had the first brutally frank conversation we'd had in years. For a moment I thought I could process everything and we could rebuild from scratch. We had blown it up and had the opportunity to start new. But then it fell apart again. I began to suspect that the Hill was damned, that no relationship could survive there.

When we finally announced our divorce and he built his own place, it was like a great burden had lifted. Justin moved back to the small town he was from and settled into a comfortable life for himself. I made it clear that he could see the boys anytime, and he stayed involved with them. I didn't ask him to leave the company; we continued to work together. I still don't wish I'd jumped in that Dodge my brother left running outside the church on my wedding day. We were meant to have those boys. They are, and always will be, my greatest accomplishment.

At first it was hard seeing so much of Justin after we'd split, but as time went by I regained my strength. I no longer felt I had to apologize for being myself and for wanting to build and create things. I didn't need to feel guilty for being an entrepreneur. I also realized it was okay to expect more from a marriage. I realized that I deserved a full partner, someone I didn't have to hide parts of myself from, someone who could love all of me for who I am.

I knew that I had a lot of love to give, and that someday maybe I would pour the same passion and enthusiasm that I had built my business with into a relationship. I vowed to do better if I ever got another chance.

I look back and realize that I conducted the divorce as a business transaction. I didn't deal with its emotional aspects. I did what I thought was best for everyone involved, without thinking too hard about what I needed or wanted. I just handled it. I didn't address the failures on my part, or the failures on his part. The fact was, in the aftermath, there was still so much pent up inside, I was afraid that one crack and it was all going to come out—all the stress, all the heartache, all the blood, sweat, and tears. The dam would break. Everyone that I felt responsible for would suffer because of it.

I did what I always do to make myself feel better. I bought a farm.

Illinois winters can be long and harsh. I'm definitely a person whose mood is affected by weather. I needed sunshine and a break from the Hill. We had fresh produce operations all over Florida. I'd acquired a house in Naples where the boys loved spending time, so we headed there to ride out the season.

One Saturday morning, I went to a land auction to purchase a piece of property bordering some land we already owned. John was in Mexico on vacation. Before leaving, he'd told me, "If you're in Florida anyway, go bid on that property."

Most of the land I'd bought was at farm auctions. They're kind of sad occasions, because often the farmers don't want to see their land sold. I slipped into the side door of the community center where the auction was being held. Like all of the auctions I had attended before, on the block was the land of yet more farmers who had gone out of business. This time, many of the orange groves had failed because of citrus greening, an insidious disease caused by bacteria and spread by insects.

I felt so sorry for these farmers. I imagined them working in the groves from sunup until sundown tending to fading trees, struggling to hold on, asking the bank for extensions and operating loans to keep farming. Without removing the diseased trees and planting new, resistant ones in their place, their situation was hopeless. Every season would yield less and less produce. I knew how they must have felt to have worked the land their whole life and poured everything they had into it, only to watch it be taken away.

Our fresh produce operations in the Southeast were expanding.

Publix, a grocery chain based in Florida, was supporting my growing beverage business. I wanted to continue to make the necessary
investments to grow that business. I went to the auction with the
intention of buying about eighty acres of land next to ours. But during the course of the bidding I looked at the maps of another tract
of land and began to wonder why it wasn't selling for more. *What am
I missing? The land should be bringing more money. Why aren't more
people bidding?*

I locked up the first tract with a winning bid and stuck around
to watch the rest sell. I kept eyeing the glossy brochure in my hands.
Listed was a 500-acre farm that I couldn't stop looking at. I had
never stepped foot on it, but from the picture and soil map I could
tell it was a good piece of land. My gut said to bid. I had never
bought land sight unseen, but I had a feeling.

The auctioneer was dragging out the request for one more bid.
He was at $2,800 an acre, trying to get to $3,000. I raised my hand
and he dropped the hammer. My first and only bid bought the
farm—a farm that I had no idea what I was going to do with. It
wasn't part of my plan. I woke up on a Saturday morning and made
a $1.5 million impulse purchase.

A man who worked for me and who lived in the area was at the
auction. He ran over to tell me he was surprised by my decision to
buy the farm—though he was not nearly as surprised as I was.

"What the hell just happened, Sarah?" he asked me, laughing.

"Well, Joey," I said, "some women buy shoes. I buy farms. Now
tell me I bought a good one."

"You did, actually," said Joey. "It's a real good farm. I thought it
was going to bring twice what you paid."

"Good," I said. "Now let's get out there and confirm that theory."

We drove out to the land I'd just bought. On the way, I prayed
that it wouldn't be a swamp.

My prayers were answered. As we drove onto what was now my
new farm, I couldn't stop smiling. It was the most beautiful piece of
Florida land I'd ever laid eyes on. Orange trees. Flocks of wild turkeys. Rock quarries. And at the center of the farm sat a ghost town,

a fifty-plus-acre plot of land that was once the heart of a community called Sears. Almost none of the buildings were still standing, but you could see the old train tracks and the remnants of the old mill. That part of the property was then and still is maintained as a nature preserve with panthers, alligators, and black bears. Florida has more things that will kill you than almost any other state, and I host many of these species on my land.

In 1926, Richard Sears, who had founded Sears, Roebuck and owned Standard Lumber, built a mill on the path of the Atlantic Coastline Railroad to produce and ship lumber for kit homes. The workers at this little factory lived in—what else—kit homes near the factory. The town grew to five hundred people, but the mill closed in 1928, and by the late thirties the town had vanished. I vowed to bring new life to this lifeless place.

Since buying the property, I've turned it into a tomato and watermelon farm. That piece of land is now worth three times what it cost me at auction. I took that as a reminder to trust my instincts. Buying land and growing things on it is what I was built to do.

Chapter 16

Field Run

S oon after my divorce, I woke to the sound of a rooster in my house. Just great. But as I emerged into consciousness, I realized it wasn't a rooster; just my brother Ted, crowing to wake us up. He was there to take the boys for breakfast at the Skillet Fork Grill and then fishing, so that I could get some work done. I also think he started dropping by the house more frequently because he knew the boys needed his presence in their life.

Harley stepped up, too. One Easter we were eating dinner when we looked out into the yard of my house and saw an eight-foot-tall Easter Bunny hopping around in the yard. Harley had rented an elaborate bunny costume and come to entertain them. The little kids all ran over, faces pressed to the glass in wonder and glee. The only thing Harley hadn't counted on was my two dogs. They ran at top speed toward him. Harley turned and ran, basket sailing into the air, eggs flying everywhere. I had to go out there and call them off so they didn't eat him up. I shooed the dogs away and got Harley into the garage. We took off his rabbit head, and I saw that he was redder than a fire engine.

"I thought they were going to kill me!" he said, out of breath, "Worse, I thought the kids were going to have to see your dogs murder the Easter Bunny!"

Many evenings my brothers gather around my dining room table joking with William and Luke and their own families: John, Andrea, and their girls. Leonard and his boy, Aidan. Ted and his girl, Grace. Despite a few attempts at lifelong partnership here and there, all of my mother's seven living children are currently single except for John. We've found comfort in one another. I cherish my perfectly imperfect family.

I was incredibly fortunate to have support from my family now that I was alone raising boys and a business. Having my own company was stressful, but thanks to my family I had built-in flexibility that most single mothers don't. I could work from home, and I could take the boys with me when I traveled.

I wanted my sons to learn how to pitch in and help the family, too. Sometimes I had to go out of my way to teach them to care for each other the way my brothers and I had, even when it would have been easier for me to step in.

When William and Luke were five and three, William shot himself in the foot with a mini-BB gun while he was up to his knees in a little pond. The tiny pellet wasn't dangerous, but I knew from experience that it really stung. When little Luke just stood there on the edge of the pond watching him cry, I was horrified. If my brothers or I got hurt, the rest of us would drop everything to run over and help.

I yelled at Luke, "Go help your brother out of the pond and give him a hug!"

"No, Mommy!" Luke yelled. "Kitty fish in there!" He was terrified of catfish and were sure they would bite him.

"You get in there right now and hold your brother's hand and help him out of that pond!" I yelled.

Yes, I wanted to run over and pull William out of the pond myself, to hug him and find him a Scooby Band-Aid. It would have taken me seconds to make everything right. But I thought Luke should be the one to help him instead of just standing there. I knew that they needed to be there for each other, which meant Luke had to go into that pond.

Luke started bawling, saying, "But *kiiiiitty fiiiiiiiish!*" I looked at those two boys wailing over nothing and I smacked my forehead. *My sons would never have survived an hour of my childhood.*

I held my ground. Finally, when he saw I wasn't budging, Luke, still crying, gingerly stepped into the pond and took William's hand, then led him out of the pond. I made them hug and tell each other "I love you." They did and the tears dried. They walked back to the house together, arm in arm, forgetting that I was even there. A Band-Aid was located. The nick was taken care of. In ten minutes they were back playing again as if nothing had happened.

One question haunts me: How do I instill an independent spirit in my children, given that they are growing up with so much more privilege than I did?

Once when William was nine and Luke was seven, we were at the grocery store and I realized they were just throwing things into the cart willy-nilly. I thought, *Oh, this might not be the best lesson in the world for the kids.* Stopping the cart before we reached the check-out, I mustered up all of my acting skills. I looked into the cart very solemnly, as if thinking, *Oh my gosh.*

William said to me, "Mom, what's wrong?"

I made a sad face and said to them, "I'm not sure we can afford everything in this cart."

Right away, the boys said, "It's okay, Mom! Don't be sad! We don't need this! We don't need that!" They started grabbing things and running around putting them back on the shelves.

The truth was, we could afford everything in the cart. But I wanted the boys to get a glimpse of what it feels like not to have enough money to buy whatever you want, and to realize in a visceral way that you care more about your family's happiness than you do about Cap'n Crunch.

I remind my children often that they are growing up with a lot more than I did, and with a lot more than most kids in this country have. I do what I can to help them learn that not everything is easy. They have to know that most people have to check the price tags on everything at the supermarket, every time they go. I'm often asked why I would sell my products to value retail chains like Aldi rather than sticking with higher-end ones like Whole Foods. My response is that everyone deserves access to fresh produce. Eating well shouldn't be a privilege reserved for the wealthy.

I also want my boys to know what it is to work hard. It's their job to make breakfast—usually bacon and eggs. I haven't made my own coffee in seven years.

I routinely drop the boys off in the fields with our workers. Once when William was five, we arrived home from kindergarten pickup to see the workers out in the field in front of the house picking pumpkins. It had been a long, hard day for them, and they still had so much to get done before the sun set. When we got out of the car, I told William to go help them.

"Out there?" he said, shocked, pointing to the fields, which I'm sure to him looked miles away even though they were basically in our backyard.

"Yeah, go," I said.

He did it. From our house, I watched from the back porch while he picked pumpkins. I was glad to see him working hard and to see the other workers being patient with him and teaching him well. When he came home for dinner, ravenously hungry, he was proud of himself, as proud as I'd ever seen him. He'd helped contribute to the household in a tangible way. And he had new respect for the workers who helped make our life possible. He'd made new friends. He'd worked up a real appetite. He had dirt under his nails. The many times I've sent him and his brother out there since, they've both gone without a backward glance.

After my divorce, I questioned whether it was possible to run a company and be a good mom at the same time. I felt insecure and unsteady at times in life and in business. The failure of my marriage left a mark. I struggled with the perception of being a single woman in business and at home. There was no retreating to one world or the other to heal. Everything was intertwined. The boys were getting older and I decided to involve them in my business even more than I had before. The more they knew about the company, the more they understood its importance to our family and to the world at large.

As I saw their enthusiasm, my entrepreneurial hunger became more overwhelming. We would talk about world events and big ideas while we cooked dinner together. I wanted to diversify the company, to continue to expand from fresh produce and beverages into other areas. With them on board, I felt freer to take risks, to pursue bolder ideas.

For years, the amount of fresh fruits and vegetables that went to waste on farms had bothered me. I knew what it was like to have very little food. I would watch at the end of a harvest when entire fields of watermelons or pumpkins were plowed back into the soil. These were perfectly good pieces of fruit that just had the misfortune of not being suited for the produce section of a grocery store. Perhaps they were a little burned by the sun, or misshapen, or smaller than normal, or just not pretty enough. Still, the fruit inside was just as wonderful as—sometimes better than—the most perfect-looking fruit in the field.

To me, our guiding principle should be what's known in farming as "field run." The field run is a crop that has not been graded or sorted for size and shape imperfections. You select fruit as it ripens naturally, celebrating the difference in each one without throwing any out because they look different. I'll tell you a secret: the best-tasting fruit never looks perfect. The ugly fruit might not go in a display bin, but if you're creative and committed to making the best out of what you have, you can turn the ugliest fruit into the tastiest dishes.

Field run means you take it as it comes. A perfect honeydew grown in ideal conditions in California looks beautiful, but it's not necessarily flavorful. In Illinois, the melon may show cracks along its skin, but the fruit is more likely to be sweet.

There's something profound in that, I've always thought. I feel a personal affection for the imperfect fruit. Perhaps that's because in my life I've often felt like a field run crop myself, one that hasn't been graded or sorted for imperfections, one whose inherent value may be invisible to people looking for outward signs of conformity. I've always identified with the "ugly fruit," the underestimated, the neglected. My brothers and I were not the same as the other kids at school. We weren't as wealthy, popular, or well-dressed as the others. We could have easily been overlooked. Our clothes and faces were often dirty. And yet inside us you'd find a beautiful heart and a desire to succeed.

As a result, I seek out the "ugly fruit" in my friendships and in business. As a boss, I routinely hire the single moms, the community or state college grads, and the applicants with no formal education. I've learned that they care. They're not entitled. They'll put in the hours. They're hungrier to climb the ladder and do the work. The hungriest "field run" worker can outwork the rarefied MBA any day trying to prove themselves. Having said that, we encourage those who join our team to continue their education, and we pay for them to do so.

I seek out those who haven't been given a head start in life. It's not because I'm doing anyone a favor. It's a business decision for me. I believe that these people possess character strengths that are important to my business: unique approaches, a strong work ethic, and a healthy dose of willpower. I dug my future out of the ground, and I want to surround myself with other people who, if given the chance, will do the same.

I was letting my female employees work from home before that was a thing. One of my employees, Wanda, has been with my company for seventeen years. I hired her over the phone without ever meeting her in person. She's traveled to Illinois fewer than ten times over the years. Another of our valued employees is a childhood neighbor named Stephanie. Before I recruited her, she worked in fast food. I ran into her one day at the convenience store and saw that she was holding a lanyard of keys. She was managing a McDonald's. It occurred to me that being a manager at McDonald's is an incredibly tough job. You have to follow procedures. You have to manage teenage shift workers and the lunchtime rush. I asked her to come to my office. I offered her a higher salary. She did everything I asked her to do, and she did it well: sales, program management, buying. She's been promoted along the way and now has built an amazing career for herself with the flexibility to live anywhere she wants to.

I've put the field run mentality to work in every aspect of my business. We started to make use of the pumpkins that ordinarily would have been wasted. We harvested them for seeds, which I sold to grocery stores as a healthy snack. I shipped semi loads of our hand-harvested but visually imperfect pumpkins to canneries for use in pies. It was a higher-quality ingredient than was collected by machine harvesting.

The same thing happened with my ugly-but-delicious watermelons. I realized that instead of tilling them back into the soil, I could turn them into watermelon juice or sell them as personal-size melons. We learned how to use new, high-tech equipment to quickly cut and process the fruit, then turn it into a semi-frozen slush right there on the farm. We were able to preserve the freshness and quality of fresh-picked fruit and to greatly reduce waste.

The launch of Tsamma watermelon juice inspired me to look at other fruits and vegetables that might otherwise be wasted.

A few months ago, I was in a meeting and a buyer asked, "What would you do to improve the frozen juice category?"

The problem they had was that no one was buying the old cans of frozen orange juice anymore. I could see why. First thing in the morning, I don't have time to get out a pitcher and a wooden spoon and spend my time melting a frozen block of concentrate.

I love a challenge, so I was thrilled to have the question before me about how I might be able to make better frozen juices.

The first thing I thought was: *The people buying frozen juice are busy women like me.* Women do most of the grocery shopping in this country, whether we're at Trader Joe's or ShopRite. I also thought that, like a lot of parents, I want cleaner ingredients in my kids' beverages—and in mixers for my cocktails. The question was, how do you create a juice that accomplishes all that—something delicious for adults, better for kids, and easy to thaw and serve?

The first step was to figure out the most efficient kind of packaging. I looked at every conceivable box and bag. I chose one that resembled the packaging inside boxed wine. I started from there, designing a variation on it that could lie flat in the freezer but which you could then thaw, add water to, and set upright in the fridge. We developed a farm-fresh frozen juice mix packed so that you could just pour water into the top, shake it up, and then dispense using the built-in spigot, whether for your kid's breakfast beverage or your evening drink.

This invention was thrilling to me. Ever since I was eight years old in that Centralia Hometown IGA, I've been obsessed with food and how it's packaged and delivered. And ever since the days of Voila! chicken, I've wondered if it might be possible to get packaged food to taste as fresh and as good as the food we ate on the farm. It was exciting to know that we would be using some of our own field run produce, juicing it just the way my brothers and I would every summer in our kitchen on the Hill.

That's how my aguas frescas found their way into the freezers of twelve hundred Walmart stores. William and Luke drink them every day. And when girlfriends come over for drinks, I thaw a few varieties in the fridge ahead of time and serve them in delicious cocktails. Those juices, for my money, are the coolest new products on the market. Start to finish, we got it done in a single season.

In doing that, I saw my mission with the Sarah's Homegrown brand: creating food that is at once healthier and easier. Too often people are asked to choose between food that is fast and cheap, on one hand, and food that is labor-intensive and expensive, on the other. I refuse to believe those are our only options.

When I look to the future, I see the challenges our world will face in feeding a growing population. The family farm will be at the center of this challenge. And if history repeats itself, the family farm will come through. Times will always be difficult, but the farmer is resilient and will rise to the occasion.

The other day, standing in one of my fields with a friend, I broke open an ugly watermelon. Flat on one side, this melon had been left there in the dirt by our pickers. Soon I'd send a team through to take these ugly melons for juice and other products; even a couple of years ago they all would have been plowed back into the soil. With my knife, I carved out a big piece and handed it to my friend, then cut another one for myself. We bit into the melon and smiled at each other. It was the sweetest fruit you could imagine.

My friend and I had both come from humble beginnings. We'd taken different paths to success but were both at the top of our industries. Sometimes the Davids beat the Goliaths. Sometimes the ugly ducklings become swans. Like that watermelon, we had been the ugly fruit, part of the field run. Others may have left us behind to rot, but here we were, smiling in the sunshine, juice dripping down our chins.

Being out in the field is still my favorite part of being a farmer. My least favorite part? Bureaucracy.

Not long ago, in a small conference room at a customer's headquarters, I took a call from an IRS auditor. It was my second IRS audit in nine years.

The auditor's first question: "How did Frey Farms start?"

"I started it when I was a teenager," I said.

"Well, who gave you this company?" she asked. Her tone was already suspicious and combative.

"No one gave it to me."

"Your dad didn't give you this company?"

"No, I started the company."

"What do you mean you started the company?"

"I started the company like people start companies. I was a teenager and I sold watermelons out of the back of a pickup truck. Before the company was a limited liability company it was a DBA, Sarah Frey doing business as Frey Farms Produce. That's how the company started."

"Well, who gave you the land?"

I thought: *My dad gave me something, all right: a pasture full of pigweed, mild PTSD, and $5,000 that I had to pay back because the government had overpaid him and then came after me for it.*

"No one gave me the land. I bought the land."

I was trying to stay cool, because the last thing you want to do is tick off the IRS.

"Well, the land where your house is—who gave you that?"

"Again: nobody *gave* me the land." I was trying to remain friendly.

Finally, she asked me about my second home, the house in Naples.

"Yes," I said. "I have two houses. My primary residence is in Illinois. My second home is in Florida. On the Florida property there is a small house that's traditionally been a rental property. There was a tenant in that little house when I moved in and I haven't kicked him out. I collect that rent."

"Well, who lives there?"

"I can't remember his name," I said. "But he pays his rent and it's reported income on my statement. I think it's somewhere around $2,400 or $2,500 a month. Whatever it is, it's on the statement. I deposit every penny of his rent. It's all accounted for."

"What's your relationship with him?"

"I don't understand what you mean by that. He's my tenant. I provide shelter for him and he pays me money. Like I said, I can't even remember his name."

"Do you have a *personal* relationship?"

By now, various employees of mine had come into the conference room and were gasping at these questions. The call was going way longer than I anticipated, and I mouthed "Sorry" to those who were waiting for me.

I regretted taking the call right before a customer meeting there. *This is what I get for trying to multitask.* My customer was going to walk through the door any minute to find me defending my honor to the IRS.

"Ew," I said. "Why would you ask me that?"

"Well, I have to ask. If you're in a relation—"

"I don't quite understand what you're getting at," I said. "Do you think we're working something out on the rent? Listen, sister, I've been hard up in my life. But never like that."

At this point, my friend Brian leaned over and hit mute on the speakerphone. "So, Sarah," he said in a goofy voice, "do you have any other places you want to 'rent'?"

We all cracked up.

"Jerk," I said, and then I hit unmute.

Calls like that are a drag, but I'm reassured by evidence that stereotypes are changing. I also know that karma is real.

The other night I was at a dinner in Orlando with my team when I ran into a ghost from my past: Howard, that Immokalee fruit market produce broker who'd told me to stay out of the sandbox and mocked me in front of the other brokers.

My first feeling was schadenfreude. Howard looked like he'd seen better days. Meanwhile, I'd been at the conference with my family. My sons were there, and my brothers. We laughed a lot, saw friends, and did a ton of business. At the restaurant I was with a huge group of wonderful people who work for my company, dining in a private room. I love cooking for my employees and family and I love buying them food, so I was in my element. We were eating a delicious meal. I was happy, and proud of what I'd built with the help of the people around me.

Howard said hello.

I stuck my hand out and smiled and said, "Nice to meet you."

I knew who he was. I vividly remembered how awful he'd been to me that day at the Immokalee market so many years earlier. *This is no place for a young girl. You're going to fail. Run on home.*

I decided not to let him know that I knew him. I considered it his get-out-of-jail-free card. If he didn't bring it up, I certainly wouldn't.

Then he said something I didn't expect to hear: "Something has bothered me for a long time. It's eaten at me for twenty years how I treated you. I have felt bad about that and have often thought of reaching out to you. I've wanted to apologize to you for a very long time. Please forgive me for how I behaved."

That really surprised me. In my head, I gave him credit for saying that to me. I could have said, "Apology accepted!" and given him a hug, reassured him that it was no big deal. But I didn't do any of those things. The truth is, I hadn't let it bother me back then, nor had I thought about him in the intervening years. I didn't need his apology to feel better. For me, I felt closure when I walked away that day he tried to humiliate me. I gave him forgiveness all those years ago when I didn't let my brother beat him up. It seemed like too much for him to ask for another apology now.

"I don't know what you're talking about," I said, smiling brightly. "I've heard a lot about you. It's nice to meet you in person. Please excuse me. I need to return to my guests." Then I walked away.

As we returned to the table, John looked anguished. He thought the guy seemed genuinely remorseful. He accused me of twisting the knife.

"Sarah! C'mon!" John said. "He's an old man. Forgive him! That guy's been carrying that around for years and he's trying to apologize. You could have given him absolution. Instead, you just made him feel worse!"

I saw John the Baptist's point. And yet, he and I handle these things differently.

"I smiled and walked away when he did it," I told John. "I'll smile and walk away now. I didn't care what he thought of me then, and I don't care today."

That was a powerful moment for me. It wasn't revenge; it was an affirmation. Years ago when he insulted me, I could have let my hurt feelings get in the way of what really mattered. I could have climbed in that truck and told Ted that we were leaving Florida for good, that there was no opportunity there. Instead, I hadn't let him get under my skin. Now I had confirmation of the value of the way I've lived my professional life. I've been told again and again I'll never win, that I'm aiming too high. Again and again, I've tuned those voices out.

That is how I choose to deal with sexism: no tears, no complaining, just the sweet satisfaction of winning, however long it takes. Whether my victory comes right away or in the long term doesn't matter. In fact, it's one of the few ways in which I'm actually very patient.

I love it when people think I'm going to be softer than the men in my company. Recently a supplier tried to go over my COO's head by cc'ing me on an email to him about pallet prices. Until I received that email, I hadn't noticed we were spending so much on pallets! I immediately became involved. The result was a win-win: that supplier learned I wasn't a soft touch, and my company is saving a lot this year on pallets.

Few things bring me more joy than mentoring young women. Sometimes I don't even know that I'm helping them. Most of the women who mentored me along the way probably didn't realize what they did for me, either. They were busy with their lives and work. To them, our time together might have been just another day, but for me these were big moments; their words mattered. As I've grown the company, I've remembered who was there for me when I needed help, and I've done my best to pay it forward.

At a restaurant near Capitol Hill called Monocle not long ago, I was out with a couple of my brothers. A young woman named Olivia was there celebrating her birthday. A year or two before, I'd met her at that same restaurant when she was working there as a bartender. We'd talked briefly about her work as a realtor and her dreams of launching a management company as a side business.

As she was leaving, she spotted me and yelled, "Sarah, Sarah!" She gave me a big hug, and then she turned around and told my brothers, "This woman is an inspiration to me. I'm successful because of the advice that she gave me. It made such an impact on my life."

Apparently I'd told her to pretend she knew what she was doing—just start the business and figure out the details later: "This is what you do. You go tell this person this, and then you go tell this person that, and then you go tell the bank this." And I told her briefly what this, that, and this were. I'd said, "It's okay to fake it until you make it as long as you're putting the hours in behind the scenes. The most important thing you can do is just get started."

Evidently, after our talk Olivia had felt inspired to begin. In just the prior year, she had become very successful. She wound up doubling her business with her realty company and she opened her own LLC, which now manages thirty-two units. She'd bought a new place near Capitol Hill and an SUV. She radiated confidence and pride.

All I'd done was give her the inspiration to take a risk. You get the win, and then you go get another win, and you go get another one. You have to get over your losses fast. If you tell people what you're trying to accomplish, you get them excited. They feel invested. When they believe in your goals, they want to help. I love the saying "Talk's cheap. It takes money to buy whiskey." Olivia was able to convince people to believe in her because she was so determined and so hardworking.

I see these sorts of diamonds in the rough everywhere I go. The other day, my car's sensor said I had a low tire. I googled the nearest tire shop. When I arrived there, a young woman with curly blond hair up in a bun and a cute face, her clothes covered from head to toe in grease, bounded out to greet me. She was probably nineteen, and she looked like a Rosie the Riveter postcard. I stood there and watched her, full of energy, rush around adding air and getting my car all checked out. In no time she was finished.

"You're good to go! No charge!" she said in a chipper voice, with a big smile.

I marveled at her. I thought, *That was me long ago. I used to feel like that—driven solely by the desire to do my job well.* I gave her $20 wrapped around my business card and told her to drop me an email. Her job was to work on tires and she did it with enthusiasm and energy. That's the kind of person I'd love to have in my company. I'd hire her in a heartbeat.

I imagine that girl's community never had huge expectations for her, just as mine didn't for me. The folks in Orchardville probably just hoped I would marry well.

Regardless of how disadvantaged I was growing up in some ways, I think all of it, ultimately, was an advantage. When I realize that someone is underestimating me, counting me out like the ugly fruit, I know the disadvantage is theirs.

Chapter 17

The Family Table

Being so bound up with my family means more hands to help out, but it also means more people to worry about. In 2016, John picked up a new hobby: cycling. While training for a ride called the Tour de Fresh, a charity that helps get fresh produce into U.S. schools, John was hit by a car going sixty-five miles an hour. It was driven by a girl who may or may not have been texting.

When I received the call about the accident, I raced to the hospital. Later my sister-in-law Andrea would tell me that a friend of hers who worked as a nurse at the hospital told her I'd terrified the staff. I was looking everywhere for him, and when the doors wouldn't open—well, I made them open. The only thing I remember is that I kept yelling, "Where is he?"

Finally I found him. I saw a leg hanging off the table and his foot pointing the wrong way. His body looked like it had been flayed alive. He had tubes in him. They were getting ready to airlift him to a bigger hospital. After it took off, I started vomiting from fear. I didn't think he'd survive the flight. When I reached Evansville, about seventy-five miles away, that night, I found that he hadn't been to surgery yet. When he rolled over, I saw that he had no skin on his backside. His memory was gone. In the days that followed, whenever Andrea wasn't there, I'd stay overnight with him. Every day I'd go to the ice cream shop G. D. Ritzy's and buy him a caramel praline milkshake.

And every day he would think it was the first time he'd ever tasted one.

"This is the best milkshake I've ever had!" he'd say. "Where did you get it?"

"You said that yesterday," I'd say. "G. D. Ritzy's."

Every day, the same conversation.

Finally I walked in one day with no shake and John said, "Where's my shake from G. D. Ritzy's?" That was the moment when I knew he'd be okay.

To me, loyalty is more important than anything else. I can forgive anything but betrayal. That's how I was raised. For all of my father's faults, he was infinitely patient with mistakes. If he thought you were sneaking, you'd be in big trouble, but honest errors were fine by him.

When I was seven, I was driving my parents' truck, a white 1981 Ford pickup. Driving through a gate, I turned too close and caved in the driver's side door on a post. Instead of stopping, I kept going and sideswiped the whole side. I thought my father would be mad, but he didn't say a thing. You'd never get in trouble for something like that. You could burn down the barn or break a double-pane window and never hear a word about it. But if the stalls in the barn weren't cleaned? Or if you were caught in a lie? Heads would roll.

I'm the same way with the kids. I was told by a neighbor lady when I was pregnant with William that not everyone would love my children. At first, I was shocked by what she said. Then I realized that it made sense. I would love them because they were mine, but if I wanted the world to love them, I would have to raise them to be loveable. I think I did that. If they forget their manners, I'm quick to remind them with a death stare. But if they broke the most valuable possession I own, I'd just shrug.

So you can imagine how I felt when I found out that one of my nieces, Ted's daughter Gracie, then fifteen, had snuck an old phone from my office drawer. She'd lost permission to have her own phone and wanted to keep talking to a boy, so she took one of mine.

I was enraged. I thought back on myself at that age. I was an adult by that point. I was doing everything myself. Here she was making selfish decisions. When she snuck that phone, that was a huge deal—not because the phone was anything special, but because of the sneaking. I had to make her understand the problem. And, because she is stubborn like me, I knew I would have to carefully orchestrate her punishment so it would stick. Her father, Ted, agreed that I should have everyone over to dinner so I could confront her with the family there. I called all my brothers and told them about what Gracie had done: "She's sneaking around. She isn't listening to her parents. And she took my old phone."

My brothers were upset. They loved Gracie so much, and they were worried about what this type of behavior could lead to. We discussed all of the reasonable approaches for talking with teenagers and trying to explain the consequences of such actions. Ultimately, we decided that the one thing that had been missing in Gracie's life so far was a real understanding of how urgent it was for us to stick together as a family. We decided that she would have to give me back the phone in front of everyone.

The moment of truth arrived. At seven on the appointed night, everyone arrived. Dinner was served. The kids were at the kids' table. The adults were at the grown-ups' table. The stage was set for the tribunal.

After dinner, the adults were playing cards when up walked Gracie.

"Hey, Sis, how are you doing?" I said, casual as can be.

She handed me the phone.

"What's this?" I said, feigning surprise.

"It's your phone," she said, looking like she wanted to be anywhere else. "I took it. I was grounded and I took your phone out of the drawer where you throw your old phones. I turned it on so that I could talk to my friends. I'm giving it back."

"What do you mean, that's my phone? What do you mean, you took my phone?" I laid it on thick, the shock and disappointment.

"Yeah, I took it. You don't use them, so I thought it was okay to take it because that's where you keep the phones that you don't use." She crossed her arms and looked at me without fear. I did not hear an apology anywhere in her tone or what she was saying.

"What do you mean, you just took it?" I said.

"Well, I just took it because you don't use them anymore." Then, finally, she said, "I'm sorry."

You know how quick kids grow. She was as tall as me now, and she had my same green, steely eyes. I realized that in many ways she was a lot like me as a teenager. I also realized that at this point in her life that resolve could go either way; it could be her deliverance or her downfall. I appreciated her boldness, except that in this case it was directed not toward building something positive but rather toward satisfying her own selfish desires. I had to make her understand the effect her actions could have had on the family.

"Do you realize what you could have done?" I said. "Do you realize the sensitive company information I keep on my phones, even the ones I'm not using right now?"

"I'm sorry," she said again. She wanted it to be over quick. She didn't want to wrap her head around what could have happened.

"You jeopardized my livelihood," I said. "That means you jeopardized your father's livelihood. You jeopardized the livelihoods of every single person sitting around you in this room tonight." Her parents and her aunts and uncles looked at her gravely.

I still felt like I wasn't getting through, so I laid it on thicker: "You could have ruined everything for this whole entire family." Still nothing. She looked at me like, *What's your problem?* Then I brought out the big guns: "I'm so disappointed in you. I thought you were smarter than this." That's what my father always said when he wanted me to feel bad.

She took a step back from me and avoided eye contact, but she still didn't look upset or remorseful. I'd had a feeling it would come to this; she was so much like me that Ted accidentally calls her Sarah sometimes. So before her arrival I'd staged a bunch of empty pots and pans at the end of the kitchen island. When I realized she still wasn't getting the message, I swept those metal pots off the counter: *bing, bang, bing, bang*, they clattered down on the hardwood floor. The sound was deafening.

I had her attention now. I had everyone's attention.

All the other kids went silent. Luke and Anna and Aidan were sitting nearby. Their eyes widened. I was glad. I wanted them to see how serious this was to the family.

Finally Gracie looked shocked. I thought, *Okay, now we're getting somewhere.* I kept laying into her. I went on and on and on about how I was disappointed and how she would jeopardize everything over some no-good Wayne County boy. That was the moment when I thought, *Okay, that was too much. I just turned into my father.*

Only one problem: I still wanted to see some evidence that she was really sorry. I marched her to the bedroom so I could talk to her without an audience.

At this point, I knew the little kids were thinking I was going to kill Gracie in the bedroom: *It's going to happen. Our beloved cousin is going to die now. This is the last time we're going to see her.*

Once we were alone, I sat her down on the bench. I asked if she understood what could have gone wrong because of her actions.

At last she started to tear up, crying, "I'm so sorry!"

I hugged her. She's a good girl and a hard worker. She's kind. And she heard what I was trying to tell her: *You're better than this. Leave the boys alone, at least for now. Go live a big life first. Keep your teens and your twenties for yourself. It's a big world. Remember that you are part of this family and we need to stick together and look out for one another.*

I want so much for the girls in my family, and in my life. I want them to be curious about the world, hungry for knowledge. Once they've gone out and done great things, then they can come back here to the Hill if they want to. But I want them to see the world first.

Even when children are naughty, they're the coolest thing in life. Everyone asks me about work-life balance. Here's my secret: True work-life balance is an illusion. You just have to ride the wave.

The number one thing that holds women back is guilt. Women tell me they feel guilty when they're working and guilty when they're with their kids, guilty about the dinner they didn't cook or the business trip they didn't take. I want to let them in on a secret: it is impossible to be great and guilty at the same time.

When I'm on business calls, I don't shush the children in the background. And when business associates come over, I don't hide the toys. I'm a CEO and a mother. I'm not going to pretend either side doesn't exist. It's important for my sanity to have *both* work and home. Business can be brutal. If all you have is your work, those dark times can eat you alive. My children keep me sane. And they keep me from taking everything so seriously.

You have to work in front of your kids without apology, and you have to love your kids in front of your bosses without apology. Blurring those lines between home and work means that my kids know how hard I work. I can have a phone and a computer anywhere. The kids overhear conversations and know when things are going badly or well.

I do not go in for detail-oriented parenting. I'm not packing their lunch every day. I'm not monitoring their precise calorie intake. I won't win the award for writing my kids' names on their lunchboxes. I've never labeled a thing. And I'm totally okay with it. I get deli cupcakes for the bake sale and I don't try to hide that when I drop them off. I know that everything ends up balancing itself out, that my shortcomings are offset by the things I do really well for my children—beginning with showing and telling them how much I love them every day.

When it comes to parenting, I try to care only about the important things. I care about manners. I care that they brush their teeth. I care that they take showers without me telling them. I have zero tolerance for teasing. I teach my kids not to make quick judgments, because you never know what other people are going through. I tell them, "Be kind. Always be kind."

I make sure they know they have an obligation to help those who need help whenever possible. I've told the boys, "If you see a girl with grubby cheeks sitting alone in the lunchroom, you think of me. Because that was your mom."

"If I see a girl like that, I'm going to go sit by her!" said Luke.

I'm blessed to have such good boys. I think maybe God thought, *We have to give her good kids because she couldn't handle hard ones.*

The boys know that I want them to stand up for people who need help.

"But I might get in trouble for fighting!" William said one time when I told him he should defend a classmate who was getting picked on.

I told him, "If I have to come pick you up from the principal's office for defending someone against a bully, I'll take you straight from the school to Dairy Queen and you can order whatever you want."

There are special challenges to raising boys. William can talk about anything for any length of time, and he says it all with such conviction that you believe him. Very few other kids challenge him on what he says, but one girl from his school always does. Her name is Savanna.

I've tried to encourage William to be okay with girls being the boss, but I see how it can be tough on him. He's used to being the kid the other kids look up to. Savanna will correct Will when he's wrong. She does it sweetly, but sometimes she will do it in front of his friends. I've encouraged William to try to see the benefit in being friends with all different kinds of kids, especially those who challenge you.

Savanna is pretty perfect in my opinion—nose in a book all the time, hair pulled back, kicking everyone's butt at academic meets, funny and warm. She is one of five children. Their dad's a police officer and their mom's a teacher. They are delightful. But William always had a problem with Savanna. He was nice to her, but you could tell that something got under his skin. At first I thought he had a crush on her. William would roll his eyes when asked about her.

One time I was taking her home after she'd been over at our house and I said, "If you could go anywhere in the world, where would you go?"

Savanna gazed out the car window, appearing to visualize something beautiful, and then said in a dreamy voice: "I'd like to go to the Louvre."

"Good answer," I said. Hearing her say that made me proud. Not long after, I flew her down to Florida, her first plane trip. In a thank-you note, she wrote, "Thank you for letting me stay in your house in Florida. (I know I'm your favorite.)" The note made me laugh; I love a girl with shameless self-confidence.

So I finally sat William down and said, "What's your issue with Savanna? Be honest."

He leaned over the kitchen island and looked me right in the eyes. He said, "Well, Mom, she steals my thunder."

I was glad that he saw that the problem was not with her but with his ability to accept the way she was. I also thought, *I've probably stolen a lot of thunder in my life.*

Stealing thunder is something girls need to do more often. And boys need to learn to accept it, and to help them.

My nieces are always impressing me with the smart things they say. For years, my mom had a Jack Russell terrier named Skipper. He was a mean little dog to everyone except Grandma. One time Luke hugged his grandmother and the dog attacked him, biting him and leaving teeth marks on his back. Under normal circumstances, that dog would not have lived to see the morning. But my mother loved the dog too much, so he got a reprieve.

After years of tormenting us all, finally death came for Skipper. He ran out of the house and was hit by a truck. Everyone felt bad that Mom had lost the dog, but we also felt relieved that he died before biting any of the children's faces off. Ted buried the dog in the backyard. After the interment, the cousins gathered at my house. They were huddled around the kitchen island while I made them cheeseburgers and tried to ask about their day at school. It was like pulling teeth. They were acting so morose.

"Why's everybody so sad?" I asked them.

"I'm sad about Skipper," William said. "Grandma really loved that dog."

The girls seemed especially unhappy.

"Cheer up!" I said. "Remember: all dogs go to heaven."

"Not all dogs," little Audrey said. "You don't go to heaven unless you're good. Skipper was not a good dog." She started explaining everything that was wrong with Skipper, how he bit and snarled and barked. Skipper, in her telling, was a terrible sinner. They'd been taught in church that you had to ask forgiveness to go to heaven. They couldn't see Skipper appealing for mercy.

I never can stand to see sweet kids be sad. I always want to fix it. But Audrey had a really good point. That dog was the worst one I'd ever known.

"Skipper is definitely in heaven," I said. "You just have to believe. Think about it: Skipper made Grandma happy! That counts for something, right?" *Yeah, they're not buying it. Super-sad faces still. Now they are looking at me like they know I'm lying. I need to take it up a notch.* "And who knows? Maybe dogs have their very own savior who died for their sins. There may be a Jesus for doggies."

No sooner had the words escaped my lips than I realized my error. My niece Anna looked me right in the eye. I noticed for the first time how identical her dark brown eyes are to my brother's. "There is only one God," she hissed. "If you went to church more often, you'd know that."

Ouch. That burns.

She was nine years old. Her hand flew up to her mouth as if she couldn't believe she'd just basically called her aunt a heathen. "I'm sorry, Aunt Sarah!" she said. Her big eyes began to fill with tears.

"Anna, it's okay!" I said. I laughed. I respected her for calling me out on Doggie Jesus. I also suspected that one prayer from someone as fiercely good as Anna could get even the evil Skipper into heaven.

Over the years it's become common for me to wake up on a Saturday morning and forget exactly how many children spent the previous night. Between the boys' cousins and friends, a typical Saturday morning includes stepping over around a dozen kids. I never put a limit on the number of children who can be at my house at any point. The more the merrier.

The other night, the boys and their cousins decided they wanted to watch *Children of the Corn*. I put the little ones in my room with me to watch a Disney movie. I knew the big ones wouldn't last long but I allowed them to try. Five minutes into movie night, the giant kids came running in and climbed into bed with me and the little ones. I fell asleep during the Disney movie. When I woke up early the next morning, I saw five kids sleeping scattered around my room. I looked around at all those snug, dreaming children, the sun filtering through the curtains onto their faces.

The image before me was familiar. I thought of when my brothers and I had slept in the living room all together to stay close to the woodstove. This was much the same—so many arms and legs flung here and there. But it was also so different. We were in my very own cozy house. There would be pancakes for breakfast. When I was a girl, this scene was something I'd dreamed of without ever quite knowing how I'd get here—a home full of children who were safe, warm, and full.

Chapter 18

Harvest Time Again

The past couple of years have given me new perspective on both my personal and professional lives. The biggest lesson of all came just this past year. After a number of such deals, I was poised to put my beverages into another large chain.

Not only were these drinks a healthier alternative to soda, but we could demonstrate that offering them would actually yield more profits. Consumers had begun to demand lower-calorie beverage options from restaurant chains, and we began to feel that we were on a noble mission to provide them. With this deal, we were going to do our part to conquer the obesity epidemic and bring a windfall to family farms. The only thing standing in our way was a multibillion-dollar global beverage company who controlled the space. *No big deal.*

With a contract in process and a commitment from our customer, we invested millions of dollars and two years working on the mission. We did all the ingredient sourcing, product innovation, consumer research, and third-party testing. We brought in tons of raw ingredients from a dozen small farms around the country.

Then at the last minute a global beverage company came in and pressured the restaurant chain to allow them to implement *our* idea with a similar product—and a lot of marketing dollars.

At a meeting, the deal changed. Our customer reluctantly told our team they had to limit the number of flavors we could offer because their global beverage partner would now be offering similar alternatives. Everyone knew our product innovation was superior. You could taste it—the flavor was so much fresher and cleaner.

But the giant had woken up. Suddenly the beverage company that had been controlling this space, our competitor, realized what was about to happen. In response, they appeared to be trying to copy our plan and pressure the chain to drop us.

"Tell me the one about David and Goliath again?" I said later on the phone to Gearry, my long-suffering CFO.

"David wins," Gearry said.

"Does the giant's head get cut off?" I asked.

"It does," he said.

"Good," I said. I pictured the competing beverage company as a giant on the ground waiting for me to finish him off with his own sword.

There was something else, too. The competitor said a small company couldn't manufacture the product on time and would fail operationally. I saw red. When I was a nineteen-year-old girl with no track record, the largest retail chains in the world trusted that I could deliver the necessary volume, and I did not disappoint them. Now, twenty years later, we had fleets of trucks and a track record a mile long of on-time, high-volume deliveries.

That meeting where I learned we were potentially losing the business was the first one in my entire career where I lost my cool. Since I was a small child, I've always prided myself on being unflappable. But, when I realized the giant's tactics were beginning to work, I had trouble staying calm.

The nights away from my family and the pressures of having to take care of everything were starting to get to me. My team had poured everything into making this successful. They'd played their A game, and I felt I'd led them down the wrong path. My enthusiasm for risk and my ego had caused me to lead my small army into a rout. Now here we were getting slaughtered.

My voice rose. I wasn't screaming, but I was louder than usual. I could feel tension spreading throughout my whole body like poison. It was the first time I had risked so much for a higher purpose and been left feeling like we'd failed. I was ashamed that I cared so much. I'd accepted the financial risk when I started the project, because to me this wasn't just some deal. We were fighting for something greater, something that would be good for families, good for small farms, and good for family businesses.

That night I had an early dinner, then went back to my hotel room and crashed. The next morning I was lying there flat in my bed, still asleep, when my hand fell on the top of my stomach and brushed the bottom of my breast. My eyes popped open. The back of my hand was pressing against something hard. It was a lump.

I catapulted out of the bed. I felt a rush of heat shoot through my body. My ears were ringing. I ran into the bathroom and threw up over and over again. I wasn't crying. My body was just staging a revolt. I was overwhelmed. And I was immediately sure that I had breast cancer. In that moment I thought, *My boys . . .*

As I was lying there on the cold tile alone in a hotel bathroom, my world was spinning. It was all just crashing down. It was like a movie reel in my head: all the things I had spent my energy on, all the deals I'd gotten obsessed with, the time spent away from my children. Time. Most important, time. *What kind of mother have I been? Who was I to ever think that I could do anything more than peddle a few melons? Why did I care so much about this one deal?*

My thoughts were completely out of control. I'd watched my half sister go through treatment for stage two breast cancer the year before. I knew the physical and emotional toll that could follow a cancer diagnosis. Memories rolled through my mind like raging water, faster and faster. I couldn't move. I couldn't calm them. Ted wasn't there to lift the heavy branch and save me. I was drowning. I lay on that bathroom floor with my face against the marble for what seemed like two days but was probably only about ten minutes.

Finally, another voice: *Are you finished?* I collected myself, changed my flight, and got myself back to St. Louis. My entire field of thought, usually going in a thousand different directions, was reduced to: *Book flight. Pack bag. Get in car. Get on plane. Fly. Land. Find car. Find doctor.*

Then, as I drove home to the Hill, to my boys, the movie started back up again: The night before I left on the trip, with Luke asking what day I was coming home, William trying to get my attention so he could ask me to sign his permission form for the track meet, both boys waiting for me to get off a conference call.

Lately I hadn't been giving so much time to them. Whom had I been giving my time to? People who didn't deserve it. Seconds, minutes, hours, days. Special time. I thought about the investment I'd made. For what? I feared it had cost me not only financially but, more important, time I could have spent with my children.

It's not unusual for me to become obsessed with getting a deal done, but this particular hunt had distracted me like no other. Not long before that meeting, I'd had a woman who helps me, Marla, pick up the boys at school and bring them to my office. I'd chatted with them about their day and then was called out of the office to look at something that took all of about five minutes. On my way back, I glanced at the clock, noticed it was 3:05, and panicked. I saw Marla again and frantically asked her when she was going to pick up the boys. She stared at me in disbelief and just pointed upward to my office, where I had just left them.

Another time during this stressful period, I called my office and asked for myself. I was on the road between our farms in Illinois and Indiana. I had a million things going on. I called the office and said, "Hey, is Sarah there? I need to talk to John." That lapse should have clued me in that I was overwhelmed, but I just laughed it off. It took the health scare to make me truly face how stretched thin I was.

Once I got back to southern Illinois after finding the lump, I called my doctor, Dr. Sweet-Friend. (That is actually her last name.) She knows me well and made sure I was seen quickly. Believe it or not, the healthcare system in rural southern Illinois is great. I went to a brand-new little hospital in Mount Vernon and the care was top-notch.

I walked up to the mammogram machine. As I was standing there, I began to feel flushed. I imagined myself fainting and hanging from the machine by my boob. I started to laugh a little. I thought, *After everything I've been through in my life, I am not going down like that.*

The nurse called a co-worker in and found me a chair. They sat me down in between images. And the two nurses stood there just in case I fainted.

The mammogram didn't look good. They brought me in a day later for a biopsy. I was able to get all the testing done there in a couple of days. I would only need to wait a few more days to get the biopsy results back.

During that wait, I told the people closest to me in my company what was going on. I asked them to step in and do what they could to salvage what was left of the beverage deal. Cancer or no cancer, I wasn't giving another moment of my energy to it.

They rallied and worked twice as hard as I ever expected them to. I turned to the young women in my company—mainly my niece Hilary. I asked her to step up and lead the rally. They were just as emotionally invested in the deal as I had been. I knew they would be ruthless. They would turn any opportunity into success. I told them they would have to fight the giant in ways that he wasn't accustomed to, ways that would surprise him. They would have to outsell, out-hustle, and outmaneuver. I told them that once the product reached the hands of the consumer, the consumer would decide who would win the battle. I told them that the giant was powerful, but even giants bleed.

The women were the warriors. They picked up the swords and shields to get a new version of the deal over the finish line. It wasn't everything the old deal would have been, but it was enough. I was proud of them. And grateful. They were the ones who fought the fight when I needed to step away. My brothers also stepped up in ways that I never imagined. They became the face of the family farm. They attended the trade shows and poured beverages. When family and team members in my organization see me down, they grow stronger. That's been one of the greatest benefits of building a family-centric company.

The test results came back. My doctor told me that the biopsy was clear but that I'd have to be checked again every year. She kept talking, but beyond that I don't know what else she said. All I heard was that I was okay. I kept thanking her. I thanked God for tapping me on the shoulder rather than hitting me over the head with a frying pan. I promised him that I would no longer take my time here on earth for granted.

That afternoon, I booked tickets for the boys and me to go to Paris for Thanksgiving. Yes, that would mean that I, the Pumpkin Queen of America, would not be hosting Thanksgiving dinner. For the first time since I was nineteen, I would not cook the turkey or bake the pies. I would leave my country at a distinctly pumpkin-y time of year. I didn't care. I felt as though I had a new lease on life. My kids had never been to Europe. That seemed suddenly like the most pressing thing, to show them the world.

"Who's going to make the pumpkin pies?" Andrea said when I told her.

"I know you'll figure it out," I said with a smile.

Luke, William, and I spent ten days in France. We went to museums, walked through cities, and ate excellent food at quaint cafés. It was the best vacation of my life. I turned off my phone. For the first time ever, I didn't think about work once.

Some of the best moments of that whole year were spent enjoying food in France with my boys. We let ourselves be carried from place to place by our appetites and our whims—except for Thanksgiving. I knew I needed to make a special plan for that. The French don't celebrate our holiday, of course, but I wanted to give the boys a turkey dinner that night.

Finding a traditional Thanksgiving dinner was harder than I thought it would be. The hotel offered to make us some Cornish hens, but that wasn't going to cut it. I went online and found an inconspicuous little café that was going to host an American-style Thanksgiving. They were booked, but I talked my way into a reservation.

When we arrived, we saw American families coming in and sitting down at long, communal-style tables. There was turkey, stuffing, sweet potato puree. The food wasn't precisely American, but the Thanksgiving spirit was authentic. We were families in a foreign land, sharing food with strangers, giving thanks for what we had, sharing the common bond of being American even though we were far from home. The room was full of warm smiles and full plates.

At one point Luke asked if they had apple cider. The waiter raised his eyebrows, but brought him a glass of it. It turned out to be a hard cider, so Luke took only a sip. We all got a kick out of the fact that the French would serve booze to a tiny ten-year-old who looks like Paddington Bear.

Hands down, it was the best Thanksgiving I've ever had. Everyone back home survived without me cooking. I used to think I had to be there, to do everything or the world would collapse. But they were fine. They even managed to make their own pies. That trip to France taught us all something about freedom.

Then and there I resolved that no matter what is going on in my life, I will block out everything for that kind of time with Luke and William. We need to explore together, to inspire and be inspired. I want to be the one to show them the world.

My boys are growing up so fast. On that trip, William was only fourteen, but over six feet tall and already wearing a size-fourteen shoe. In France some people actually thought he was my husband—*not creepy at all.* They'll be in college before I know it. Now is the time to enjoy them, to teach them what I know, and to make sure they find out how big and wonderful the world is.

Thanksgiving in France also inspired one of the best ideas I've had in years. At the end of our holiday dinner, the café served a pumpkin pie. It tasted a little different than the traditional American version. It was light and fluffy, and tasted almost like a snickerdoodle cookie. It was the best pie I've ever eaten in my life. They had bought the pie from a street vendor, so I couldn't chase down the exact recipe. But what I could do was sit there, savor every bite, and make mental notes.

Bite by bite, I decoded what was in it. *Definitely a French varietal. Heirloom. One more bite. Got it.* I decided to make that flavor profile the inspiration for a Sarah's Homegrown product. I had been growing French pumpkins for the last decade. Then I thought: why not sell pies inspired by the flavor of that street vendor's pie?

Back in the United States, I hit the ground running. A retail chain asked me to put together a line of Sarah's Homegrown beverages for their stores. I said, "Why not also pumpkin muffins? And how about desserts? And if we're going to do that, why not a whole new menu straight from the farm?"

As I rushed to get the new beverage and pumpkin products ready, all the business drama of the past weeks melted away. Maybe, I thought, all of that disappointment was meant to happen, to bring me to Paris and to that French café. I needed to be reminded that what matters is spending time with my sons, eating delicious meals, and working on projects that bring me joy and that help families like mine enjoy the best food the land has to offer.

The land continues to be so good to me. At dawn, a thick spring fog rolls in over the same fields I worked in as a little girl. I prop myself up on my elbows in bed and squint at the window, listening to the birds talking to one another. In my warm bed, I roll over and pull the blankets over my head to get a little more sleep. Down the hall, my sons, taller by the day, dream on in their own rooms. We will wake up soon to go to school and work, but not yet. In the kitchen, the fridge and countertops are full of good food—a carton of just-collected eggs, a big bowl of fresh fruit, a loaf of homemade bread.

We left the dishes unwashed last night after a big dinner of fried chicken and gravy shared with my brothers and their families, with business associates and friends. In the guest room downstairs and the carriage house out back are friends and colleagues visiting from hundreds of miles away. They sleep under fluffy down blankets. In every single room, I've made sure that a thermostat hangs on the wall.

That moment when I decided to buy the farm, I believed that forces greater than myself were making me stay. I saw my future playing out in front of my eyes, and it felt like a life of sacrifice. Now I see how staying on the Hill has given me great gifts. I count my blessings daily. I've seen the world and spent time with wonderful people. At my little rural schools, I was taught by teachers with big hearts. I believe deep in my soul that everything I've been through prepared me for what I was put on this earth to do. I may not know exactly what that is all the time, but I do believe in a higher purpose for my life. And I believe that forgiveness and redemption have set me free.

As a child, I couldn't wait to get off the Hill. Now it's where I go to sleep soundly, focus, reflect, and regroup. And my commute to the Frey Farms headquarters in Orchardville, Illinois, is just a five-minute drive. My home and office are a little anchor for me in the middle of nowhere. When people ask what I do for a living, I still to this day say, "I'm a farmer." I do a lot more than that, of course, but that's still the core of who I am, and I'm proud to say it.

Business colleagues don't always understand why I've kept our headquarters here in southern Illinois. We have many facilities around the country that are big and modern. They could handle everything we're doing here. But I can't bring myself to leave Orchardville entirely. I feel a responsibility to the people here. For as wild and free as I may be, this is where my roots took hold. I love and appreciate this community.

The Frey company employs countless numbers of people I care about; among them: Al, the boy whose cap I used to knock off every day in study hall; Jenny, who's been one of my best friends since high school; and Renee, who I hired as the head of sales twenty years ago.

She's stood on the floor of every trade show we've ever had. She earned the nickname "The Warden," because she's always by my side, guarding me.

When we think of the family farm, we think of the obvious physical parts of it—corn growing tall, horses grazing, silos filling up, the farmer in overalls, his wife in her apron, and their kids hard at work on chores. But most farms are much more complicated than that, just as most families are more complicated than their neatly framed portraits. First of all, farmers aren't all men. Women have been cultivating land for thousands of years. Thinking back over my life in the course of writing this book, I was reminded how I took over the farm to save my family. But now I see that our connection actually transcends this patch of earth. Our past and our love unite us. That bond will never die, no matter what happens to our farm. I see that now.

Writing this book has forced me to live in something other than the future for the first time. Exploring the past has made me more thoughtful, and I've realized that the core of who I am hasn't changed. I was a hunter back then. I'm a hunter now. I see each coming season as a new beginning.

My father died in 2000. His girlfriend had moved him around to different care facilities, so for several years we didn't know where he was. She thought he had money and so she kept him away from us. Unfortunately for her, he died with nothing. His one last hustle.

Not long before that, though, I found out which nursing home he was in. On a Sunday afternoon I slipped in to see him. Entering his room, I saw that he was near death. He had a trach tube in his throat, so he couldn't speak, but when he saw me his eyes grew wide. His hands flew up off the bed. I told him that I loved him and that I knew he loved me. Looking into his wide green eyes, I thought of all he had given me. I'd held him in such high regard growing up. I'd feared him and I'd worshiped him. I couldn't forget how much damage he'd done—to my mother, to my brothers, to my half siblings, to his first wife, to his own parents, to me. And yet, sitting there by the side of his bed, I forgave him. I thanked him. And I said goodbye. When I walked out of that room, I knew that would be the last time I ever saw him. But I left that room at peace.

When I think of my father now, I don't feel angry. I feel love. He taught me to value myself as we did the field run crops—as worth no less for being rough around the edges. To him, I was his prodigy and then his rival. In the end, I hope he came to see me as part of his positive legacy. My father was a difficult man in so many ways. But he trained me to be fearless. He made me believe I'd killed a rabbit and caught a fish. He made me see that I could take on a snapping turtle. He prepared me for a life that he knew wouldn't be easy. He and my brothers wanted me to believe I was great. If I *felt* like I was great, they knew I could *become* great—great enough to survive our rough way of life and to transcend it. There is no better gift for a child, especially a young girl, than that sense of innate power.

My mother is nearing eighty. She lives down the road and drops by often. A light went out in her when she lost her little girl Lana. After having my own children, I can't begin to imagine her pain. It's taken a long time for that light to come back on in my mother's eyes. Now that she's a grandmother, she has brightened. My boys adore her. With the help of her grandchildren, she still runs a melon delivery route to a few stores every summer.

My mother tells me I look just like my father, that we have the same green eyes, and she does not say it as if it's a good thing. "You have to be in charge, just like your father did," she likes to say.

The difference, I hope, is that I use my power for good. I've made my living bringing cheer and fresh food into people's homes. I could have gone down a path like his. I could have used my power in other ways. I could have skipped town after I led that last horse off the farm. Instead, I put my family above my own desires. And I do not regret it for a second.

I believe in redemption. All I can do is try to be a force for good and to change the things that I can change. I need to look out for my children and for all the other young people in my life, for my brothers and for my employees. I'm proud that I've raised the boys to take care of themselves, and that they love the land like I do.

It's been a few years since my divorce and I've come to see Justin as a fundamentally good person, easygoing, a loving dad. He still works with the company. My brothers still get along with him. And how can I ever regret that relationship when it brought me Luke and William?

I've also come to see that I didn't need marriage to make me normal. Now I'm not even sure what normal is or if it even exists. If I ever do meet someone, he will have to accept me as Rowdiest Girl, and he should probably be okay with getting his thunder stolen from time to time.

A few months ago, William went hunting and brought back a rabbit. I taught him how to make rabbit pot pie. The boys ate it and loved it all the more because they'd fed their family that night. When the fireflies came out last year, I made the boys run outside with me. I showed them how if you spin slowly you can feel the lightning bugs gently tapping your arms.

William has his learner's permit now. As soon as it was in his wallet, he started asking me every hour to take him driving.

One morning he woke up early and started in on me before I'd even had coffee. "Let's go do something!" he said. "Let's go drive somewhere!"

I had a cold. I was tired. I didn't want to go anywhere, but I also knew he wasn't going to stop asking me. "Fine," I said. "You want to drive? Take us to St. Louis." He smiled.

We all got in the car, with him driving. At the end of the country roads, he stopped at the four-way at Potter's Corner and said, "Okay, very funny. You can take over now."

"I'm not joking," I said. "Get on the interstate."

William looked shocked. He had never driven on a highway, much less the interstate, nor had he ever driven in a city.

"Let's go," I said. He looked at me, and I looked back at him.

I was my dad and this drive was William's snapping turtle. When I'd dropped William off for his first day of high school the week before, I bawled like a baby. But I'd faced facts: he wasn't a baby anymore. He was a good driver. If he wanted to drive, he should drive.

"This is the Frey way," Luke said from the backseat, with resignation and a trace of fear. Luke is usually asleep five minutes into a car ride. His eyes were saucers that entire drive. But we made it there in one piece. I didn't let them know, but my nerves were shot. I don't know if it was the two-hour drive with a fifteen-year-old or the fact that he drove so far under the speed limit that I thought we'd never get there.

At the restaurant we went to in St. Louis, I read the list of cocktail specials.

"Mom!" Luke said, shocked to see his mother considering a drink in the middle of the day.

"Hey," I said, "I have a designated driver now."

Looking back, there were so many people who helped me along the way. Most of them probably didn't even know what they did for me. But I will never forget John Dorsey's contagious laugh; Mrs. Leyva's class and grace; the store manager at Tractor Supply who gave a smart-ass kid a shot at his job; Stanley Greenspan, who stood up for me at the produce market; all the farmers who sold me fruit on credit; all the produce managers who ever left their air-conditioned stores to help me unload melons in the hot sun.

I think about the farmer who wished he would never see me again for my own good, and the one who didn't think I was crazy to plant pumpkins. The women who used their positions of power working for the largest retailers in the world to help another woman get started. The retail buyers who put my products on their shelves and gave them time to catch on. The mechanic who helped me hide thousands of watermelons in the middle of the night. The truck drivers who believed me when I said getting the load delivered on time was the most important thing in the world. The men and women who took on more than just jobs when I asked them to join my business. The sheriff's deputy who trusted me to handle a family situation. So many people who changed the course of my life. I owe them all.

Orchardville is the same as it ever was, with only a few changes. There are more mobile homes now than there used to be. There's a new megachurch, so on Sundays the population swells from dozens to hundreds. The convenience store just opened a little backroom with legalized gambling, so now you can buy a set of pliers, a bag of Friskies, and some power steering fluid, then play video roulette.

Going forward, I want to keep taking on new adventures, to invest my time in the places where my creativity can grow. When something feels right, I trust that it's worth going for. No matter what I do, I know I'll always have that entrepreneurial fire. Most of all, I want to watch my sons continue to grow into fine men. They already know how to cook and clean and work. They play the piano. They can hunt and fish. They also have friends and are part of sports teams. I'm trying to show them the plants at their feet but also the stars in the sky.

I get asked if the boys will want to take over the company someday. Maybe. Or maybe one of my nieces and nephews will want to. I hope they respect the sacrifices that were made to provide that opportunity to them, and that they grow the business. I hope they pass the land and the tradition of stewardship down to their children and their children's children, on down the line. Regardless of what the next generation may or may not want to do, I hope they see the greatest value in our close family. I hope they lean on one another as much as my brothers and I do. I hope they see that the company is a result of that love and mutual support.

. . .

When people in this business meet me for the first time, they often say something like: "You're sure not how I pictured you."

What that tells me is that they've made assumptions and I've surprised them. It delights me when they say I've made them reconsider what they thought they knew about my part of America. It gives me hope for all of the other girls I know who are growing up like I did. They might have the same chance someday to show the world how much more they can do and be.

Crops die and they're harvested and then there's new life. You sow seeds and hope for the best. You pray for good weather. If you have good weather, you have higher yields. But you don't always get good conditions. No two summers are alike. Everything is seasonal. You have dark times and bright ones. For human beings, every season can be a growing season—the ones that are fallow can teach you as much as the ones that are bountiful.

In life and in business, I continue to ask this question: What do you do with the ugly fruit? Life is a field run harvest. Do you discard the ugly fruit and till it back into the earth? Or do you see past the imperfections? Do you look for the good in it and cherish that? Do you find its greater purpose?

Acknowledgments

Writing this book nearly killed me. After one long session of working on the book last spring, I was briefly catatonic. It didn't help that I thought memoirs were something that you did when you got old—after your give-a-damn had gotten up and left. I thought very seriously about just writing a cookbook and calling it good.

What changed my mind was running into a young acquaintance named Olivia. She shared the story of how my words in a chance meeting a year earlier had given her the courage to take a risk that changed her life. I suddenly realized how much power words and examples can have, and how much other people's stories have contributed to where I am today.

Walking away from that encounter, I thought, *If she only knew more about my life and experiences.* I felt selfish and, frankly, a bit cowardly for not having shared more with her and others along the way. I asked myself, *What if something about my story could inspire just one more Olivia?* In that moment, I knew I had to write this book.

Of course, that's not to say that super scary monsters didn't keep popping up throughout the process. In fact, they almost ate me. But with the help of those I love and trust, I was set free. Here are the people I would like to thank for helping me fight off those beasts and get these stories out of me and into the world:

First and foremost, I would like to thank my agent, Mollie Glick, and her colleagues at CAA. Thank you for putting life, work, and family into one bucket to make this book a reality. You are the epitome of what I believe it means to be a Boss.

Ada Calhoun—words cannot express the gratitude that I feel for the patience and understanding that you gave not only to this book but to me. I can't think of another human being I would rather crash weddings with or bare my soul to.

Endless thanks to Susanna Porter, my editor, for taking a chance on the "Rowdiest Girl" and believing this story deserved to be told. When I visited Ballantine's offices I walked out, looked at Mollie, and said, "I want it to be them." Susanna's amazing team includes Sarah Breivogel, Joseph Perez, Sarah Horgan, Emily Hartley, Kara Welsh, Kim Hovey, Elizabeth Rendfleisch, Cindy Berman, Jennifer Garza, Amelia Zalcman, Debbie Aroff, and Taylor Noel. Thanks to all of you for taking such good care of this book.

I would also like to thank all of my friends and compatriots in business and in life, especially:

Lisa Wagner, thank you for being my truth teller and sister.

Richard Porter, thank you for always taking my calls even when you know it's because I'm in trouble.

Jim Keyes, I still think I pay you too much for advice but, hey, some of it has been good.

Gearry Davenport, thank you for your loyalty, hard work, and friendship. I will never let you retire.

Thank you to the fantastic and dedicated team at The Frey Company—and, of course, my entire family. My brothers: Leonard, Harley, John, and Ted—for smiling when I steal thunder and making me believe I can kill giants. Mostly for always sticking together no matter what. My mother for opening up her heart for this book and sacrificing so much of her life so that we could have the chance at a better one. You don't get to choose your family, but I would have still picked all of you.

Finally, thanks to William and Luke, for making me coffee every morning, making me laugh every day, and making everything I do worthwhile. You are the best sons I could have asked for, the best men I know; and, no matter what I may do, you will always be the greatest accomplishment of my life.

ABOUT THE AUTHOR

SARAH FREY has been described by the *New York Times* as "the Pumpkin Queen of America." She sells more pumpkins than any other producer in the United States. Her family business, Frey Farms, plants thousands of acres of fruits and vegetables in Florida, Georgia, Missouri, Arkansas, Illinois, Indiana, and West Virginia. With a mission to end food waste in the fresh produce industry, the family makes natural food products and beverages from imperfect or "ugly fruit." Inspired by her humble beginnings and early life on the farm, she continues to create opportunities for those living and working in rural communities. Frey lives in Southern Illinois and is raising her two sons, William and Luke, on the same family farm where she grew up.

freyfarms.com
Instagram: @freyfarms

ABOUT THE TYPE

This book was set in Caslon, a typeface first designed in 1722 by William Caslon (1692–1766). Its widespread use by most English printers in the early eighteenth century soon supplanted the Dutch typefaces that had formerly prevailed. The roman is considered a "workhorse" typeface due to its pleasant, open appearance, while the italic is exceedingly decorative.